Power by Design

POWER BY DESIGN

Constitution-Making in Nationalist China

Suisheng Zhao

University of Hawai'i Press, Honolulu

96 97 98 99 00 01 5 4 3 2 1

Library of Congress Cataloging-in-Publication Data
Zhao, Suisheng, 1954–
Power by design : constitution-making in Nationalist China / Suisheng Zhao.
p. cm.
Includes bibliographical references and index.
ISBN 0–8248–1721–4 (alk. paper)
1. China—Politics and government—1895–1945. 2. China–
–Constitutional history. I. Title.
JQ1522.Z43 1996
320.951'09'041—dc20 95–23127
CIP

University of Hawai'i Press books are printed on acid-free paper and meet the guidelines for permanence and durability of the Council on Library Resources

Book design by Kenneth Miyamoto

For my wife
Ren Yi

and for our children
Lillian, Sandra, and Justin

Contents

Note on Romanization ix
Abbreviations x
Acknowledgments xi

1. Introduction: Institutional Design in Authoritarian Settings 1
2. The Rise of Constitutionalism 20
3. Power Resources and Authority Relationships 38
4. Relative Power Positions of the Major Players 57
5. Institutional Preferences of the Major Players 74
6. The Succession Struggle: From Cabinet to Presidential Government, 1925–1928 87
7. The Grand Anti-Chiang Coalition: From Presidential to Cabinet Government, 1928–1931 106
8. The Destruction of Chiang's Major Rivals: From Cabinet Back to Presidential Government, 1931–1937 126
9. Conclusion: A Comparative Perspective 143

Notes 157
Selected Bibliography 199
Index 211

Note on Romanization

Pinyin is used as the primary romanization system for Chinese characters throughout this book except in the quotes, where original spelling stands unchanged. The Wade-Giles romanization system is used occasionally for names and organizations long familiar in the West. Examples include Kuomintang (Guomindang in the *pinyin* system), Sun Yat-sen (*pinyin* Sun Yixuan), Chiang Kai-shek (Jiang Jieshi), and Chiang Ching-kuo (Jiang Jingguo).

Abbreviations

CCP	Chinese Communist Party
CEC	Central Executive Committee
CPC	Central Political Council
CSC	Central Supervisory Committee
KMT	Kuomintang (Nationalist Party)

Acknowledgments

THIS BOOK is based largely on my dissertation research. Although my primary area of interest is contemporary Chinese politics, my dissertation focused on a historical period because I think an in-depth historical knowledge of Chinese politics is important for understanding contemporary Chinese politics. It was fortunate that my dissertation advisor shared my belief and helped me devise a historical topic with contemporary significance and comparative value. I would like to acknowledge those at the University of California, San Diego, who guided my graduate work and dissertation. The support, advice, and constructive criticism of Susan Shirk guided my graduate study and my intellectual growth. My scholarly role model in the Department of Political Science was Arend Lijphart, whose dedication to scholarship, passion for teaching, and profound knowledge of comparative politics greatly helped my research from its inception and have been a constant source of inspiration in my academic career ever since. I am indebted, too, to Richard Madsen, Paul Pickowicz, Mathew McCubbins, Teng-jen Cheng, and Victor Magagna for their extensive suggestions concerning my research. My gratitude goes also to a number of my fellow graduate students, in particular John Carey, Kathy Underwood, Hendrik Spruyt, and Dabbi Avant, for their intellectual support for the research.

This research would not have been possible without access to a number of libraries and archives. I would especially like to thank the East Asian National Resource Center at Stanford University for a travel grant that allowed me to make use of the archival collections at the Hoover Institution and the libraries at the University of California, Berkeley. A research trip sponsored by the Cultural Foundation of the United Daily News Group in Taipei made it possible for me to access the archival collections in the National History Archival Museum, the KMT Party History Commission, and the Institute of Modern History of Academia Sinica in Taiwan.

In the course of revising the manuscript, I benefited greatly from the suggestions of a number of scholars. I am especially grateful for the comments of Andrew Nathan and Ramon H. Myers. The written comments of two anonymous readers were extremely helpful in sharpening the argument. I would also like to express my appreciation to the editors at the University of Hawai'i Press, in particular to Patricia Crosby for her efficient work style and personal attention to the manuscript during the usually impersonal initial stages of the publication process, and to Mr. Don Yoder who copyedited the manuscript swiftly, consistently, and with a very sharp eye. My colleagues at Colby College provided a supportive environment that made revision of the manuscript enjoyable. Valuable technical assistance from Patricia D. Kick, the Government Department secretary, Duc Buu Truc and June Chan, my research assistants, and Grace Von Tobel at Colby's Faculty Manuscript Service allowed me to put the final touches to the manuscript.

Finally, I would like to thank my wife, Ren Yi, and my three children, Lillian, Sandra, and Justin, for their love, tolerance, and encouragement during the prolonged process of research, writing, and revision. Their understanding and support have been beacons of light during times of flagging energy and wavering resolve in my struggle. To them, this book is dedicated.

Power by Design

Chapter 1

Introduction: Institutional Design in Authoritarian Settings

There is a growing comparative politics literature that explores the political consequences of alternative constitutional designs and analyzes the processes of constitution-making. This literature evinces great interest in the institutional choice between parliamentarianism and presidentialism in democratic countries.[1] Little attention, however, is devoted to the study of different constitutional frameworks in authoritarian settings. Indeed, there is a general tendency to ignore constitutional and institutional issues in the study of authoritarian regimes. Because of the difficulties in determining the relationship between individual leaders' power positions and their institutional incentives in authoritarian countries where there are noncompetitive elections or no elections at all, scholars tend to assume that authoritarian leaders are not constrained by formal institutional procedures and rules. Hence they rarely bother to examine different incentives and strategies of the political leaders who are responsible for the formal institutional design of the presidential or the cabinet system in these countries. Conventional wisdom holds that formal institutions are of little importance in nondemocratic regimes.

Nevertheless, political leaders operating in nondemocratic regimes often seem to think otherwise. Indeed, they pay quite a bit of attention to institutional design and are willing to fight for their preferred designs. A review of constitutional development in contemporary authoritarian states reveals that, after the presidential and the cabinet systems were introduced, seasoned political leaders in authoritarian states of Asia, Africa, and Latin America certainly found that it was to their benefit to make use of the constitutional form of government and to take advantage of institutions to their liking rather than simply ignoring them. They also clearly showed their institutional preferences and designed government institutions that could enhance their power and positions. In the contemporary world, most authoritarian regimes have adopted the presidential system. After independence, for example, nearly all African states redrafted their constitutions to "enhance presidential power."[2] In Asia, most modern authoritarian regimes emerged after World War II. The Philippines, Indonesia, South Korea, Taiwan—all were structured in the presidential form of government, although that system has been undermined in recent years and presidential power has been constrained in the process of democratic transition.[3] In most Latin American countries, as well, the presidential system was retained when the democratic regimes changed into authoritarian regimes.[4] In recent transitions toward democracy, one controversial issue has fascinated not only political scientists but also politicians in many Latin American countries: is the viability of presidentialism as a system able to accommodate the transition process? This debate has formed part of the "new institutionalism" literature in comparative politics that has produced provocative hypotheses about the effects of institutions on the transition toward democracy.[5]

In this context, it is especially interesting to investigate constitution-making and the political causes and consequences of the alternative constitutional designs, especially those of the institutional choice between the presidential and cabinet systems of government—one of the major institutional differences in democracies—in nondemocratic settings. The following questions have not been addressed but deserve an answer in the study of authoritarian regimes: What is the functional difference between the constitutional form of government in an authoritarian setting and the same form in a democratic setting? How are political institutions utilized by authoritarian leaders? What is the political logic of institutional design in an authoritarian setting? Why is the presidential system, rather than the cabinet system, chosen in most authoritarian regimes in spite of the fact that both systems were introduced from Western democracies in the early twentieth century? What political incentives are presented by the presidential versus the cabinet forms of government in an authoritarian setting? Given the authoritarian rule of such regimes, how are the institutional preferences of political players shaped? And how is the outcome of the struggle among political leaders for their preferred designs of government institutions determined?

Defining the Contrasting Systems

This book tries to answer the foregoing questions by examining the design of the Nationalist government of China during 1925–1937. This period is an especially promising case because major changes took place in a relatively short time. When the Nationalist government was first established in Guangzhou in 1925, it was designed to be a cabinet system. Then a presidential system replaced the cabinet system in 1928 when a unified Nationalist government was organized in Nanjing. Then the cabinet government was restored in 1931 and prevailed until the presidential system was again installed by the 1936 constitution.

Why did presidential and cabinet systems exist alternately during the formative period of the Nationalist government? Why was the presidential system finally adopted in 1936? To answer these questions, we must clarify the institutional differences between the presidential and cabinet systems.

Presidential and Cabinet Systems in a Democratic Setting

One of the fundamental problems in the institutional design of democratic government is the authority relationship between the executive and the legislative branches. The two most prevalent formal arrangements of executive/legislative relations in modern democracies are the cabinet system and the presidential system.[6] The cabinet system, also known as the parliamentary system in the political science literature,[7] has been defined by Leon D. Epstein as "the form of constitutional democracy in which executive authority emerges from, and is responsible to, legislative authority."[8] In contrast to the cabinet system, the tenure of the office of president in the presidential system is independent of the will of the legislature.[9] In other words, the president has a fixed term in office.[10]

Political scientists have noted many institutional differences between the presidential and cabinet systems. Indeed, Douglas Verney has described as many as eleven criteria by which to distinguish the presidential system from the cabinet system.[11] Matthew S. Shugart and John M. Carey, however, believe that Verney's criteria "overlap considerably" and have therefore distilled his eleven criteria into six.[12] In Arend Lijphart's definition, only three are essential: first, the chief executive in the cabinet system is dependent on legislative confidence but is elected for a fixed term in the presidential system;[13] second, the chief executive in the presidential system is elected by popular vote but is selected by the legislature in the cabinet system;[14] third, the president is a one-person executive whereas the cabinet is a collective body.[15] Of Lijphart's three institutional distinctions, the first two are accepted by most scholars. A few scholars, however, argue that the third criterion should not be considered a crucial distinguishing characteristic. Shugart's and Carey's work on presidential government contends that the third criterion "contradicts the spirit of the first two criteria described by Lijphart himself" because "both of these criteria emphasize the relative independence of the legislative and executive branches."[16] It is not my intention here to join the debate over how to distinguish presidential from cabinet systems in democratic countries. But I would like to start from these well-established definitions to investigate the presidential/cabinet contrasts in an authoritarian setting.

Presidential/Cabinet Contrasts in Authoritarian Settings

While there is an emerging scholarly discussion of the institutional and behavioral differences between the presidential and the cabinet systems in the context of modern democratic settings, virtually no attention is given to the fact that these two constitutional forms of government have been adopted by many modern authoritarian regimes in Asia, Africa, and Latin America. Influenced by Western democracies, these countries have not only promulgated a constitution—a notion that was totally foreign to them—but have also established, at least in name, separate executive and legislative organs. The top political leaders in these countries are no longer kings or emperors; now they are presidents or prime ministers. Politicians have also argued about installing the "cabinet" or the "presidential" form of government, even though these modern forms in authoritarian settings never perform the same functions as their counterparts in democratic regimes. From this perspective, what distinguishes the authoritarian regime from the democratic one is not the constitutional form of government but the functional substance of government.

At least three substantial characteristics of constitutional government in authoritarian settings can be cited to distinguish it from its counterpart in democratic settings. First, the constitution in authoritarian settings sets a "legal order" that legitimizes and organizes the roles of a political elite rather than constrains the power of the ruling elite. It establishes the superior purpose of power holders over individuals and groups and consolidates their position. Second, constitutional government in authoritarian settings is often characterized by a one-party system in which a revolutionary or nationalist party monopolizes the authority of the political system and, hence, political competition is not among political parties but among individual political leaders within the ruling party.[17] Third, there are no genuine competitive elections or no elections at all. Therefore, political leaders are accountable not to their citizens but to the party's central authority. Often, too, the military is one of the key resources utilized by political leaders for the purpose of power.

Nevertheless, constitutional government in modern authoritarian states, after all, is different from absolute monarchies. The constitutional form of governance is a political phenomenon of modernization and a product of the convulsive processes of social, economic, and political changes. These changes were most evident during the nationalist revolutions and constitutional movements that occurred in traditional societies during the early twentieth century.[18] There are at least two political arrangements that distinguish modern authoritarian governments from absolute monarchies. First, modern authoritarian states are governed not along hereditary family lines but by competing political elites. Second, rival political elites in these states compete for secular political power rather than traditional sacred authority.

In view of the fact that constitutional government was adopted from Western democracies, the formal institutional differences between the presidential and the cabinet systems in authoritarian settings are usually prescribed, in many aspects, just as they are in democratic settings. The president is prescribed as a titular head in the cabinet system, for example, but a true chief executive in the presidential system. But because of the substantial distinctions between authoritarian and democratic regimes, the definition of the presidential/cabinet differences in a democratic system cannot be automatically applied to an authoritarian setting. At least Arend Lijphart's first two differences—namely, the head of government's dependence on legislative confidence versus his election for a fixed term and the chief executive's election by popular vote versus his selection by the legislature—become irrelevant. This is because there are no competitive elections (or no elections at all) and the legislature can never be really independent of the executive in an authoritarian regime.

Nevertheless, Lijphart's third presidential/cabinet contrast—namely, one-person leadership versus collective leadership—offers a clue in our investigation of the presidential/cabinet contrasts in an authoritarian setting. Because the president is selected neither by the majority of citizens nor the majoritarian party, but by the revolutionary party or the military junta, the characterization of the presidency as a one-person executive in the presidential system produces a strong incentive for the leader of the party or the head of the junta to assume the president's role. In this situation, when the leader of the revolutionary party or the military forces occupies the presidency, he not only wields the ultimate executive power but also seizes the ultimate authority of the regime, since the party, the military, and the government powers are all concentrated in the hands of a single person.[19] The president thus becomes a strongman who wields not only the executive power but also the ultimate authority of the government. In contrast, the cabinet system grants executive power to a collegial executive body and creates the possibility of a collective leadership among a group of top power elites such as leaders of different political factions or heads of different government institutions. Because the ultimate authority of the regime is shared by a group of power elites, the collective leadership becomes the norm of institutional arrangement.

This distinction is comparable to Aristotle's distinction between "rule by one" and "rule by the few." The institutional arrangement of the singular leadership in the presidential system appears analogous to Aristotle's "rule by one." The collective leadership in the cabinet system occurs as Aristotle's "rule by the few." Significantly, "rule by many" (or "democracy"), Aristotle's third form of politics, does not enter the realm of political possibility in authoritarian settings.[20] Although both "rule by one" and "rule by the few" in their own interests depict the substance of authoritarian regimes, they are involved with two different forms of government. Aristotle labels the former "tyranny" (or "kingship") and the latter "aristocracy" (or "oligarchy").[21] This distinction can be expressed through the different constitutional arrangements of the presidential and cabinet systems in an authoritarian setting.

It is the different power consequences proceeding from the two forms of institutional arrangement (rule by one versus rule by the few) that lead seasoned politicians in authoritarian regimes to fight over the choice between the presidential and the cabinet system. What they are interested in is not executive/legislative relations, or different modes of elections, but who wields the ultimate authority: a single person or a group of elites. From this perspective, politicians in modern authoritarian regimes have indeed borrowed the constitutional form of government from Western democracies, but they have vested it with very different substances.

The Presidential/Cabinet Contrast in Nationalist China

The design of government institutions preoccupied competing leaders of the newly established Nationalist regime throughout the period 1925–1937. After the first Nationalist Government Organic Law *(guomin zhengfu zuzhi fa)* was promulgated on July 1, 1925, five revisions of the Organic Law were adopted by the KMT Central Executive Committee: on March 30, 1927, February 11, 1928, October 3, 1928, November 17, 1930, and December 30, 1931, respectively. A provisional constitution and a draft constitution were promulgated on May 12, 1931, and May 5, 1936. The central controversy among the constitution-makers was the choice between presidential and cabinet systems. Some preferred the presidential form of government; others preferred the cabinet form. In the authoritarian setting of Nationalist China, the focus of these competing leaders was to see who would wield the ultimate authority in the regime: a single person or a group of power elites. As a result of this power struggle, the two forms of constitutional government alternated until a presidential form of government was established by the 1936 constitution.[22] Study of the different institutional arrangements prescribed in the six versions of the Organic Law and several drafts of the constitution during the period

1925–1937 confirms that the alternative designs of the presidential and the cabinet systems were related to the variations of the singular versus collective leadership analyzed above.

When the cabinet form of government was adopted during the periods 1925–1928 and 1931–1936, the president was selected from and by a group of power elites—namely, the members of the National Government Council. He was not allowed to hold any other government, party, or military post concurrently, nor did he control the group of top elites by being empowered to appoint members of the National Government Council. The presidency by law was not a unitary executive but only a figurehead of state. In this instance, the National Government Council was an institution of collective leadership and the president was only a figurehead (or, at most, shared power with other council members).

In contrast, when the presidential system was adopted during 1928–1931 and again in 1936, the president was prescribed as both head of state and chief executive of the government. He concurrently held the posts of commander-in-chief of the Nationalist army and chairman of the Nationalist Party (Kuomintang or KMT). The president was selected by the Central Executive Committee (CEC) of the KMT, which he chaired himself. Moreover, he was empowered to appoint the heads of other branches of government. In this situation, the president was the singular leader of the regime.

The Political Logic of Institutional Choice

Given the different institutional norms of the presidential and cabinet systems, how would individual politicians choose between them? Borrowing ideas from public choice theory,[23] this study assumes that political actors who design government institutions are driven by power maximization strategies just as business firms are driven by wealth maximization strategies. In short, they prefer the design that enhances their personal power. In this case, the presidential system, which tends toward singular leadership, can best satisfy the ambitions of a single political leader who anticipates himself becoming dominant in the regime. For politicians in weaker positions, seeking their share of power by promoting collective leadership in the cabinet system rather than pursuing one-person dictatorship in the presidential system is a rational choice. The power maximization assumption does not deny that political leaders may have other long-term goals to pursue. Nor does it mean that politicians have no policy preferences. For politicians designing government institutions, interest in the maximum growth of their personal power usually converges with their interest in achieving policy goals. The same institutions that widen their chance of overcoming the political competition will also improve their chances of achieving policy goals.

Proceeding from these assumptions, this book argues that the institutional preferences of political actors are shaped by their relative power positions in the regime. If a political actor in an authoritarian regime possesses more power resources than his rivals and anticipates himself becoming dominant in the regime, he will choose the presidential system. If a political actor is in a weaker position and does not anticipate becoming dominant, he will prefer the cabinet form. The ultimate design is determined by the outcome of power struggles among leading political contenders in the regime. If a balance of power exists and no single political leader prevails, the cabinet form of government will be chosen. Only when one political leader defeats his major political rivals and faces no strong political challenge in the regime will the presidential form of government be chosen. Different designs therefore represent different strategic choices that political leaders must make to enhance their power. The institutional design becomes an outcome of the power contest.

The singular and collective leadership variation in an authoritarian setting is not a new discovery in the field of comparative politics. Many scholars have studied the contrast between personal dictatorship and collective oligarchy in the former Soviet Union and other Soviet-style Communist countries. Nevertheless, most of these studies have taken the two different forms of leadership as an independent variable and use them to explain policymaking outcomes rather than focus on the political logic of institutional design itself. Very few scholars take the variation of singular and collective leadership as a dependent variable and explore the incentives, strategies, and problems confronting authoritarian leaders when they choose a certain form of government institution. Samuel P. Huntington, for example, distinguishes two policymaking processes: "legislative" and "executive." According to Huntington the legislative process embodies a collective leadership, since "the units participating in the process are relatively equal in power" and "consequently must bargain with each other"; but the executive process could be a one-person rule, because "the participating units differ in power" and "are hierarchically arranged."[24] Ellen Comisso, in her study of the political process in postwar Eastern Europe, finds that politics took two basic forms: "patrimonialism" and "collegiality." She believes that "patrimonialism appeared as charismatic leadership," whereas "collegiality, in turn, has occurred as collective leadership."[25] Neither Huntington's nor Comisso's study explores the factors that affected the choice of the two distinctive forms of leadership. They are interested in policy outcomes rather than institutional consequences. Philip G. Roeder, in a study of the Soviet political process and its foreign policy, has tried to link the distribution of power within the Soviet government to what he calls decision-making regimes. He identifies five distinctive regimes—"pluralistic," "directive," "primatial," "oligarchic," and "cartelistic"—that form a continuum between one-person rule at one end and collective leadership, consolidated authority, and dispersed authority at the other.[26] For Roeder the "regimes" were not a dependent variable but an intervening variable used to explain different patterns of Soviet foreign policymaking.

Thomas Baylis, by way of contrast, takes different forms of government as a dependent variable. He contrasts collegial leadership with what he calls "monocratic" leadership and discusses this distinction with regard to both democratic and nondemocratic governments. His cases of nondemocratic governments were the former Soviet Union and several East European countries. Explaining the determinants of the collegial and monocratic leaderships, Baylis lists six organizational and societal variables such as peculiar history, cultural predisposition, and the presence of class, linguistic, ethnic, regional, and religious divisions.[27] While Baylis tries to explain why one country adopted collegial leadership and others adopted monocratic leadership, his variables are too general to tell us why the two forms of leadership alternated in the same country in different periods. To fully understand the logic of institutional choice, we must enter the realm of power competition at the individual level. The theoretical model presented in this book is a modest effort in this regard.

The Case of the Nationalist Government in China

The institutional design of the Chinese Nationalist government during its formative period tests these theoretical assumptions. The empirical study takes four steps. The first step defines three important power resources in the possession of major political leaders by exploring the political environment and the authority relationship in the Nationalist regime. The second step compares relative power positions of leading political players in Nationalist China by analyzing their power resources. The third step examines the relationship between the relative power positions of the players and their institutional preferences. The last step explores the relationship between each institutional design and the outcome of each episode of the power struggle among the competing leaders during the entire period 1925–1937. We turn now to the the major findings in each of the four steps.

The First Step. A hybrid pattern of authority relationship combining the hierarchical and anarchic principles characterized the KMT regime during the period of the study. The two types of authority relationship were based on whether or not there existed a mutually recognized central authority. Because there was a hierarchy in which the KMT monopolized the supreme authority of the Nationalist regime, political leaders had to compete for the top position within the party. Because the competition among several equally powerful KMT leaders often ended in deadlock, which in turn resulted in anarchy, the power positions of political leaders were often ordered by ad hoc negotiations or violent battles, and the political leader who commanded military forces or possessed other effective negotiating resources (say, the support of strong factional groups) was in a powerful position.

In light of the hybrid authority relationship, politicians in the Nationalist regime cultivated three important power resources:

1. *Formal positions in the top organ of the KMT pyramid.* The Nationalist regime was characterized by a one-party system in which political competition was carried out not among political parties or interest groups, as in a democratic regime, but among individual leaders of the KMT. The outcome of their power struggle was formally determined within the party's decision-making organ. Powerful political leaders usually occupied the positions at the apex of the party hierarchy,

namely, the leading posts in the top decision-making organs of the KMT: the Standing Committee of the Central Executive Committee (CEC) and the Standing Committee of the Central Political Council (CPC). Revolutionary seniority or proximity to the founding father of the KMT, Sun Yat-sen, could also be intangible power resources.

2. *Support of factional groups.* After the death of Sun Yat-sen in 1925, the succession struggle among several strong personalities in the KMT resulted in the fragmentation of authority among faction leaders.[28] To claim leadership, each contender had to rely on the support of one or more factions.[29]
3. *Military capacity.* Some political leaders of the KMT were themselves the commanders of military forces. Moreover, some civilian leaders were backed by powerful regional militarists who had just recently declared allegiance to the Nationalist Revolution and were financed not by the central government but by their own local resources. Hence military forces were important power resources for competing political leaders.

In the political environment of Nationalist China, therefore, political power belonged to those leaders who not only occupied formal positions in the top decision-making organs of the KMT but also led powerful factions and had the capacity to command military forces.

The Second Step. The second step compares the relative power positions of four leading political players in the KMT regime: Chiang Kai-shek, Wang Jingwei, Hu Hanmin, and Sun Ke. All four figures held top positions in the KMT's Central Executive Committee and the Central Political Council. Chiang Kai-shek, Wang Jingwei, and Hu Hanmin assumed the chairmanship of the CEC or the CPC in different periods. Sun Ke was a member of the Standing Committee of the CEC during most of the period 1925–1937. Their support from factional groups and their military capacity, however, varied dramatically.

Chiang Kai-shek entered KMT politics with a strong military background. As commander-in-chief of the Nationalist army, he gained the most powerful capacity to command military forces.[30] Chiang Kai-shek also established and led several well-structured factions both inside and outside the KMT's formal organization, such as the Blue Shirt Society and the Organization Group.[31] He was therefore supported by powerful clientele groups. Wang Jingwei's political influence came at first from his revolutionary seniority, but he was also supported by an influential left-wing faction, the KMT Reorganizationalist Comrades Association. Although he aligned with powerful regional militarists from time to time, Wang Jingwei was a civilian politician and did not directly command military forces. Hu Hanmin owed his eminence to his past association with Sun Yat-sen and to his authority as an exponent of the KMT ideology. Hu Hanmin was the spiritual leader of an extreme right-wing faction in the KMT, the Western Hill Group, but he never formalized his connections to the group. Hu Hanmin was also a civilian politician and did not have the capacity to command military forces. Sun Ke savored political prominence because he was the only son of Sun Yat-sen. Nevertheless, Sun Ke did not lead a well-structured faction and his relations with the military were weak.

A comparison of the relative power positions of the four leading players shows that Chiang Kai-shek was the only political leader who could anticipate becoming dominant in the Nationalist regime. Neither Wang Jingwei, Hu Hanmin, nor Sun Ke enjoyed the extensive support of factional groups or had the capacity to command military forces to the extent that Chiang Kai-shek did. They were in weak positions and could not expect to become predominant in the regime. In light of this comparison, one would expect Chiang Kai-shek to prefer a presidential system whereas Wang Jingwei, Hu Hanmin, and Sun Ke would prefer a cabinet system for the design of the Nationalist government.

The Third Step. Empirical study of the CEC meeting minutes, proceedings, and other archival sources confirms the preceding assumption. Chiang Kai-shek was indeed the only leader in the KMT regime who expressed a consistent preference for the presidential form of government. Neither Wang Jingwei, Hu Hanmin, nor Sun Ke showed any interest in the presidential system: all three advocated the cabinet form of government.

Chiang Kai-shek's preference for the presidential system was expressed for the first time in 1928 when he formally rose to the top position in the regime. At the Fourth Plenary Session of the Second CEC held in February 1928, Chiang Kai-shek assumed the chairmanship of both the Central Military Commission and the Central Executive Committee of the KMT. Confident in his power position, Chiang Kai-shek called for the Fifth Plenary Session, which was convened in August 1928. It was at this session that Chiang Kai-shek requested the revision of the Organic Law and assumed the chairmanship of the Organic Law Drafting Committee. This revision resulted in the first presidential system in Nationalist China. Chiang Kai-shek made his institutional choice for presidentialism once again in the provisional constitution drafted in Nanjing in 1931. The provisional constitution empowered the president of the national government to appoint and dismiss the presidents of five *yuan* (branches of the Nationalist government) and heads of ministries. Chiang Kai-shek, for the third time, expressed his preference for a strong presidency at the Fifth Plenary Session of the Fourth CEC, held December 10–14, 1935. He sponsored a resolution that dismissed the cabinet system designed by Sun Ke in a preliminary draft of the permanent constitution and ordered a rewriting of the draft to design a presidential form of government.

Hu Hanmin's preference for the cabinet system was expressed on at least two occasions. In a formal proposal submitted to the KMT's Central Executive Committee immediately after the death of Sun Yat-sen in 1925, Hu Hanmin aimed at creating collective responsibility by proposing a cabinet system to replace the generalissimo system established by Sun Yat-sen.[32] Hu Hanmin's second expression of institutional preference was in 1927 when he and Sun Ke submitted a formal proposal to the CEC suggesting that the national government be formed as a cabinet led collectively by the heads of the five *yuan*. The president of the national government was to be selected from and by the members of the National Government Council.

Wang Jingwei's preference for a cabinet system was expressed systematically in a letter he sent to Chiang Kai-shek in October 1931. At that time Wang was supported by a grand anti-Chiang coalition composed of Wang Jingwei, Hu Hanmin, Sun Ke, and several powerful regional militarists including Feng Yuxiang, Li Zhongren, and Yan Xishan.[33] Wang Jingwei's letter asserted that Chiang Kai-shek should be only a figurehead of state and take no political responsibility if he wanted to hold the post of president of the national government. Wang's letter also suggested the abolition of the post of commander-in-chief of the Nationalist army.

Sun Ke's preference was first expressed in 1928 when he and Hu Hanmin cosigned the proposal for a cabinet form of government in Paris. But the most systematic expression of his institutional preference was in the first four drafts of the permanent constitution, written during the period 1932–1934. Sun Ke was then president of the Legislative Yuan and led a constitution-drafting group. These drafts of the constitution clearly designed a cabinet form of government. Not only was the president of the national government a figurehead, but power sharing among the top elites was guaranteed by diffusing ultimate authority among several organs of the government.

The Fourth Step. The last step of the empirical study examines the relationship between the alternation of the presidential and cabinet systems and the outcomes of the power contest among the KMT leaders during the period 1925–1937.

From 1925 to 1928 a balance of power among Chiang Kai-shek, Wang Jingwei, and Hu Hanmin was maintained and the cabinet form of government prevailed. The presidential system replaced the cabinet form of government in 1928 when the balance of power dissolved as a result of two events: Chiang Kai-shek's Nanjing government defeated Wang Jingwei's Wuhan government, and Hu Hanmin was temporarily squeezed out of KMT politics because of his implication in the assassination of Liao Zhongkai, one of his political rivals. Chiang's victory, however, was only momentary. The emergence of Chiang Kai-shek induced self-interested cooperation among those threatened by their competitor's prospective dominance. A grand anti-Chiang coalition, formed in 1931–1936, consisted of Wang Jingwei, Hu Hanmin, and Sun Ke, as well as several powerful regional militarists. When the grand coalition blocked Chiang's efforts at domination and restored the balance of power, the cabinet form of government was chosen once again in 1932. Military resources were Chiang's trump card—one that Hu Hanmin, Wang Jingwei, and Sun Ke could never come close to topping. But legitimacy within the party remained important and distinguished the Nationalist government from that of the warlords. It was always important for Chiang to ally himself with either Hu or Wang in the period of this study. When he tried to go against both at the same time, he inevitably lost his prominent position in the regime. The same happened in his confrontation with the anti-Chiang coalition.

Chiang's strategy was to shift the playing field by constantly defining the situation in terms of military conflict with the warlords and the Communists in order to draw attention to the resources that Chiang himself possessed and away from those he did not (that is, ideological authority and seniority in the party). Chiang's success in strategic maneuvering was accompanied by the self-destruction of the anti-Chiang coalition during the period 1932–1936. When Chiang Kai-shek ultimately eliminated all his major rivals and finally achieved a dominant position in the regime, the presidential system was installed by the constitution of 1936. Thus Chiang Kai-shek was forced to accede to the wishes of his rivals during periods of relative weakness and adopt a cabinet form of government. But this institutional arrangement never did what its advocates hoped it would: restrain Chiang's ambition. When Chiang was able to accumulate power over his rivals, he eventually overturned the institutional arrangements. Ultimately, constitution-making became a political process and the alternative institutional designs in Nationalist China reflected the change in the relative power of the contestants rather than constraints on the struggle for power.

The preceding findings support the argument that politicians in nondemocratic countries are not indifferent to the formal design of government institutions. The different forms of these institutions are not only a product of a natural evolution, or simply driven by socioeconomic forces or cultural traditions, but also a product of a political process in which leaders make rational choices based on their power positions and fight fiercely for their institutional choices through strategic interactions. The relative positions of political leaders shape their institutional preferences. The outcomes of the power contest among these leaders determine the design of government institutions. In other words, the design of government institutions reflects both the personal ambitions of political actors and the outcomes of power struggles among themselves. Those who advocated a presidential system and those who supported a cabinet system were really arguing over the age-old Aristotelian distinction between "rule by one" and "rule by the few" in their own power interests.

Plan of the Book

Although this book represents a reinterpretation of the political twists and turns in Nationalist China, it is not merely a political history. Its chief objective is to explain the political logic of the institutional design in an authoritarian setting. In doing so, this work seeks to make contributions to two fields of scholarship: political science and the study of Chinese politics.

In the discipline of political science, there is an emerging literature on constitution-making, institutional design, and democratic transitions associated with the names of a number of comparativists such as Arend Lijphart, Alfred Stepan, Juan Linz, Matthew Shugart, and John Carey. This literature displays an overlapping interest in the political consequences of alternative constitutional designs and in behavioral analysis of the process of constitution-making. This book addresses both of these foci by explaining how the different institutional preferences of political leaders were shaped and how the outcomes of institutional design were determined in authoritarian settings. Although the book concentrates mostly on Nationalist China, the concluding chapter offers a comparative perspective by examining constitutional reform in Taiwan and constitution-making in the Philippines, Indonesia, and South Korea. Furthermore, the book carries out an experimental development in political science and history. History is not just the richly descriptive storytelling or subtly self-conscious historiography that may best be conducted by historians. Rather, historical details are explored here to test political science theories.

The second field to which this book seeks to contribute is the study of Chinese politics. Amid the thriving expansion of studies on China in the United States in recent decades, one area that has conspicuously lagged behind is the study of the Nationalist era. While Communist politics in China have been the subject of much scholarly scrutiny, the politics of the Nationalist government have been pretty much neglected. Indeed, KMT politics, especially prior to the founding of the People's Republic of China, is a poorly researched area.[34] There have not been many studies of Nationalist politics conducted by political scientists per se in recent decades, although historians such as Lloyd Eastman have given us sophisticated historical analyses of the era.[35] Even in recent debates over the reform of the presidential system in Taiwan, little attention has been paid to the origin of presidentialism in Nationalist China. It is therefore necessary to look back at history—exploring the causes of the changes in the constitutional design and why the presidential system was adopted in early twentieth-century China. In view of this fact, the historical study of the political dynamics of institutional design in Nationalist China has a significance that transcends the Nationalist period, because the consequences of institutional choices in the 1920s and 1930s continue to reverberate in post-1949 Chinese politics on Taiwan and the mainland as well. In fact, the presidential system designed in the 1930s was retained in post-1949 Taiwan. On the mainland, the behavior patterns of political actors in their power struggles of the 1920s and 1930s can still be found.[36] From this perspective, the theoretical model established in this book casts light on current political events in China and other authoritarian regimes.

The book's nine chapters are structured to produce and test the theoretical argument about the political logic of institutional design in authoritarian settings by analyzing individual political leaders' political behavior in association with the process of constitution-making in Nationalist China. Chapter 1 introduces the political logic of institutional design. Chapter 2 presents a historical background of constitutionalism as a driving force in early twentieth-century China and elaborates the alternative designs of the presidential and the cabinet systems throughout the entire period from 1925 to 1937. Chapter 3 analyzes the three important power resources and the authority relationship of the Nationalist regime. Chapter 4 compares the relative power positions of the four leading players in the Nationalist regime: Chiang Kai-shek, Wang Jingwei, Hu Hanmin, and Sun Ke. Chapter 5 examines the different institutional preferences of these four players and the relationship between their preferences and their relative power positions. Chapters 6, 7, and 8 elaborate the relationship between the three alternative designs of the cabinet and the presidential systems and the three episodes of power competition among the KMT leaders during the period 1925–1937. Chapter 6 examines the establishment of the cabinet form of government in 1925 and shows how Chiang Kai-shek's rise to the top of the KMT hierarchy resulted in the replacement of the cabinet system by the presidential system in 1928. Chapter 7 analyzes how the grand anti-Chiang coalition blocked Chiang Kai-shek's ambitions and restored the cabinet form of government in 1931. Chapter 8 analyzes the destruction of Chiang Kai-shek's leading political rivals and the adoption of the presidential form of government in the 1936 constitution. Chapter 9 concludes the book by presenting a comparative study of constitutional reform in Taiwan and the development of constitutionalist authoritarian regimes in the Philippines, Indonesia, and South Korea.

A Note on Sources

The data used in this book are drawn mainly from three sources. The first source is historical archives and documents including various versions of the Organic Law of the Nationalist government, various drafts of the constitution, and the *jilu* (minutes and proceedings) of meetings of the KMT National Congress, its Central Executive Committee, and the Central Political Council during the period 1925–1937. These historical records were found mostly in the National History Archival Museum (Guo Shi Guan) and the KMT Party History Commission (Dang Shi Hui) in Taiwan and in the Hoover Institution Library, the Eastern Asia libraries of the University of California at Berkeley and Los Angeles, Columbia University, and the Library of Congress in the United States. The second source is the reminiscences of elders of the KMT and the Nationalist government, including the records of the KMT oral history project conducted by Columbia University as well as recent publications in Taiwan and mainland China. The third source is the newspapers published in Nanjing, Guangzhou, Wuhan, and Beijing from 1925 to 1937. Many reports in these newspapers provide firsthand information about the operation of political institutions and the interaction of major political figures in the KMT regime.

Chapter 2

The Rise of Constitutionalism

Ever since the constitutional form of government was introduced into China in the early twentieth century, one of the central controversies among politicians was the choice between the presidential and the cabinet systems. While the institutional approach of studying politics has been developed largely by students of Western democracies and advanced economies, it is not difficult to find seasoned politicians throughout modern Chinese history who have deemed it more convenient to take advantage of political institutions than to totally ignore them. Chinese politicians have exploited the presidential system for the purpose of "rule by one," but they have also made use of the cabinet system to accommodate "rule by the few" ever since the two constitutional forms were introduced into China. Indeed, Paul M. A. Linebarger, in a study of modern Chinese government and politics, argues that the choice between the presidential and the cabinet systems, along with the choice between a federal versus a unitary state, have been the two major institutional controversies troubling Chinese politicians since the early Republican era.[1]

Institutional Choices in the Republican Era

During the Republican era (1911–1925), which preceded the formative period of the KMT regime (1925–1937), politicians in China were already concerned with the institutional choice between the presidential and the cabinet systems. Immediately after the 1911 revolution that overthrew the Qing dynasty and established China's first republic, all politicians were busy formulating constitutions and designing government institutions to their own liking. Including the so-called Nineteen Articles of November 2, 1911, seven different versions of a constitution were promulgated during the period from 1911 to 1925: the provisional constitution of March 11, 1912; the "temple of heaven" draft of October 13, 1913; the constitutional compact of May 1, 1914; the Peking New Parliament draft of August 12, 1919; the constitution of October 10, 1923; and the draft constitution of December 11, 1925.[2] The pattern of institutional preferences and the choices made by constitution-makers during the Republican era were very similar to those of the formative period of the Nationalist government. The dominant political leader always tried to promulgate a constitution that provided the presidential form of government; the weaker political players demanded a constitution containing the cabinet form.

The first republican form of provisional government, established in Nanjing by Sun Yat-sen following the collapse of the Qing dynasty, was a "presidential government" with Sun Yat-sen himself serving as president.[3] It survived only one year, from 1911 to 1912. Facing a military threat from Yuan Shikai, an ambitious warlord in North China, Sun Yat-sen was forced to resign and yield the presidency to Yuan Shikai in 1912. Having thus fallen to a weaker position, Sun Yat-sen abandoned the presidential system and, together with his KMT comrades, made great efforts to impose a responsible cabinet system on his successor. The provisional constitution, completed under the leadership of Sun Yat-sen in March 1912, provided that the provisional president could not act on his own authority without the concurrence of State Council.[4]

Yuan Shikai himself, anticipating becoming dominant, could not tolerate such arrangements. The result was the creation of Yuan's own constitutional compact promulgated in May 1914.[5] This constitutional compact provided a strong presidency in which the president "combines in himself all powers of government."[6] The government designed by Yuan Shikai in the constitutional compact was "unmistakably presidential in form."[7] After Yuan Shikai died on June 6, 1916, Li Yuanhong succeeded to the presidency. Li Yuanhong was such a weakling that he was given the nickname "Buddha," while his premier, Duan Qirui, had strong military support as leader of the Anhui Clique *(wan xi)*. Thus the president was deprived of executive power and the premier and his cabinet were granted ample powers by the draft constitution promulgated in August 1919.[8] When Duan Qirui himself became provisional chief executive *(zhizheng),* he "changed the government into the presidential form in his 1925 draft constitution and dropped the cabinet form which he himself had previously advocated."[9] The alternative institutional designs in the Republican era, just as during the formative period of the Nationalist regime, were related to the shifting power relations among the major political leaders.

The Rise of Constitutional Government

There is an essential reason why both Republican-era and Nationalist-era politicians found it important to take advantage of political institutions and concern themselves about their designs: the prevailing constitutionalism in the early twentieth century forced politicians to legitimize their governing authorities under the constitutional form of government. Therefore, to fully analyze constitution-making in Nationalist China, it is necessary to start with an examination of the rise of constitutional government in China. The constitutional form of government in twentieth-century authoritarian regimes, as noted earlier, was an outcome of the constitutional movement influenced by Western democracies. The Nationalist government of China, born after a nationalist revolutionary movement led by Sun Yat-sen and the KMT, was such a constitutional form of government. The Nationalist Revolution of October 10, 1911, not only overthrew the Qing dynasty but also exposed the pervasive decay of China's traditional monarchy and introduced a Western form of government: the republic. After a decade of military and political conflict between warlords and the Nationalist armies, the KMT established a Nationalist government in Guangzhou in 1925.[10]

Ever since the 1911 revolution, the constitutional form of government has been maintained in China. Although several attempts were made to restore the monarchy, none of them succeeded. The best-known example was Yuan Shikai's attempt to make himself emperor in 1915. Yuan Shikai was the chief military modernizer among the imperial forces and used his position to deceive both the monarchy and the republic during the revolutionary period. On the one hand, he persuaded the infant emperor to issue an imperial edict ordering the revolutionaries to set up a republic. On the other hand, he assured

Sun Yat-sen that the republic would survive if Yuan were made its first president. As soon as the revolution succeeded, Yuan Shikai took the presidency of the Chinese Republic on March 10, 1912. Nevertheless, Yuan Shikai still dreamed of becoming emperor of China. In the summer of 1915, Frank J. Goodnow, an American political science professor from Columbia University, wrote an essay for Yuan Shikai exploring what kind of political system was best suited to Chinese conditions. "It is of course not susceptible of doubt that a monarchy is better suited than a republic to China," Goodnow told Yuan. "China's history and traditions, her social and economic conditions, her relations with foreign powers all make it probable that the country would develop . . . constitutional government . . . more easily as a monarchy than as a republic."[11] But as Andrew Nathan points out, "Goodnow's advice proved disastrous."[12] In an ill-considered bid for the throne, Yuan Shikai announced, in October 1915, that he would accept "the overwhelming popular demand" for the reestablishment of imperial rule. Yuan fixed the date for his own enthronement as January 1, 1916. When resistance to restoration of the monarchy came strongly from all over China, however, Yuan was forced to cancel all his monarchical plans and restored the republic on March 22, 1916. The reign of a dynasty that was to be called "Hongxian" (Dynasty of Glorious Constitutionalism) lasted less than three months. It left behind it "nothing more than some extremely rare proof coins for the delectation of numismatists."[13]

Why was the constitutional form of government championed in twentieth-century China? This question has no simple answer.[14] The conflict between borrowed Western political systems and indigenous political and social structures has been one of the most complex and fascinating problems confronting Chinese society and students of Chinese politics. Although the first response toward the West by the elites representing traditional Chinese culture was essentially one of rejection, political values and institutions conceived and developed in the West were paradoxically discovered and subsequently championed by avant-garde elements and at some point became "an essential part of the inevitable development" and "article of faith of Chinese intellectuals" in the twentieth century.[15] When the KMT came to power in the mid-1920s, the traditional monarchical system had already been abandoned.[16] Indeed, there was a dramatic trend toward the extension of democracy in most of the world at that time.[17] This trend, which Alexis de Tocqueville had foreseen in 1835 and James Bryce had documented in 1920, appeared to be irreversible if not necessarily universal.[18] Scholars of Chinese political history also found that "the dominant strand of Chinese political thinking in the early twentieth century was democratic."[19]

A study conducted in the 1940s by Pan Wei-tung on the constitutional movement of China during the Republican and Nationalist periods found that the clamor for a constitution in China began as early as the 1880s. He indicates that the constitutional movement began "when the nation was in the throes of both foreign and domestic disturbances in which the political machine came to a standstill."[20] At the beginning of the twentieth century, even the Qing dynasty itself was making reforms leading toward constitutional monarchy. William L. Tung has pointed out two major forces that propelled China toward constitutionalism in the early twentieth century: "the unceasing revolutionary movement and the world-wide trend toward democracy and constitutionalism."[21] A study of monarchical restoration activities in the early Republic of China indicates that after the constitutional form of government was set up in 1911, constitutionalism was so strong that no restoration could ever be accepted by Chinese intellectuals and politicians.[22] "For complex, historical reasons," Lloyd Eastman observes, "the term democracy had acquired a strong positive connotation for most educated Chinese and it had become a shibboleth in the political discourse" ever since the founding of the Republic of China in 1911.[23]

On all accounts, then, the constitutional form of government was championed in early twentieth-century China. All attempts—first by Yuan Shikai and then by Zhang Xun—to restore the traditional monarchical system had failed by the mid-1920s when the Nationalist government was established.[24] The victory of constitutionalism left the politicians with no other choice but to play with different forms of constitutional government and to exercise authoritarian rule through the modern political institutions introduced from Western democracies.

The Legacy of Sun Yat-sen's Doctrine

Sun Yet-sen is regarded as the founding father of both the Republic of China and the Nationalist Party. Although he may have had a genuine desire to practice democracy and build a constitutional government, he was in reality more paternalistic than democratic.[25] In his book *Minquan Chubu* (Primer of Democracy), written in 1917, Sun Yat-sen suggested that China should learn "the good sides of representative governments" in Europe and America. What he called "parliamentary law" should be used to guide the conduct of public affairs. He believed that Chinese citizens ought to learn parliamentary procedure in the practice of democracy.[26]

In his endeavor to develop a system of government that would reflect modern thought, Sun Yat-sen made various attempts to frame the political institutions of the new Republic of China upon the patterns adopted by Western democracies. Indeed, he elaborated a whole set of doctrines in this regard. The key element was the "five-power constitution" doctrine proposed in his *Jian Guo Da Gang* (Fundamentals of National Reconstruction).[27] Sun Yat-sen distinguished *quan* (power) from *zheng* (function), or sovereignty from governing. *Quan* was "the right to rule as sovereign"; *zheng* was "the right to administer as an official."[28] According to Sun Yat-sen, the people should exercise four sovereign powers—election *(xuanju),* recall *(bamian),* initiative *(chuangzhi),* and referendum *(fujue)*—and the government should exercise five governing powers: administration *(xingzheng),* adjudication *(sifa),* legislation *(lifa),* examination *(kaoshi),* and control *(jiancha).*[29] These two sets of powers were clearly different from each other, he thought, and should therefore be completely separated.[30]

The system of government to be set up according to Sun Yat-sen's five-power constitution doctrine consisted mainly of five *yuan,* or branches: the legislative, the executive, the judicial, the censoring (or control), and the examination.[31] The essential function of the Legislative Yuan was to make laws; the Executive Yuan was to enforce the laws; the Judiciary Yuan was to interpret their meaning and apply them to particular cases; the Control Yuan was to supervise the conduct of government officials; the Examination Yuan was to recruit government officials through a system of public examination. For each of these *yuan* there was a head, later called president, directing the activities of his own *yuan.* Provision was also made for a chief of state: the president.[32] Sun Yat-sen contemplated a National Assembly, as well, consisting of delegates from districts into which the provinces were divided, one delegate from each district. The president of the nation and the presidents of the five *yuan* were all to be elected at the National Assembly, the representative organ of the electorate, and were to be responsible to it. Since the National Assembly was an organ of public opinion through which the popular political powers of election, initiative, referendum, and recall were exercised, it was the reservoir of national sovereignty.[33]

The five-power doctrine was obviously an elaboration of the traditional Western democratic theory of three powers long ago enunciated by Aristotle, Cicero, and Polybius, elaborated by Montesquieu at a later time, and adopted by the framers of the U.S. Constitution as a fundamental principle of their government toward the close of the eighteenth century. Yet it was also rooted in two native Chinese institutions, centuries old, namely, the civil service examination and the censorial system, which were realized in two of the five *yuan,* the Examination Yuan and the Control Yuan. Examination was separated by Sun Yat-sen from administration because he was fascinated by the examination system of ancient China. For a similar reason, control was separated from legislation: in Chinese history there is a long list of famous officials in charge of impeachment who even admonished the emperors for their misdeeds.[34]

Sun Yat-sen died on March 12, 1925. But the Nationalist government, established soon after his death, followed Sun's doctrine and maintained its form of republic. The five-power structure of government was erected in light of the Organic Law of the Nationalist government in 1928, a provisional constitution was promulgated in 1931, and a permanent draft of a five-power constitution was made in public in 1936. Although Sun Yat-sen accepted democracy as a normative solution for China's problems, he was not a democrat in any normally understood sense of the word.[35] Sun never had the militaristic characteristics of Chiang Kai-shek or the totalitarian tendencies of Mao Zedong, but he was very paternalistic at best.[36] The Nationalist government he left behind was an authoritarian regime. First of all, it was a one-party government in which the KMT exercised supreme authority during the period of tutelage described in Sun Yat-sen's doctrine.[37] Second, there was no popular electoral participation and political participation was limited to a small group of elites. Third, the politics of the Nationalist government was characterized by personal competition and pervasive factionalism. Fourth, military forces played a crucial role in the political competition.[38]

The failure of democracy in China has been attributed to a variety of causes. Some scholars condemn Chinese cultural resistance; Lloyd

Eastman, for example, believes that the "authoritarian-oriented culture" was responsible for China's failure to establish a democratic system.[39] Other scholars, such as Andrew Nathan, blame the country's socioeconomic backwardness.[40] Still others, Barrington Moore, Jr., for instance, trace the origin of dictatorship in China to the weakness of urban classes.[41] Although I do not intend to get involved in the debate over the origin of the modern Chinese authoritarian system, it does seem necessary to address the question why Sun Yat-sen's seemingly democratic inclination did not produce a democratic government in Nationalist China.

There is no doubt that Sun Yat-sen's political doctrine was seriously influenced by democratic theories of the West. As Paul M. A. Linebarger indicates, "Sun was in all probability a more assiduous and widely read student of political science than any other world leader of his day except Wilson."[42] Yet it is also evident that his doctrine was influenced by Chinese political thought and by certain antidemocratic theories from abroad. Lloyd Eastman claims that Sun Yat-sen's doctrine was "pestered by the bugaboo of inconsistency."[43] Certainly different views have been expressed about Sun's political thought. Linebarger observes: "A German Marxian showed Sun to be a forerunner of Bolshevism; an American liberal showed Sun to be a bulwark against Bolshevism. A Chinese classicist demonstrated Sun's reverence for the past; a Jesuit father explained much by Sun's modern and Christian background."[44] Discussing Sun Yat-sen's ideas about the design of government institutions for Nationalist China, Linebarger further points out: "It is not, therefore, extraordinarily strange to find the ancient institutions of the Empire surviving by the side of the most extreme methods of popular government. The censorate and the referendum, the examination system and the recall, all could work together in the democracy planned by Sun Yat-sen."[45]

Applying Sun's doctrine to the design of a democratic government, therefore, raised knotty if not insoluble questions. First of all, having separate executive and legislative branches is one of the fundamental characteristics of modern democratic government. But the National Assembly, which Sun Yat-sen designed as the reservoir of the people's sovereignty, did not make laws. Legislative power belonged to the Legislative Yuan. Thus the relationship between several branches of government, especially between legislative and executive powers, was vague. Indeed, defining relations between the government's executive and legislative powers in accordance with Sun's doctrine became one of the most hotly disputed issues for the later design of Nationalist institutions.[46]

Second, while Western democratic theorists from Montesquieu on assumed a conflict of social interests and advocated checks and balances as a guarantee of political freedom, Sun Yat-sen's principle of *minquan* (democracy) was the "self-rule of the Chinese race-nation" as a whole primarily and "a government by the mass of individuals making up the people secondarily."[47] When the founders of Western democracy were trying to design political systems as vessels to contain irrepressible conflict, Sun Yat-sen, influenced by traditional Chinese thinking, aimed to design a system in which no such conflict would be engendered. Sun's design started from the assumption that harmony is natural in the Chinese people. He therefore did not design a government composed of different interests represented by a series of institutional chambers and baffles, such as the American government designed by the authors of *The Federalist Papers*. Instead, according to Sun's design, the five organs in possession of power would work in unison and the five *yuan* of the Nationalist government would bear the national interest in mind and resolve disputes, if any, by a collective effort of the council consisting of the heads of *yuan* and the president of the republic.[48] Third, Sun failed to define how the president holding an office that Sun envisaged as one of importance could resist the temptation to interfere with certain *yuan* or even to dominate all of the *yuan*. Nor did he suggest any effective means by which the people could exercise their political power to check an excessively powerful or despotic government. And fourth, Sun Yat-sen explicitly put forward a three-stage program for the Nationalist Revolution: first a military government, then a political tutelage, and finally a constitutional government.[49] Although Sun Yat-sen did not say how long the military and the political tutelage periods would last, he clearly envisioned military campaigns and one-party dictatorship as a means to establish the constitutional form of democratic government. Sun Yat-sen did not live long enough to preside over the transition from dictatorship to constitutional democracy. His sudden death in 1925 left an ambiguous political program for his successors to carry out.

Inconsistencies both in Sun Yat-sen's political doctrine and in his political practice had a strong impact on the design of the Nationalist government. While he was dedicated to the eventual achievement of constitutional democracy, Sun believed that political tutelage was a necessary stage in which the KMT would serve as the vanguard of the people. Military dictatorship was to be just a transient phase in Sun's doctrine. Yet the use of military power to seize political power for revolutionary goals had been legitimized by Sun Yat-sen himself. And the KMT, which was to take responsibility for political tutelage, was primarily Sun's creation and was dominated by his personal charisma. As George Yu, son of Yu Yuren (president of the Judicial Yuan for many years and an elder of the KMT), has indicated, Sun Yat-sen "ruled the KMT party almost single-handedly. The party became merely an institution for Sun's personal power and a grouping of his personal followers."[50]

Presidential/Cabinet Differences in Nationalist China

Since the Nationalist government established after the death of Sun Yat-sen was not democratic, the presidential system could not be distinguished from the cabinet system simply by the differences in the formal arrangement of executive/legislative relations one finds in democratic settings. While the KMT leaders fought over the choice of a presidential versus cabinet form of government, they were not interested in executive/legislative relations or different modes of elections but in "rule by one" versus "rule by the few." In other words, they were interested in who would wield the ultimate authority of the KMT regime: a single leader or a group of KMT elites. In view of this observation, the presidential/cabinet contrasts in Nationalist China can be analyzed in terms of the four dimensions of institutional arrangement: the selection of the president, the location of executive power, the appointment of the heads of the five *yuan*, and the status of the president. Table 1 summarizes the four dimensions. Accordingly the two forms of government institutions in Nationalist China can be distinguished as follows.

The *presidential form* of the Nationalist government (1928–1931 and 1936–) consisted of an executive chief in the person of the president (who was not the titular head of state but the true executive of the government) and heads of the five *yuan* who were appointed by and responsible to the president. The tenure of the president was not dependent upon popular elections as in democratic countries but upon his selection by the Central Executive Committee (CEC) of the

TABLE 1
Presidential/Cabinet Distinctions in Nationalist China

DIMENSION	PRESIDENTIAL SYSTEM	CABINET SYSTEM
Selection of president	By CEC of the KMT.	By and from National Government Council.
Location of executive power	President was true executive and issued executive orders.	National Government Council or Executive Yuan was highest executive organ and issued executive orders.
Appointment of heads of the five *yuan*	By president.	By CEC of the KMT.
Status of president	Head of both state and government and concurrently KMT chariman and commander-in-chief of Nationalist army.	Figurehead of state and not allowed to hold concurrent posts.

KMT, as stipulated by the Organic Law, and, very often, with the support of the military. Under the president there was a National Government Council composed of standing councillors and councillors chosen by the KMT authorities. Since the president was selected by the KMT rather than elected by the councillors, his power was not delegated by the National Government Council but by the KMT. Thus the council had no effective power to force its will on the president. Furthermore, the president was vested the power to appoint and remove the heads of the five *yuan*. As a result, the Executive Yuan was merely his secretariat and the other four *yuan* were subordinate to him as well. As the head of both state and government, the president seized the authority to represent the national government both at home and abroad. Whatever orders and other actions the national government might adopt, they were to be done with the president's signature. Since the Organic Law and the constitution allowed the president to hold concurrently the posts of KMT chairman and commander-in-chief of the military forces, he could easily wield the ultimate authority of the regime. The presidential system in Nationalist China consequently was characterized by singular leadership. With a strong party and a military leader like Chiang Kai-shek as president, the concentration of all executive power in the hands of one person often tended to turn the presidency into a dictatorial power that was utterly incompatible with power sharing.

The *cabinet form* of the Nationalist government (1925–1928 and 1931–1936) was structured to favor power sharing among a group of KMT power elites. In contrast to the presidential system, the nominal executive—the president of the Nationalist government—assumed no political responsibility and was only a titular head in the cabinet system. He was chosen by and from the National Government Council according to the Organic Law. The president of the Executive Yuan was a true executive—just like the English prime minister, the French premier, or the German chancellor. But instead of being chosen by the parliament and of necessity commanding the support of the majority of the legislature, as is the case with prime ministers in a democratic cabinet system, he was selected by the KMT's Central Executive Committee and bore no legal and immediate responsibility to the Legislative Yuan. As the prime minister was not necessarily the head of the KMT and did not hold the concurrent post of commander-in-chief of the military, he was checked by both the KMT authorities and the military. The tenure of his office depended largely on his relationship with the KMT. As long as they worked in harmony, he continued in office. If the KMT's Central Executive Committee should oppose him, the best course for him was to resign.[51] Furthermore, in the cabinet form of government, the National Government Council was organized as an organ of collective leadership. It consisted of the presidents and vice-presidents of the five *yuan,* all appointed by the CEC of the KMT. Although the president of the Executive Yuan was the chief executive of the government, he and the heads of the other four *yuan* were collectively selected by, and hence accountable to, the KMT authorities. Moreover, the president of the Executive Yuan was assisted by a vice-president who was similarly chosen. They and the ministers formed a sort of cabinet, though neither the Organic Law nor the constitution made provision for such an organization but merely for conferences of the Executive Yuan composed of the president, vice-presidents, and the heads of ministries and commissions. According to the Organic Law, any controversy between the heads of the five *yuan* was to be settled by the National Government Council. Since the president of the national government became a figurehead of state and could no longer dominate the council in a cabinet form of government and since the councillors were collectively appointed by the KMT, the council enforced its decisions on each of the councillors.

In the sense that the Executive Yuan was only one of five *yuan* and each *yuan* exercised its independent power, the heads of *yuan* were obliged to share power. This was the most important institutional feature of the cabinet form of the Nationalist government distinguishing it from the presidential form.

Alternative Designs of the Nationalist Government

Having defined the cabinet and presidential forms of the Nationalist government, we can now explore how these two forms alternated during the formative period of the KMT regime. Four alternative designs of the presidential and cabinet forms can be identified by studying the different versions of the Organic Law of the Nationalist government during the period 1925–1932 and several draft constitutions made public by the Nationalist regime between 1932 and 1937. Table 2 summarizes the four alternative designs.

The Cabinet Form (1925–1928)

When the Nationalist government was first established in Guangzhou in 1925 after Sun Yat-sen's death, it was designed to be a cabinet form of government in which the president was a figurehead and members of the National Government Council shared the ultimate authority. According to the first Organic Law of July 1, 1925, the president was a presiding officer elected by and from the members of the National Government Council.[52] This can be seen from the statement that:

> The national government is composed of several state councillors and one president who is chosen *by and from* the councillors; and the national government shall have five standing councillors who are chosen *by and from* the councillors.[53]

In light of the Organic Law, the president was merely an agent of the council and not a chief executive of government. The council's power was concentrated in the standing committee of the council rather than in the president. All laws and orders issued by the national government had to be cosigned by the members of the standing committee.[54]

TABLE 2
Alternative Designs of Presidential and Cabinet Forms of Government

Institutions Designed in Organic Law and Constitution				
ALTERNATION	SELECTION OF PRESIDENT	LOCATION OF EXECUTIVE POWER	APPOINTMENT OF HEADS OF FIVE *YUAN*	STATUS OF PRESIDENT
Cabinet system (1925–1928)	From and by National Government Council.	National Government Council issued executive orders.	n/a	Figurehead of state.
Presidential system (1928–1931)	By CEC of the KMT.	President issued executive orders.	By president.	Head of both state and government; concurrently held top posts of KMT and army.
Cabinet system (1931–1936)	By CEC of the KMT.	Executive Yuan issued executive orders.	By CEC of the KMT.	Figurehead of state; no political responsibility.
Presidential system (1936–)	By National Assembly (which did not convene until 1948).	President issued executive orders.	By president.	Head of both state and government; concurrently held top posts of KMT and army.

The president was not granted the authority to command the armed forces.

Wang Jingwei was the first president of the Nationalist government established in Guangzhou in 1925. The National Government Council was composed of sixteen state councillors and five standing councillors. Wang Jingwei, Xu Chongzhi, Hu Hanmin, Tan Yankai, and Lin Shen were members of the standing committee. Sun Ke was a councillor. Chiang Kai-shek was not yet able to enter the council. After the open split between Wang Jingwei and Chiang Kai-shek, the revised Organic Law adopted by Wang's Wuhan government on

March 30, 1927, while retaining the mechanism of the standing committee, even dispensed with the president. It stated:

> The national government is composed of several councillors who are chosen by the CEC of the KMT. There should be five standing councillors appointed by the CEC.[55]

This president-less cabinet system continued until the revised Organic Law of February 11, 1928, reverted to the earlier system of having both the president and the standing committee.[56] There could be no question, however, that under all these laws the presidency, whenever that office existed, was not a one-person executive and the government was characterized by a collective leadership.

The Presidential Form (1928–1931)

When the five-power system was first set up in 1928, a presidential system was gradually introduced. At first the Organic Law, approved by the Fourth Plenary Session of the Second CEC on February 4 and promulgated on February 11, 1928, was ambiguous about the form of government. It provided that the members of the National Government Council should exercise the powers of the government in the council of state. It stated that:

> The national government should conduct national affairs through the state council [*guowu huiyi;* literally, "the state meeting"].[57]

This wording suggests that the president was still only a presiding member of the council. But the Organic Law dropped an old provision contained in the first version, written in 1925, stipulating that "the president should be selected by and from the members of the council." The Organic Law only stated that:

> The national government is composed of several state councillors who are selected by the KMT Central Executive Committee. There shall be five standing councillors who are chosen from the councillors and a president who is chosen from the standing councillors.[58]

The Organic Law of October 3, 1928, contained conflicting provisions regarding the command of the armed forces. In one provision it said that the national government commanded the armed forces:

> The national government shall have supreme command of the land, naval, and air forces.[59]

In another provision it appointed the president as commander-in-chief of the armed forces by stating:

> The president of the national government shall concurrently be the commander-in-chief of the land, naval, and air forces of the Republic of China.[60]

When Chiang Kai-shek became president immediately after the promulgation of the Organic Law, he assumed the command personally. While the Organic Law of October 1928 conferred the power of issuing executive orders to the president, it required a countersignature of the heads of the five *yuan*.[61] After Chiang Kai-shek assumed the presidency, the revised Organic Law of November 17, 1930, dropped the countersignature by the heads of the five *yuan*. Henceforth all laws and mandates were to be issued upon the signature of the president of the national government.[62]

On May 12, 1931, Chiang Kai-shek promulgated a provisional constitution in which the presidential system was further confirmed by empowering the president to appoint and dismiss the presidents of the five *yuan* and the heads of ministries. Article 74 of the provisional constitution stated:

> The presidents of the five *yuan* and the heads of the ministries and commissions shall be appointed or dismissed in accordance with law by the national government at the instance of the president of the national government.[63]

From this description, then, it is apparent that beginning with the revised Organic Law of October 3, 1928, the presidential system gradually replaced the cabinet system established in 1925.

The Cabinet Form (1931–1936)

About six months after the promulgation of the provisional constitution, a revised Organic Law was passed by the KMT's Central Executive Committee on December 30, 1931. It put forward several articles obviously contradictory to the provisional constitution. Executive power was vested almost exclusively in the hands of a lower organ, the Executive Yuan, by stating that: "The Executive Yuan shall be the highest organ of the national government."[64] The Organic Law stipulated that the president of the national government was only a figurehead and did not have real executive or political responsibility. He was forbidden to hold any concurrent post. This is evident in the following assertion:

> The president of the national government shall be the head of the Republic of China and shall represent the national government both internally and externally, but he shall *not have actual political responsibility*. . . . The president of the national government *shall not hold any government post concurrently*.[65]

Moreover, orders and mandates were signed by the president, "but they do not become effective until they are finally countersigned by the presidents of the *yuan* and the ministers concerned."[66] The heads of the Executive Yuan and other four *yuan* were no longer appointed and removed by the president. The president and the heads of the five *yuan* were selected and appointed by the Central Executive Committee of the KMT and were held collectively accountable to the KMT's central authority. The revised Organic Law provided that:

> The national government shall have a president and from twenty-four to thirty-six state councillors and each *yuan* shall have a president and vice-president, who shall be selected and appointed by the CEC of the KMT. . . . Pending the promulgation of a permanent constitution, the Executive Yuan, the Legislative Yuan, the Judicial Yuan, the Examination Yuan, and the Control Yuan shall be collectively responsible to the Central Executive Committee of the KMT of China.[67]

By distributing the collective leadership among the heads of the five branches of government, the revised Organic Law of 1931 clearly replaced the presidential form with the cabinet form of government.

The Presidential Form (1936–)

The cabinet form of government was maintained until 1936 when the draft constitution of the Republic of China was promulgated. The 1936 constitution "provided for a strong presidency," although "not for a dictatorship."[68] One draft published in October 16, 1934, already stated that "the president shall exercise the supreme executive power."[69] The final draft promulgated in May 5, 1936, restored the power of the president to appoint and dismiss the president of the Executive Yuan:

> In the Executive Yuan there shall be a president, a vice-president, and a number of executive members to be *appointed and removed* by the president.[70]

The heads of the Control Yuan and the Examination Yuan were appointed and removed by the president as well.

Furthermore, the constitution of May 5, 1936, provided that "the president should command the land, sea, and air forces of the whole country."[71] In other words, the president held the concurrent post of commander-in-chief of the armed forces. The president also exercised the power of promulgating laws and issuing mandates.[72] He was even conferred the power to issue emergency orders "in event of national emergency or great national economic crisis which calls for urgent measures."[73] The declaration of an emergency should be made by the Executive Council—a body comprising the head of the Executive Yuan and the government ministers. Since all members of this Executive Council would be appointed and removed by the president, "such a limitation on the presidential powers would have been little more than a formality."[74] The only constraint on the extraordinary presidential power was a provision that to remain in effect, all presidential decrees required the ratification of the Legislative Yuan within three months of being issued. Because of the subsequent outbreak of the Sino-Japanese War, however, which called "for a greater concentration of executive power," this important constraint never became effective.[75] After the outbreak of the war, Chiang Kai-shek established his one-person executive by creating the Supreme National Defense Council and exercising wartime military rule.

Chapter 3

Power Resources and Authority Relationships

In the preceding chapter we saw how the various versions of the Organic Law and the constitution distinguished the institutional arrangements of the presidential system from the cabinet system and help to explain their alternating predominance during the formative period of the Nationalist government. Such volte-faces took place to a great extent because of political maneuvering among the KMT leaders contending for power. Each of these leaders had his own preferred form of government institution—a preference determined by his relative power position. But how can we determine the relative power positions of different political leaders? The political science literature views power as a relationship between political players and compares power positions based on each player's resources. Thus it is possible to list the resources and attributes that permit some to possess greater power than others. Robert Dahl lists such tangibles as money, information, time, political allies, official position, and control over jobs and such intangibles as personality and leadership qualities.[1]

The Three Power Resources

Robert Dahl's distinction between tangibles and intangibles is an important dimension of power resources, but more significant to our understanding of power politics is the relevance of the resources to the political environment of the regime.[2] In a democratic setting, for example, official positions, voter support, and perhaps money are more effective than personality, political allies, and military connection in the exercise of power; in an authoritarian setting, the opposite is true because of the relevance of these power resources to the different political systems. From this perspective, the three power resources most relevant to the political environment of the Nationalist regime may be identified as follows.

Formal Positions in the Top Organs of the KMT Pyramid. The Nationalist regime was hierarchically structured so that the KMT held supreme authority. The outcome of a power struggle among the KMT leaders was formally determined within the party's decision-making organs. Political leaders holding top positions in the party's formal hierarchy certainly possessed one of the most significant power resources. Powerful political leaders usually occupied positions at the apex of the party hierarchy, namely, the leading posts in the top decision-making organs of the KMT: the Standing Committee of the Central Executive Committee and the Standing Committee of the Central Political Council. Decisions on key political issues and policies, including the design of government institutions, were formally made in these organs. Seniority or proximity to the founding father of the KMT, Sun Yat-sen, were certainly intangible power resources. These qualities were usually reflected in the formal hierarchical positions of the party organization.

Support of Factional Groups. Factional competition was a common practice in the Nationalist regime. After the death of Sun Yat-sen in 1925, several strong personalities in the KMT competed for the role of being Sun's successor and leader of the party. The factions in the KMT regime were "an odd assortment of temporary allies held together by a series of dyadic ties."[3] The factional relationship in KMT politics was what Andrew Nathan has called a "clientist tie."[4] Its interest lay mainly in acquiring and holding onto power, rather than in establishing and maintaining an ideological position, although ideological rhetoric persisted.[5] Two types of faction provided powerful clientele support for competing political actors. The first type formed around certain functional organs of the KMT, such as the Organization Department and the Propaganda Department; the second type formed outside the formal KMT structure, such as the Blue Shirt Society, the Reorganizationalist Comrades Association, and the Western Hill Group. Whether or not a leader was supported by these factions to a great extent determined his relative power position in the Nationalist regime.

Military Capacity. Military forces were powerful resources in the possession of competing political actors in Nationalist China. Some political leaders of the KMT themselves were the commanders of military forces, and other civilian leaders were backed by one or more regional militarists. As military forces participated in the political process, the capacity to command armed forces or align with powerful regional militarists became a crucial power resource in the Nationalist regime.

A Hybrid Pattern of Authority

To elaborate on these three power resources, we must examine the pattern of authority relationships in the Nationalist regime, since power is always exercised in the context of certain relationships. Two different patterns of authority relationship existed in the Nationalist regime during the period 1925–1937. One was a hierarchical relationship; the other was anarchic. Political actors stood "in relations of super- and sub-ordination" with respect to the hierarchical pattern.[6] In the anarchic pattern, political actors related to each other in a way characterized by the absence of mutually recognized central authority.[7] According to Kenneth N. Waltz,[8] a political scientist studying international systems, the "ordering principles" of the two patterns of authority relationship were different.[9]

When hierarchy was the ordering principle, the authority relationship could be very simple, since political actors merely competed for the top position of the mutually recognized power center. Once the ranks were settled, the relative power positions of political leaders were ordered. This hierarchical authority pattern existed so long as the KMT monopolized the supreme authority of the Nationalist regime and the KMT was structured hierarchically. In this case, whoever occupied the top position of the KMT would be the most powerful leader in the regime. But when anarchy was the ordering principle, the authority relationship could be so vague and organizational sanctions so tenuous that conflicts between competing political actors could "not be reliably resolved through recourse to some set of recognized superiors" or through an institutional mechanism.[10] Often the power positions of political actors were ordered by the ad hoc outcome of negotiations or even violent battles if necessary. In this political environment, the leader who commanded military forces or possessed other effective negotiating resources (say, the support of strong faction) was in a powerful position.

The pattern of authority relationship in the Nationalist regime during the period 1925–1937 was neither entirely hierarchical nor entirely anarchic. A hybrid pattern of authority relationship, combining both hierarchical and anarchic principles, prevailed. In the one-party state, the KMT monopolized the legitimacy of the political system, the recruitment of political leadership, and interest aggregation and policymaking.[11] It was a hierarchical environment in which political actors fought for power by occupying the formal positions in the party structure.[12] The final decisions on the key political issues were made formally within the KMT hierarchy. The anarchic dimension of the authority relationship, nevertheless, was manifested in the fact that competition among equally powerful KMT leaders often ended in a deadlock that in turn resulted in the diffusion of party authority into competing centers around a few strong personalities. In a polity with fragmented authority, the conflict among competing clusters could not be resolved by appealing to a recognized supreme authority or even through an institutional mechanism. The competing leaders in this situation had to rely on the support of their faction and often the military forces under their command as the court of last resort. The following sections elaborate the three power resources in the context of this hybrid authority relationship.

The KMT and Its Hierarchy

A formal position at the top of the KMT hierarchy was one of the three key power resources. To understand the importance of the formal positions, it is first necessary to discuss the nature of the KMT and its monopoly of power in Nationalist China.

The KMT was born as the Xingzhonghui (Revive China Society) in 1894 and was renamed the Tongmenghui (Common Alliance Society) in 1905. It was named the Kuomintang (Nationalist Party) after the 1911 revolution that overthrew the Qing dynasty and founded the Republic of China. The KMT had a hybrid nature combining a Western democratic party and a Leninist-style revolutionary movement in its early phase. Influenced by Western democracies, it had a genuine democratic inclination. The party was dedicated to two basic political principles: nationalism and republicanism.[13] Yet, born and organized as a revolutionary movement, the KMT and its leaders were also committed to a one-party dictatorship.

In the early years after the 1911 revolution, the KMT wholeheartedly espoused Western-style parliamentarianism, strongly supported immediate constitutional government, and willingly competed in the political arena with other parties.[14] Nevertheless, Chinese parliamentarianism was crippled by corruption, military intervention, and chaotic factionalism within and among all political groups after the founding of the Republic of China in 1912.[15] Constitutionalism became a mockery. Without military strength or a mass political base, the KMT lay at the mercy of men like Yuan Shikai, the warlord in North China who forced Sun Yat-sen to resign as president of the new Republic of China and took over the presidency himself. The KMT, led by Sun Yat-sen, sought to check Yuan's personal ambition by means of a parliamentary majority and a responsible cabinet. The KMT controlled the majority in both houses of parliament in the election of the winter of 1912–1913. Although the parliamentary leader of the KMT, Song Jiaoren, was prepared to head a KMT cabinet, he was assassinated by Yuan at the railway station in Shanghai on March 10, 1913. To ensure his personal power, Yuan Shikai even declared he would dissolve the KMT and unseat its members in parliament on November 4, 1913.[16]

It was in this historical context that Sun Yat-sen conducted a thorough reorganization of the KMT in 1924,[17] a reorganization that owed its beginning to the spreading influence of the Soviet revolution and the rise of the Communist Party in China. Since its inception in 1894 the revolutionary movement led by Sun Yat-sen had always sought foreign assistance. In 1921, for example, Sun appealed to the president of the United States to help China by recognizing his Guangzhou government. The United States and other Western countries turned a deaf ear to Sun's requests.[18] Thus when Russia extended the hand of friendship to Sun Yat-sen and the KMT, Sun welcomed Russian aid to reorganize the party and reconstruct China. The first Soviet advisor, in the person of Michael Borodin, arrived in Guangzhou in August 1923. By October he had convinced Sun and the KMT leaders that "party reforms must be undertaken immediately."[19]

With the help of representatives from the Soviet Union, Sun held the First National Congress of the KMT at Guangdong in January 1924. With members of the Chinese Communist Party participating, the congress enacted a party statute, set up an organization, both central and local, and issued a manifesto that looked forward to close cooperation with the Soviet Union.[20]

While the reorganization marked the emergence of the KMT as a much more effective force, it was influenced strongly by Communist organizational skills and the Leninist line of a revolutionary party. The two emphases of the reorganization were party discipline and the role of the military. The KMT was now closely modeled after the Russian Communist Party with its hierarchical structure. The Huangpu (Whampoa) Military Academy, set up in May 1924, was modeled on the academy for Red Army officers in the Soviet Union. The party's commissar in the Huangpu Academy was to have sole charge of the political training of cadres and was to oversee general administration with the president of the academy. Chiang Kai-shek, who had been in Moscow in the summer of 1923 to study the organization of the Red Army, was appointed president of the academy; Liao Zhongkai, another man who had intimate dealings with the Communists, was the party commissar. When Liao Zhongkai was assassinated in August 1925, Chiang Kai-shek became the supreme authority in the academy in his capacity as president.

Thus when the KMT established its dominion over China through military force in 1927, its hybrid nature was seriously skewed toward a one-party dictatorship. In April 1927, the Nationalist regime led by Chiang Kai-shek in Nanjing abandoned party competition and declared the Communist Party illegal. Then came a severe purge of the Communists from the ranks of the Nanjing regime, resulting in widespread persecution and murder of Communist Party members in the lower Yangtze valley.[21] A few months later, in August 1927, the Nationalist government in Wuhan conducted a severe purge of the Communists from its own ranks.[22]

Following the suppression of the Communists, the KMT regime in 1928 formally declared the beginning of the political tutelage period described in Sun Yat-sen's *Fundamentals of National Reconstruction*. Political tutelage meant one-party dictatorship and gave the KMT a monopoly position. The principal aim of political tutelage, according to Sun Yat-sen, was to enable the KMT "to instruct the people in the pursuit of constructive work of a revolutionary nature."[23] This principle was interpreted by the *Xunzheng Yuefa* (Essentials of Political Tutelage), adopted by the Standing Committee of the KMT's Central Executive Committee on October 3, 1928, to mean that the KMT should possess supreme authority in the regime during the period of political tutelage.[24] The chief point of the "Essentials" was to proclaim that the KMT, through its congress or the Central Executive Committee or the Central Political Council, on behalf of the People's National Assembly, was to exercise the sovereign power of the nation during the period of tutelage. Article 1 of the "Essentials" stated:

> The Republic of China shall, during the period of political tutelage, have the KMT's National Congress to guide the people, on behalf of the People's National Assembly, in the exercise of their political power.[25]

Article 2 said:

> The KMT National Congress shall, at the close of its session, delegate the power to its Central Executive Committee.[26]

Article 5 asserted:

> The guidance and supervision of the national government in carrying out important state affairs shall be entrusted to the Central Political Council and the Central Executive Committee of the KMT.[27]

The beginning of the political tutelage period marked the establishment of the one-party system in China. Political tutelage meant that the KMT exercised the sovereignty of the nation and that its major rival, the Communist Party, had to be suppressed by the Nationalist government. Because the one-party system gave the KMT monopoly power in the Nationalist regime, KMT leadership positions conferred legitimacy on political leaders and became an important power resource in Nationalist China.

The hierarchical structure of the KMT organization made the formal positions at the top important. During the period of this study, the KMT was organized hierarchically with four tiers of authority. At the apex of the pyramid were the central organizations: the Party National Congress, the Central Executive Committee, the Central Supervisory Committee, and the Central Political Council. Below these were the provincial organizations, the county organizations, and the district organizations. Each level of the organization also maintained an executive committee. At the lowest level of the hierarchy, the KMT, like other revolutionary parties, was composed of formal members.

The organization of the KMT was formally laid down in its statute. The first statute was adopted at the First National Congress in 1924, which reorganized the KMT under the heavy influence of Russian Communist organizational skills. Minor changes of the statute were made at the Second National Congress in 1926 and the Third National Congress in 1929. No amendments were adopted by the Fourth and the Fifth National Congresses in 1931 and 1935 respectively. Thus during the period of political tutelage, the prevailing party statute was the one passed at the Third National Congress in 1929.

According to the party statute of 1929, the highest organ of the KMT was the National Congress, which met every two years.[28] When it was not in session, the highest authority of the party was vested in the Central Executive Committee and the Central Supervisory Committee (CSC). The CSC was an agency the KMT had adapted from two sources: the Bolshevik pattern of an independent intraparty control system and a native *jian-cha* (supervising) power. Similar in function to the Party Control Commission employed by the Communist Party in the Soviet Union and later in Communist China, the CSC was in charge of an inspection system. Because of the relative laxity of the KMT organization, the work of this committee was far less important than that of the CEC, which was a formal policymaking arena.

The position of *zongli* (director general) of the party was designed for Sun Yat-sen, the charismatic leader of the KMT, at the First Party Congress of 1924.[29] When Sun Yat-sen was alive, the supreme authority of the KMT was in fact vested in the hands of the *zongli* personally. According to the statute adopted in 1924, both the party congress and the CEC were to be called into session by the *zongli*, who presided over both meetings.[30] A Chinese scholar observes that "as the Leader of the Party and concurrently Chairman of the two committees (CEC and CSC), [Sun Yat-sen] even had the power to veto the decisions of the National Congress."[31]

After Sun Yat-sen's death, the Second Party Congress in 1926 decided to retain in the party statute the provision concerning the office of *zongli* with the declaration that, to do him honor and reverence, Sun Yat-sen, the "Founder of the KMT," would always remain *zongli* of the party. Thus the CEC and its standing committee became the highest organ of party authority when the party congress was adjourned.[32] The party statute required that the CEC meet at least every six months.[33] These sessions, the plenary sessions of the CEC, were supposed to be the most crucial decision-making loci of the KMT. Thus important decisions about leadership selection, institutional design, and policy choice would be formally decided in the CEC.

Under the CEC, according to the party statute, there was a Central Political Council *(zhongyang zhengzhi huiyi)* that had the power of formulating important policies to be executed by the Nationalist government. The CPC was a party body designed to link the CEC of the party with the Nationalist government. The Political Council had its origins in the Political Committee *(zhengzhi weiyuanhui)* established in 1924 as a personal advisory body to Sun Yat-sen and consisting mainly of the members of the CEC and the CSC. Chiang Kai-shek was among the first twelve members of the Political Committee appointed by the *zongli* (Sun Yat-sen) and one of only three who did not at that time hold a position in the CEC or the CSC.[34] The CPC became a party organ only after the death of Sun Yat-sen. It was done by a resolution, passed by the CEC in June 1925, which stated:

> The Political Council is to be established in the party's Central Executive Committee to guide the progress of national revolution; political goals will be determined and executed by the Political Council in the name of the party-state.[35]

In July 1926, the CEC passed another resolution officially establishing the Political Council as the formal party organ.[36] In January 1926, nine members of the CPC were selected by the CEC from among the members of the CEC and the CSC. In April 1927, the CPC was expanded to thirty-four members, including all members of the CEC's standing committee and others selected by the CEC from among the CEC and the CSC.[37] The standing committee formed the core of the CPC. In 1927, the committee was composed of only three top leaders in the KMT: Chiang Kai-shek, Hu Hanmin, and Wang Jingwei. They were selected from and by the CPC members according to the statute. The CPC was the most powerful organ of the KMT. According to the "Provisional Regulation of the Central Political

Council," passed by the CEC on April 15, 1929, the CPC virtually directed the national government and formulated all the important national policies, foreign and domestic, to be executed by the national government. All central government officials were appointed by the CPC and could be dismissed by the CPC.[38]

Based on the hierarchical relations of the KMT organization described here, membership in the CEC and the CPC was obviously the most important formal position in the KMT regime. The political leader who formally held a post in the CEC and CPC, especially in their standing committees, therefore possessed a key resource of power in Nationalist China.

Authority Relationships under Anarchy

If the hierarchy were the only ordering principle of authority relationship in the Nationalist regime, one would simply need to look at the formal posts of KMT leaders to compare their relative power positions: the political actor at the apex of the KMT hierarchy would hold the most powerful position in the regime. But the authority relationship in the Nationalist regime was not characterized merely by the hierarchy. There was an anarchic pattern as well. Thus while the formal positions within the KMT hierarchy were one crucial power resource, the other two resources—relations with factional groups and the capacity to command military forces—were significant also.

The anarchic pattern of authority relationship emerged whenever a stalemate among factional leaders of the KMT resulted in the diffusion of the party's authority into competing centers around several strong leaders. These factional leaders did not stand in a relationship of superior and subordinate. Each claimed to hold the central leadership and did not recognize the others' positions. As there was no mutually recognized central authority in this situation, the conflicts among them could not be resolved by appealing to a recognized central authority or through a centralized institutional mechanism. To claim the leadership each leader had to rely on the strength of his factions and, very often, on his military capacity.

The anarchic situation that resulted from the diffusion of the KMT's central authority arose at least twice during the period 1925–1937. The first occasion was in 1927, two years after the death of Sun Yat-sen, when the succession struggle between Chiang Kai-shek,

Wang Jingwei, and Hu Hanmin resulted in the emergence of two Nationalist governments and three KMT Central Executive Committees. Wang Jingwei led one Nationalist government and held one CEC in Wuhan; Chiang Kai-shek established a rival Nationalist government and rival CEC in Nanjing; the extreme right-wing Western Hill faction had another CEC in Shanghai.[39] The second occasion arose in 1930. The deadlock among Chiang Kai-shek, Wang Jingwei, and Sun Ke produced no fewer than three Fourth National Congresses of the KMT, held separately at different locations. Chiang Kai-shek convened the Fourth National Congress in Nanjing on November 12–13, 1930; Sun Ke held one in Guangzhou on November 18 to December 5, 1930; and Wang Jingwei held one in Shanghai on December 7, 1930.[40] Each leader claimed the legitimacy of his congress as well as control of the KMT's central authority.

This kind of power diffusion took place in response to two peculiar features of the KMT's central authority. One was the lack of institutionalization; the other was the uncompromising factional conflict. In the first case, while the KMT was organized hierarchically, its central authority was never institutionalized. The party's central organs never operated as required by the party statute. Prior to 1925, the KMT was dominated by one person, Sun Yat-sen, who "ruled the party, at least what remained of it, almost single-handedly. The party became merely an institution for Sun's personal power and a grouping of his personal followers."[41] After the death of Sun Yat-sen, the function of the KMT's central authority was still characterized by the lack of institutionalization, which manifested itself in three dimensions. First, according to the KMT statute the National Congress was the highest decision-making body of the party. Nonetheless, it was never regularly convened. Indeed, only four congresses were held between 1925 and 1937 (Table 3)—one every three years instead of one every year as required by the party statute of 1924 and one every two years as required by the party statute of 1929. Moreover, the National Congress became too big to make decisions effectively. The First Congress in 1924 was attended by 165 delegates; in the following three congresses the membership increased to more than 600.[42]

Second, the Central Executive Committee plenary sessions were not always held regularly—one session every six months as required by the party statute. The First and Second CECs convened frequent and regular plenary sessions. But thereafter the CECs held sessions

TABLE 3
KMT National Congresses and Plenary Sessions of the CEC: 1924–1937

Congress and Session	Date	Place
First Congress	Jan. 20–30, 1924	Guangzhou
First Session	Jan. 21–Feb. 6, 1924	Guangzhou
Second Session	Aug. 15, 1924	Guangzhou
Third Session	May 18–25, 1925	Guangzhou
Second Congress	Jan. 4–19, 1926	Guangzhou
First Session	Jan. 24–25, 1926	Guangzhou
Second Session	May 15–22, 1926	Guangzhou
Extraordinary Session	July 2–7, 1926	Guangzhou
Third Session	Mar. 10–17, 1927	Wuhan
Fourth Session	Feb. 3–7, 1928	Nanjing
Fifth Session	Aug. 7–15, 1928	Nanjing
Third Congress	Mar. 18–27, 1929	Nanjing
First Session	Mar. 28–Apr. 4, 1929	Nanjing
Second Session	June 10–18, 1929	Nanjing
Third Session	Mar. 1–6, 1930	Nanjing
Fourth Session	Nov. 13–18, 1930	Nanjing
First Extraordinary Session	May 1–2, 1931	Nanjing
Fifth Session	June 13–14, 1931	Nanjing
Second Extraordinary Session	Nov. 9–11, 1931	Nanjing
Fourth Congress	Nov. 12–23, 1931	Nanjing
First Session	Nov. 22–29, 1931	Nanjing
Second Session	Mar. 1–6, 1932	
Third Session	Dec. 15–22, 1932	Nanjing
Fourth Session	Jan. 20–25, 1934	Nanjing
Fifth Session	Dec. 10–14, 1934	Nanjing
Sixth Session	Nov. 1–6, 1935	Nanjing
Fifth Congress	Nov. 12–22, 1935	Nanjing
First Session	Dec. 2–7, 1935	Nanjing
Second Session	July 10–14, 1936	Nanjing
Third Session	May 15–22, 1937	Nanjing

Source: *Zhonghua Minguo Zhengzhi Fazhan shi* (History of the political development of the Republic of China) (Taipei: Jingdai Zhongguo Chuban She, 1985), vol. 2.

less and less regularly. For example, the Third CEC held five irregularly scheduled plenary sessions and two extraordinary sessions during the three years between 1929 and 1931. The Fourth CEC held six sessions in the four-year period between 1931 and 1935. The Fifth CEC held only three sessions during the three years between 1935 and 1937. (For a list of CEC sessions see Table 3.) Moreover, when the CEC did convene to discuss various issues and pass resolutions, it often discussed only trivial matters rather than crucial political decisions. According to the minutes of the Fourth Session of the Third CEC in November 1930, the agenda included such items as debates on where the foreign embassies in Nanjing should be located, how much teachers should be paid, how to arbitrate the dispute between employees and employers in factories, and how to design the colors of the passport to differentiate ordinary citizens and ranking officials.[43]

Third, the effective functioning of the CPC and its standing committee was undercut as a result of fast-growing membership. The CPC was originally designed to be composed of only a small group of top KMT leaders. Nevertheless, its membership was expanded dramatically in order to bring in more factional leaders after it was formally established. In March 1927, the CPC was composed of only fifteen members: nine CEC standing committee members and six others selected by the CEC. It was increased to thirty-four in April 1927 and to more than one hundred in 1929. The Fourth Party Congress of November 1930 attempted to cut the CPC's size in order to improve its efficiency. But by the end of the congress, the CPC's membership had instead grown to 172, including all regular and alternate members of the CEC and the CSC.[44] Moreover, the standing committee of the CPC, originally composed of only three top leaders, Chiang Kaishek, Wang Jingwei, and Hu Hanmin, was also expanded. In the Third Plenum of the Fourth CEC in 1932, it was expanded to include all nine members of the CEC standing committee, who were leading figures of the party-state representing various factions.[45] As more and more factional leaders attended the CEC and CPC, factional bargaining and compromise became more and more difficult and these organs had more and more trouble performing their normal function. As a result, the standing committee of the CPC, even with such a small membership, rarely met to discuss major issues of party and state in the mid-1930s.[46]

The lack of institutionalization handicapped the formal authority of the KMT and encouraged factional bargaining. Indeed, it became common practice that if a decision on a major issue (such as leadership selection) could not be made within the formal organs of the party, each political leader, supported by strong factional groups, would act upon his own will and claim leadership based on the consent of his followers. As a result, several centers of authority appeared simultaneously. Yet factionalism itself need not result in the anarchic authority relationship that emerged in the Nationalist regime. Factionalism has appeared in many societies where a central authority is maintained. Traditional societies provide fertile ground for factional conflicts; so too do certain modern political systems. Factionalism is not a special product of any particular culture or society. As a structure of conflict, factional politics is commonly recorded in African and Indian tribes, in Thai bureaucracy, in China's early Republican government and the Communist regime, in other Soviet-type Communist regimes, in early American politics, and in contemporary Japanese political parties.[47] The diffusion of authority into an anarchic relationship occurs only when factional bargaining is conducted under a consensus rule and when the factional leaders hold out instead of compromising on the issues.

Andrew Nathan's factional model, derived from the study of Chinese Communist politics, finds that political decisions usually "were made by consensus among the factions."[48] In the case of the Nationalist regime, decision making at both the CEC and the CPC was similarly based on consensus instead of the formal voting procedure. The KMT statutes did not have an article to regulate decision-making procedure for the Party Congress or any other decision-making apparatus. The party statutes required the CEC to meet twice a year and to cast votes for decisions. But neither the party statutes nor the organizational regulations of the CEC specified the voting procedures for decision making. Reading the minutes of CEC meetings, one finds that almost all bills were passed unanimously and opposition votes were rarely recorded—a typical manifestation consensus decision making.

Nevertheless, the consensus rule did not mean that consensus could be easily reached. Attaining consensus on routine policy decisions might not be difficult, but it could be a protracted process. And arriving at a consensus on decisions like the succession issues was extremely difficult to achieve. The constant dispute and discord among KMT leaders are a testament to the lack of consensus in the KMT regime. From this perspective, it is evident that the minutes of CEC sessions recorded only decisions that reached consensus and deliberately omitted difficult disputes that failed to achieve consensus.[49] It was the lack of consensus that led to the formation and reformation of political alliances among competing leaders to engage in political maneuvers to beat their opponents. The competing factional leaders of the KMT were hardly able to agree upon who among them should be leader of the party and the state. It was stalemate—in other words, lack of consensus—on this kind of issue that resulted in the diffusion of the KMT's authority into competing centers. The authority relationship in this case was characterized by anarchy: factional support and military capacity, instead of formal positions in the party organs, became crucial power resources.

The Support of Factions

Under the anarchic authority relationship, conflicts among factional leaders could not be resolved through a recognized central authority or an institutional mechanism. In this case, the support of factional groups became extremely important for political contenders who wished to claim leadership in the power struggle of Nationalist China.

Generally speaking, two types of faction provided the most powerful support for competing political leaders. The first type formed around the KMT's functional organs. One example of this type, formed around the party's Central Organization Department, was called the CC Clique or the Organization Group.[50] This was a powerful faction that provided one political leader, Chiang Kai-shek, with strong support in his political career. When the KMT was reorganized in 1924 after the Russian Communist Party, the Organization Department played a dominant role in the appointment and control of party and government personnel.[51] Not only was the Organization Department in charge of the organization of the party branches and the management of party cadres, but it also picked the delegates to the party congress and nominated party candidates to posts in party and government institutions. Ever since the days of the split with the Communists in 1927, Chiang Kai-shek and a single group of his people had been in more or less full control of the Organization Department. Attempts to dislodge them had no success. Other than controlling party organization and personnel appointments, the Organization Group's pivotal position in the KMT was further strengthened by its affiliation with the party's secret service, innocuously called the Bureau of Investigation and Statistics, which kept an eye on the thoughts and activities of people outside as well as inside the party.

The Organization Group thus could influence decision making within the CEC or CPC not only by controlling official appointments but also by physically eliminating Chiang Kai-shek's opponents through assassination.[52] This is why Chien Tuan-sheng, in his classic work on the Nationalist government, asserts that "whoever controls the Organization Department controls the Party and the Nationalist Government."[53] The support of the Organization Group gave Chiang Kai-shek a great advantage in competing with his rivals in the Nationalist regime. By factionally controlling the Organization Department of the party, the two crucial functions of the department—personnel power and internal investigation power—became the personal power of Chiang Kai-shek.

The second type of faction that provided powerful support for competing political leaders was formed outside the KMT's formal organization—for example, the Blue Shirt Society, the Western Hill group, and the Reorganizationalists. These factional groups will be analyzed in the next chapter.

Military Capacity

The third power resource was the capacity to command military forces. When the anarchic pattern of authority relationship emerged, military forces could be utilized by politicians as the last resort in their power contest. Indeed, the stalemate among factional leaders often had to be settled by armed conflict on the battlefield.

In Nationalist China, some political leaders of the KMT were themselves commanders of military forces, and other civilian leaders were usually backed by one or more regional militarists. The top military positions that political leaders could assume were chairman of the Military Commission of the Nationalist government and commander-in-chief of the Nationalist army. A politician holding these positions was not only in charge of the nation's military affairs but also had a final say about political decisions in the regime.

The Military Commission was first established in July 1925, a few days after the establishment of the Nationalist government in Guangzhou. It was put directly under the KMT's authority and entrusted with the administration and command of all the armed forces and military organizations.[54] When the Northern Expedition began, the Military Commission was reorganized and put under the government.[55] The beginning of the Northern Expedition also saw the creation, on July 7, 1926, of the post of commander-in-chief of the Nationalist Revolutionary Army, outside the Military Commission. Chiang Kai-shek was appointed to this post and authorized to act concurrently as chairman of the Military Commission. Two years of the Northern Expedition culminated in Chiang's military supremacy. He became president of the Nationalist government in 1928 while he still held his post as commander-in-chief and chairman of the Military Commission—demonstrating the importance of the capacity to command military forces for a politician in the Nationalist regime.

For those political leaders who were not military commanders, one way to gain the support of military forces was to play to regional militarists. The continuing warlordism that existed even after the victory of the Northern Expedition made it possible for civilian politicians, such as Wang Jingwei, Hu Hanmin, and Sun Ke, to ally with strong regional militarists in their opposition to Chiang Kai-shek who himself was a military commander. As one study of Nationalist politics indicates: "The territorial bases of the militarists and their relative independence from Nanjing offered Chiang's factional opponents a secure place for political retreat. . . . Some provincial militarists became natural allies of Wang and Hu in their opposition to Chiang's authority."[56]

Although Chiang Kai-shek's military efforts and political maneuvers enabled him at the end of the Northern Expedition to incorporate almost the whole body of Chinese armies into the Nationalist Revolutionary Army, with himself as commander-in-chief, Chiang was never in full control of the armies. The army was divided into four corps, and Chiang Kai-shek was only the commander of the First Army Corps, which was regarded as the "central army" *(zhongyang jun)*. The commanders of the other three army corps, Feng Yuxiang, Yan Xishan, and Li Zhongren, controlled their own territorial bases and resisted Chiang's growing penetration. In the north, Yan Xishan held Shanxi province and Feng Yuxiang ruled Chahaer and Hebei provinces. In the south, Li Zhongren controlled Guangxi and Guangdong provinces. Their armies were regarded as "regional armies" *(difang jun)*. The central government in fact controlled only part of China, and more than half of the provinces remained in the hands of the regional militarists. In the Nationalist era, these regional militarists became new warlords.[57] This was not only because they had recently declared allegiance to the Nationalist Revolution and "had little or no commitment to the ideological goals of the movement,"[58] but also because they were financed not by the central government but by their own local resources and were hence independent, to a varying degree, of the central government.[59] After the establishment of a "unified" Nationalist government in 1928, these regional militarists "were now simply indulging in political maneuvers, which they hoped would result in the preservation, if not the enhancement, of their personal and regional power."[60]

The new warlordism was evident at the Reorganization and Disbandment Conference *(bian qian huiyi)* held in 1929 by the Nationalist government. The participants included Chiang Kai-shek and regional militarists. They all agreed that the army had to be greatly reduced in number and improved in quality after the victory of the Northern Expedition. Nevertheless, nobody expected the ax to fall on his own forces. It was natural for Chiang Kai-shek to place greater trust in the units commanded by graduates of the Huangpu Academy and to argue that these units should be kept and improved. But the heads of the other groups maintained that their military achievements during the expedition should not be ignored, and all of them rejected the proposal to disband the army units under their command. The conference thus not only dragged on without any result but also engendered suspicion and eventually conflict among these militarists.[61] And in addition to militarists within the Nationalist army, there were a number of militarists in the northeast who had not yet been brought under the Nationalist army when the Northern Expedition was complete. For example, Zhang Zuolin and his son Zhang Xueliang, known as *shaosuai* (Young Marshal), still controlled four provinces in the northeast and were in an independent position to affect political events.[62]

The fragmented military forces left great room for maneuvers of the competing political leaders. Chiang Kai-shek, as commander-in-chief of the Nationalist army, enjoyed enormous power in KMT politics. In the meantime, Chiang's factional opponents could also benefit from the strength and territorial bases of the regional militarists and their relative independence from Chiang Kai-shek. Both Hu Hanmin and Wang Jingwei enjoyed the support of quite a few regional militarists and utilized regional military forces in their opposition to Chiang's attempt at domination. In fact, there was a reciprocal relationship between these prominent civilian politicians and the regional militarists. The civilian politicians benefited from the military strength and territorial bases of regional militarists; the militarists, in turn, needed the prestige and influence of the prominent political leaders in the KMT and the Nationalist government to legitimize, preserve, and enhance their own interest.

The new warlordism meant that civilian political leaders could now play to the regional militarists in the anarchic power relationship whenever there was a diffusion of the KMT's authority. Factional conflicts were more easily settled on the battlefield than in the party's formal apparatus: a winner could be clearly determined after a battle and the extremely difficult process of consensus building was avoided by a simple trial of strength on the battlefield. Consequently, whenever a deadlock among factional leaders appeared, not only did the politician who was himself the commander of military forces, Chiang Kai-shek, tend to bring in military forces but the civilian politicians, Wang Jingwei and Hu Hanmin, tried to do the same. For the politician who was a militarist himself, the military forces were a convenient instrument to carry out his political ambitions. For the prominent civilian politicians, the territorial bases of regional militarists could at least safeguard their survival. Moreover, the support of regional militarists often strengthened their bargaining power in factional conflicts. It was under these circumstances that military capacity became one of the key power resources in the Nationalist regime.

Chapter 4

Relative Power Positions of the Major Players

Having elaborated the three power resources in the context of authority relationships in the Nationalist regime, we can now compare the relative power positions of the KMT leaders by examining their power resources. Chiang Kai-shek, Wang Jingwei, Hu Hanmin, and Sun Ke were the major players in the constitution-making game of the Nationalist government during the period 1925–1937. They owed their eminence to the possession of different power resources and competed with one another for leadership of the KMT regime. Table 4 illustrates their relative power positions in accordance with their different resources.

We cannot compare these leaders simply by looking at their formal positions in the KMT hierarchy, however, because all four players held formal positions in the KMT's top organs: the Central Executive Committee and the Central Political Council. Chiang Kai-shek, Wang Jingwei, and Hu Hanmin were each made chairman of the CEC or the CPC at different times. Wang Jingwei was chairman of the CEC in 1925–1926; Hu Hanmin assumed the chairmanship of the CPC for a short period in 1927. While Chiang Kai-shek was a latecomer who first became a member of the standing committee of the CEC in 1926, he quickly climbed to the top and took over the chairmanship of both the CEC and the CPC in 1928. Sun Ke was a long-term member in both the CEC and the CPC. Because all four leaders held top positions in the formal decision-making institutions, the other two power resources—the factional support and military capacity—became especially important.

TABLE 4
Power Sources of the Major Players

	Power Resources		
PLAYERS	POSITION IN TOP ORGANS OF KMT	FACTIONAL CONNECTIONS	MILITARY CAPACITY
Wang Jingwei	Chairman of CEC and CPC (1925–1926)	Spiritual leader of Reorganizationalists	Aligned occasionally with regional militarists
Hu Hanmin	Chairman of CPC (1927)	Spiritual leader of Western Hill Group	Aligned occasionally with regional militarists
Chiang Kai-shek	Chairman of CEC and CPC (1928–)	Head of Blue Shirt Society and Organization Group (CC Clique)	Commander-in-chief of Nationalist army
Sun Ke	Longtime member of CEC and CPC	No close relation with any well-structured faction	Aligned occasionally with regional militarists

Chiang Kai-shek entered KMT politics with a strong military background and hence based his power primarily on his capacity to command military forces. But Chiang also led several well-structured factions both inside and outside the KMT, such as the Blue Shirt Society and the Organization Group. Wang Jingwei's influence in KMT politics came first from his revolutionary seniority and then from the support of a left-wing faction, the Reorganizationalist Comrades Association, within the KMT. Wang also aligned himself with a number of powerful regional militarists from time to time. Hu Hanmin owed his eminence mostly to his past associations with the KMT and with Sun Yat-sen, to his authority as an exponent of Sun's doctrine, and to his appeal to a sense of prestige, dignity, and stability. Hu was the spiritual leader of one right-wing faction in the KMT, the Western Hill Group, for only a short period of time. He did not have the capacity to command military forces, and his relations with regional militarists were weak. Sun Ke savored political prominence as the only son of Sun Yat-sen, a birthright that gave him powerful influence he could not have won by dint of talent alone. Sun Ke did not lead any well-structured factional organization, and his relations with military forces were fragile. This chapter analyzes the power resources possessed by each of the four leading players and, based on these analyses, presents a comprehensive comparison of their relative power positions.

The Power Resources of Chiang Kai-shek

Although Chiang Kai-shek was a latecomer to the political scene in Nationalist China, he quickly became the most powerful political leader during the formative period of the Nationalist regime.[1] Chiang did not get involved directly in the Nationalist movement until the victory of the 1911 revolution. He met Sun Yat-sen for the first time in 1912. Despite his lack of longevity in the movement (compared with Wang Jingwei and Hu Hanmin), he improved his position considerably by the loyalty he displayed to Sun Yat-sen at the time when Chen Jionming, a warlord in Guangdong province and once Sun's follower, turned against Sun in 1922.[2] Chiang Kai-shek was exceptionally skillful at manipulating political events and gaining the support of party elites. The most important power resources he possessed were his capacity to command military forces and the support of well-structured factions. Chiang Kai-shek's power was attributed also to his firm control over the Nanjing government's financial resources and support from the business class in the big urban areas such as Shanghai, Jiangsu, and Zhejiang provinces. Nevertheless, these financial resources were maintained basically by his military forces. Parks M. Coble's study of the relationship between Chiang's Nanjing regime and the Shanghai capitalists suggests that neither Shanghai's capitalists nor any urban social class served as a political base for the Nanjing regime. Chiang Kai-shek's power rested principally on his military capacity.[3]

Military Background

Chiang Kai-shek's rise to political power started from his military career. Even those who praise Chiang Kai-shek agree that he was essentially a military man. Hu Puyu's biography of Chiang Kai-shek, for example, views Chiang primarily as a leader of military forces.[4]

Hollington K. Tong, in an authorized biography published in 1937, also regards Chiang Kai-shek, first of all, as a soldier.[5]

Chiang Kai-shek had his first military training in the Imperial Military Academy at Baoding, Hebei province, at the age of eighteen. Aloof and ambitious, he was so successful that within a year he was sent to the Shinbo Gokyo (Preparatory Military Academy) in Tokyo, where he met Chen Qimei, the well-known leader of the Zhejiang and Jiangsu factions of the Zhonghua Geming Dang (Chinese Revolutionary Party), one of the political bodies that later merged to form the KMT. Through Chen Qimei, Chiang Kai-shek got involved in the Nationalist Revolution. Chiang's military studies were terminated by the outbreak of the Republican Revolution in 1911. Chiang returned to Shanghai and began a vigorous military career. It was there that he met Sun Yat-sen in 1912 and took part in the abortive Second Revolution in 1913.[6]

Chiang Kai-shek emerged as a potential leader in the KMT when Sun Yat-sen appointed him president of the newly created Huangpu (Whampoa) Military Academy in 1924. This academy was set up to produce an army dedicated to the KMT's revolutionary goals. In the early period of the Nationalist regime in Guangdong and later the Northern Expedition, Chiang's few but well-disciplined Huangpu soldiers proved to be his greatest political asset. Following a successful military campaign against Chen Jiongming, Chiang was made commander-in-chief of the KMT's Party Army *(dangjun)* in April 1925, garrison commander of Guangzhou in June, and a member of the Military Commission of the Nationalist government in July. When the post of commander-in-chief of the Nationalist Revolutionary Army was created in July 1926, Chiang immediately seized this post. As Chien Tuan-sheng puts it: "Two years of the Northern Expedition culminated in Chiang Kai-shek's military supremacy."[7] Facing first the threat of the warlords and later the Communists, the military forces became more and more necessary for the survival of the KMT regime. Consequently, Chiang Kai-shek became more and more important in the politics of Nationalist China.

Since Chiang Kai-shek's rise to power started from his presidency at the Huangpu Military Academy, Huangpu graduates and staff members became a solid base for Chiang's political career. The armies—especially those units over which Huangpu graduates had sole or even partial control—were strongholds of Chiang's military as well as political power. One study of the politics of Nationalist China indicates that "as long as the Huangpu group could be held together, Chiang Kai-shek had a formidable personal army in his struggle for the leadership of the KMT Party-state."[8]

Rise to the Top of the KMT Hierarchy

Although Chiang Kai-shek arrived at the political center of Nationalist China through the military, he was not simply a militarist. Chiang skillfully manipulated KMT politics and cultivated supporters within the KMT structure. Indeed, it was Chiang Kai-shek's political skill that finally moved him to the top of the KMT hierarchy.

Chiang Kai-shek's political skill was manifested in his success at manipulating political events and taking the winning position in the severe left/right struggle that developed within the KMT after the death of Sun Yat-sen. He was always able to stand with the prevailing side. Sun Yat-sen's collaboration with the Communists and the reorganization of the KMT in 1924 on the Leninist model generated severe left/right antagonism within the KMT. The left wing took a reformist line in favor of alliance with the Communists; the right wing distrusted the Communists and saw the 1924 reorganization as a major threat to the KMT's survival. Sun Yat-sen's collaboration with the Communists helped the leftists prevail for a while: in the Second National Congress of the KMT on January 1, 1926, the left wing dominated the CEC and the rightists were at bay. Indeed, the congress passed a resolution expelling the Western Hill Group simply because of its open denunciation of the leftists.[9] Chiang Kai-shek stood with the left wing at the Second National Congress. He criticized the Western Hill Group and proclaimed that the KMT revolution could not succeed without the collaboration with the Communists.[10] As a supporter of the party's left wing, therefore, Chiang Kai-shek was elected for the first time as a member of the Central Executive Committee at the Second National Congress.[11] When the right wing gradually gained strength after the death of Sun Yat-sen, Chiang Kai-shek moved to a centrist position. After 1927, when the rightists prevailed in the KMT, Chiang quickly shifted to their side and finally became leader of the party's right wing.

Chiang's artful handling of the left/right antagonism gathered around him an ever-growing group of supporters and sent him steadily to the top of the party hierarchy. Upon his election to the CEC at the Second National Congress, Chiang quickly joined the five-member standing committee of the CEC at the First Plenary Session of the Second CEC on January 22, 1926, and thus became one of leading figures in the KMT hierarchy. At the Fourth Plenary Session of the CEC on February 4, 1928, Chiang Kai-shek was finally made chairman of the Central Political Council, the highest post in the KMT.[12]

Factional Support

Chiang Kai-shek's success in manipulating KMT politics was enhanced by his ability to maintain the powerful support of factions both inside and outside the KMT. The Blue Shirt Society (Lan Yi She) was formed outside the KMT's formal hierarchy; the Organization Group (better known as the CC Clique) was formed within the party's Central Organization Department.[13] Besides these two factional organizations, Chiang Kai-shek also led a less structured group known as the Political Study Clique (Zheng Xue Xi)—a collection of experienced politicians, militarists, and industrialists who saw great benefit in their association with Chiang Kai-shek. Since the Political Study Clique was not as well organized as the other two groups, the discussion of Chiang's clientele support in this chapter focuses on the Blue Shirt Society and the Organization Group.[14]

The Blue Shirt Society, organized mainly by the graduates and staff of the Huangpu Military Academy, was also known as the Huangpu Faction. The Huangpu graduates at large were in fact a loose group, but certain men affiliated with the academy began to achieve political importance and built Chiang up as the leading figure to control the party-state through the Blue Shirt Society. The faction's name was explained in Liu Liqun's proposal for the creation of this organization: "The blue shirt is one kind of cloth that Chinese intellectuals, workers, and peasants love to wear. It is simple but useful. The name of the 'Blue Shirt Society' means a revolutionary group formed by young intellectuals who would like to combine with ordinary people. This is a simple and honest group."[15] The Blue Shirt Society was an informal but well-structured political machine with definite goals and an initial core drawn from the right-wing segment of Huangpu graduates.

Historically the Blue Shirts can be traced as far back as the establishment of the Sun Yat-senist Study Society on the Huangpu campus in 1924–1925 by a group of anti-Communist students and their staff supporters. By June 1926 the Study Society had more than three hundred members. But as the Northern Expedition proceeded, the society began to disintegrate. Then the Huangpu Alumni Association was founded with Chiang Kai-shek as its titular head. The most dramatic organizational development involving the Huangpu graduates came about in 1931 and 1932. Alarmed by the condition of the nation and shocked by Chiang's temporary resignation from the government, Liu Liqun, a former instructor at the military academy, sent Chiang a patriotic proposal in the fall of 1931 and suggested organizational measures against what he called major threats to the republic.[16] The major threats listed by Liu Liqun included the Japanese invading Chinese territory, the Communists surviving in the interior, and the KMT leaders clashing bitterly among themselves.[17] Chiang immediately called upon Liu and other Huangpu men to form a secret organization based on three principles:[18]

1. Chiang himself should be regarded as their supreme and permanent leader.
2. The Huangpu alumni should form the basis of the organization.
3. The members should follow the precepts of the People's Three Principles, should practice the Communist Party's organizational techniques, and should cultivate the spirit of the Japanese samurai.[19]

The Blue Shirt Society thus came into existence in March 1932 with its headquarters in Nanjing.[20]

There were both military and nonmilitary cadres among the Blue Shirts. The professional military men commanded units directly loyal to Chiang Kai-shek; the nonmilitary members performed a variety of functions in intelligence, sabotage, and espionage. Operations of the Blue Shirt Society were centered in the Military Commission, the highest governing body in the military: virtually every administrative bureau of the council was headed by a Blue Shirt. Moreover, all of the Nanjing-oriented military schools and training camps and most party organizations in the army units on the Nanjing payroll were controlled by the Blue Shirts. The Blue Shirt Society's budget was never sanctioned or regulated by the legitimate procedures set forth in the statute of the party and the constitution of the republic. Funds came either from Chiang's personal financial sources or from institutions that he directly controlled.[21] Thus the Blue Shirt Society became one of Chiang Kai-shek's major political assets in his fight for personal power and his dream to unite China through military means.[22]

Another powerful faction that supported Chiang Kai-shek within the party hierarchy was the Organization Group (CC Clique). This group's power lay in its control of the KMT's Central Organization Department. Chen Guofu and Chen Lifu, two brothers and loyal followers of Chiang Kai-shek, succeeded him to head the Organization Department and the CC Clique. The Chen brothers' intimate relationship with Chiang Kai-shek and their rise to powerful positions in the KMT regime originated in Chiang's special relationship with Chen Qimei, their uncle. Robert Payne's biography of Chiang Kai-shek provides a detailed account of the relationship between Chiang Kai-shek and the Chen family, including the early letters Chiang sent to Chen Qimei and how Chiang adopted Chen Qimei's nephews after Chen was murdered.[23] S. I. Hsiung's 1948 biography of Chiang Kai-shek even claims that Chen Qimei was Chiang Kai-shek's sworn brother.[24]

Chiang Kai-shek's relationship with the Chen brothers became significant in 1924 when Chiang was appointed president of the Huangpu Military Academy. Upon Chiang's recommendation, Chen Guofu was made the party's representative in the Zhejiang–Jiangsu–Anhui region and was put in charge of recruiting cadets for the academy. At the Second Party Congress in 1926, with the strong support of Chiang Kai-shek, Chen Guofu was elected to the party's Central Supervisory Committee. Later in the same year he became head of the party's Organization Department. Meanwhile Chen Lifu, the younger brother, had returned from the United States in 1926 and served as Chiang Kai-shek's confidential secretary. Later, in 1928, he was appointed head of the party's secret service, the Statistical and Investigation Bureau affiliated with the Organization Department. From 1929 to 1931, he was secretary-general of the party's central headquarters in Nanjing. In 1932, Chen Lifu succeeded his brother as director of the Organization Department.

The Chen brothers and the CC Clique worked hard to consolidate and strengthen Chiang's position in the party and government. Through the Organization Department, they assigned Chiang's followers to various party branches in the government, the military, and even social organizations and then supervised their performance through the Statistical and Investigation Bureau. The CC Clique also recruited its members in high-level party organs as well as lower-level party bureaucracies. Formal admission to membership was through a quasi-official organization in Nanjing, the Central Club, which was based on the Zhejiang Revolutionary Comrades Association created by Chiang Kai-shek in 1926. The Chen brothers headed the Central Club; only those party cadres who had demonstrated their loyalty to Chiang Kai-shek could join. Through this kind of organizational development, the CC Clique penetrated to all key positions in the KMT regime. A study of the CC Clique shows that at the Third Party Congress in March 1929, the clique was represented by forty delegates, mainly from Shanghai, Nanjing, Jiangsu, and Zhejiang provinces, who organized to provide support for Chiang Kai-shek within the party structure. In 1931, some 15 percent of the 72 newly elected members of the CEC belonged to the CC Clique; in 1935, some 50 of the 180 CEC members were reportedly affiliated with the clique. At the peak of its strength in the 1930s, the CC Clique had over ten thousand members, most of them middle-level and lower-level party bureaucrats and cadre members.[25] Hence Chiang Kai-shek not only held the highest formal position within the party hierarchy himself but also had followers controlling the party's powerful Organization Department and thereby received the powerful clientele support of the military and the government, as well as the party.

The Power Resources of Wang Jingwei

Wang Jingwei was a leading political rival of Chiang Kai-shek. One of his major power resources was his revolutionary seniority in the Nationalist movement. Wang Jingwei was also regarded as the leader of a factional organization in the party called the KMT Reorganizationalist Comrades Association (Kuomintang Gaizu Tongzhi Hui). Wang Jingwei himself did not have a military career and never directly commanded any military force. But he did enjoy support of the military from different regions by allying frequently with powerful regional militarists.

Revolutionary Seniority

In the opening paragraph of a study of Wang Jingwei's checkered career, Howard L. Boorman offers this profound observation: "Man's addiction to wishful thinking and uninhibited hindsight makes it hardly surprising that the history of any people tends to be a volatile blend of myth and reality. In China the triumph of Mao Tse-tung and the Communists at the mid-century has obscured earlier developments, even as the apparent triumph of Chiang Kai-shek and the Nationalists in the nineteen-thirties blurred earlier chapters in the evolution of the Chinese Nationalist movement."[26] Boorman concludes that Wang Jingwei, "who a generation ago ranked as one of the most prominent figures of the Republican period, is also obscured, his memory shrouded by both Nationalists and Communists with the darkest of drapes, that of 'national traitor'."[27]

Indeed, Wang Jingwei was well known as a hero in the early phase of the Nationalist movement. But this same man later cast his lot with the Japanese and caused his name to be sullied as a national traitor. During the early, secret-society phase of the modern Chinese Nationalist movement, Wang Jingwei was an eloquent spokesman for Sun Yat-sen's cause and indeed risked his life in 1910 in a bold attempt to assassinate the Manchu prince regent at Beijing. When the assassination failed, Wang Jingwei was arrested and sentenced to life in prison by the government of the Qing dynasty. He was freed after the victory of the 1911 revolution overthrowing the Qing dynasty.[28] Wang remained close to Sun Yat-sen after the 1911 revolution and became chairman of the Central Executive Committee of the KMT and president of the newly established Nationalist government in Guangzhou immediately after Sun Yat-sen's death in 1925.[29] Both his inspiring revolutionary background and his seniority in the party were important power resources that Wang Jingwei could depend upon in his effort to claim leadership of the KMT.[30]

Support of the Reorganizationalists

Apart from his revolutionary seniority, Wang Jingwei's influence derived from his relationship with the KMT Reorganizationalist Comrades Association. The group's name reflected its advocacy of the revolutionary principles adopted at the time of the KMT's 1924 reorganization. Since this was a group within the party that opposed the growing power of Chiang Kai-shek, it was denounced as heretical by Chiang's supporters.[31]

The Reorganizationalist Comrades Association originated from the early left/right antagonism within the party. At this time Wang Jingwei was a leader of the left-wingers in the struggle. After the right wing became dominant in the party in 1927, Wang Jingwei and his followers were bitterly denounced by Chiang Kai-shek and the right-wingers as Communists and some of them were even excluded from the party and government. Facing the prospect of suppression, several of Wang's supporters, including Chen Gongbo, Wang Leping, and Gu Mengyu, met in Shanghai and organized this faction in the winter of 1928.[32] In the "Statement of the First National Conference of the KMT Reorganizationalist Comrades Association," Wang Jingwei was praised as their leader. Wang himself was ambivalent about the association, viewing himself as the leader of the entire party rather than merely a faction. Chiang Kai-shek and the Nanjing regime were accused of having betrayed Sun Yat-sen's principles, and both democracy and a radical program of socialist changes were demanded in the group's statement. This group demanded further reorganization of the party to purge the reactionaries and unfaithful so that the spirit of the KMT's 1924 reorganization might again prevail.[33] Thus they were known as the Reorganizationalists.

Wang Jingwei's supporters were able to find followers among the intelligentsia, who were disaffected by Nanjing's undemocratic tendencies. According to documentary sources published in Mainland China, this group developed very rapidly.[34] It established branches in more than ten provinces and several overseas countries (Japan, Vietnam, France, Singapore, and others) and had members in many universities and major cities. Indeed, its membership expanded to more than ten thousand just within Shanxi province.[35] In the meantime the group was subjected to calumny and denunciation. At the Third Congress of the KMT held in Nanjing in March 1929, its leaders were punished by party discipline. In a resolution passed by the congress, Chen Gongbo, Gu Mengyu, and Gan Laiguan were expelled from the party and Wang Jingwei was given a warrant *(jinggao)* within the party.[36] But these sanctions only drove them to seek further means to overthrow Chiang Kai-shek.

Alignment with Regional Militarists

Wang Jingwei's opposition to Chiang Kai-shek evoked responses from several regional military leaders who were dissatisfied with Chiang Kai-shek's policies, suspicious of his intentions, and jealous of his rising star. Among these regional military leaders were Feng Yuxiang and Yan Xishan, who controlled substantial armed strength in North China and had begun a brief but destructive civil war against Chiang's Nanjing government. In 1930 Wang Jingwei joined these men in an attempt to establish a rival national government in Beijing. Several telegrams were exchanged between Wang Jingwei, Yan Xishan, and Feng Yuxiang in early 1930 in which Wang Jingwei discussed his anti-Chiang plan. In the telegram dated February 18, 1930, for example, Wang Jingwei encouraged Yan Xishan to fight Chiang until victory.[37] In another telegram dated February 24, 1930, Wang Jingwei pushed Yan Xishan to organize a new government as soon as possible.[38] Wang also sent a telegram to Feng Yuxiang on March 16, 1930, showing his determination to fight Chiang to the end.[39]

Backed by the regional militarists, Wang Jingwei called an expanded session of the KMT's Central Executive Committee at Beijing in July.[40] Both a new CEC and a new national government were set up with Wang Jingwei and Yan Xishan as their respective heads. Like the government in Nanjing, the Beijing government claimed to govern in the period of the KMT's tutelage.[41] Thus two KMT headquarters and two nationalist governments stood side by side in Nanjing and Beijing. In July 1930, the armies commanded by Chiang Kai-shek and the armies allied with Wang Jingwei met on a battlefield in Central China.[42] For quite some time, neither side could win. The turning point came when the Young Marshal, Zhang Xueliang, who controlled Manchuria (northeastern China), suddenly declared his support of Chiang Kai-shek and the Nanjing regime in September 1930.[43] The armies allied with Wang Jingwei were then attacked from the rear and quickly collapsed.

Following the collapse of his military forces, Wang moved south and became the senior KMT leader active in a new opposition movement at Guangzhou—a movement that was sparked by Chiang Kai-shek's house arrest of Hu Hanmin in Nanjing in 1931 and sustained by the political ambitions of Guangdong and Guangxi military leaders. This alliance with Guangdong–Guangxi militarists, though not strong enough to dislodge Chiang Kai-shek, nevertheless restored Wang's position and paved the way for his later rapprochement with Nanjing.

The Power Resources of Hu Hanmin

Although Hu Hanmin was a prominent leader of the KMT during the early period of the Nationalist regime, he had less control of factional groups and military forces than did either Chiang Kai-shek or Wang Jingwei. The most important resources in his possession were his seniority in the KMT's revolutionary movement and his authority as an exponent of Sun Yat-sen's doctrine.

Disciple of Sun Yat-sen

Hu Hanmin was a scholar in the accepted literary tradition and also an old disciple of Sun Yat-sen.[44] He was successful in his classical training and won an advanced degree under the old examination system.[45] He had been a KMT leader of prominence ever since the days of the Tongmenghui (an early organization that later merged into the KMT). When studying at Tokyo Law College in Japan, he met Sun Yat-sen and joined his revolutionary movement. Shortly after Sun organized the Tongmenghui in the autumn of 1905, Hu Hanmin was given the responsible post of secretary of party headquarters. While continuing to study for his law degree, which he received in 1906, Hu supported the Nationalist movement chiefly as an editor and writer for *Minbao,* the party organ that first appeared in Tokyo in November 1905.

Melville T. Kennedy, a Western biographer of Hu Hanmin, observes that "as a student, academic administrator, editor, writer, and ideologue, he considered himself and was considered by some others as a leading representative of the intelligentsia."[46] Kennedy also indicates that "Hu Hanmin appeared not to be ambitious for power himself... while he was closely identified with revolutionists who seized and used power."[47] This impression emerged from the fact that Hu Hanmin owed his prominence in KMT politics not to his ability to manipulate political events within the party or command military forces, but mostly to his authority as an exponent of Sun Yat-sen's doctrine and to his personal prestige. He exercised this authority in the name of the KMT's path and its ideology.[48] Hu Hanmin himself described his role in the party simply: to serve as Sun Yat-sen's faithful scribe while he lived and to gather his writings for posterity after his death. Hu Hanmin edited a five-volume collection of Sun Yat-sen's writings, *Zongli Xuanji* (1930). He also wrote extensively on Sun's political thought in the journal *Sanminzhuyi Yuekan* (The People's Three Principles Monthly), which Hu founded in early 1933.[49]

Political Ambition

To say that he was an ideological leader does not mean that Hu Hanmin lacked ambition for political power in the KMT and the Nationalist government. In fact, Hu Hanmin had been deputized by Sun Yat-sen as the generalissimo of the Guangzhou Military Government when Sun Yat-sen left for Beijing in November 1924. Hu Hanmin enjoyed this position but failed to keep it and was defeated by Wang Jingwei in the competition over the chairmanship of the Nationalist government after the death of Sun Yat-sen. One historian maintains that Hu Hanmin was very "disappointed when his colleagues picked Wang Jingwei, instead of him, to be the successor to Sun Yat-sen in 1925."[50] To express his disappointment, Hu Hanmin went to Europe for a visit until 1927 when he was invited by Chiang Kai-shek and the right wing of the KMT to rejoin the government.[51] He became chairman of the Central Political Council of the KMT at a meeting of the CPC held in Nanjing on April 17, 1927.[52] These actions show that Hu's interest in political power was as strong as that of any other politician in the Nationalist regime.

Relations with Factional Groups

Although there is no evidence that Hu Hanmin formally led any factional organization, he was well regarded as the spiritual leader of the right wingers of the KMT in the late 1920s. The Western Hill Group (Xishan Huiyi Pai) was a right-wing faction in the KMT formed by several decidedly anti-Communist CEC and CSC members in the party's central authority including Lin Sheng, Zou Lu, Ju Zheng, Xie Chi,[53] and Zhang Ji. Because these people held a session of the CEC and CSC on the Western Hill of Beijing in December 1925, the faction became known as the Western Hill Group.

Hu Hanmin did not join any of the Western Hill Group's organizational activities, but he did maintain close personal friendships with several of its leaders.[54] In fact, to avoid suspicion of his involvement in factional activities, Hu Hanmin even sent a telegram to Wang Jingwei opposing the divisive activities of the Western Hill Group.[55] Hu Hanmin did not begin working with this faction until 1927 when Chiang Kai-shek openly broke with the Communists. Nevertheless, he never formally led the Western Hill Group.[56]

Relations with Regional Militarists

Hu Hanmin's relationship with military forces was very subtle. Even though he was deputized by Sun Yat-sen as generalissimo of the Guangzhou Military Government for a short period in 1924, he never personally commanded any military forces. Nevertheless, Hu Hanmin's personal prestige within the KMT was so influential that several regional militarists were ready to safeguard him whenever he got into serious trouble in KMT politics—not because they had any personal commitment to him or saw him as a leader of their regional forces but simply because they needed his personal influence and ideological authority in the KMT to gain legitimacy and block Chiang Kai-shek in their struggle to secure personal and regional power. The regional militarists in Guangdong and Guangxi provinces, for example, strongly protested Hu Hanmin's arrest when he was taken into protective custody by Chiang Kai-shek in March 1931. Moreover, Hu Hanmin was welcomed to Guangdong by Chen Jitang, the provincial military leader, upon his release from custody. Nevertheless, once Hu Hanmin finally arrived in Guangdong in 1932, although Chen Jitang initially showed him respect, he made every effort to control Hu's political activity and ensure that Hu could not intervene in his policy in Guangdong.[57]

The Power Resources of Sun Ke

Similar to Hu Hanmin, Sun Ke owed his eminence mostly to his special relationship with his father, Sun Yat-sen, the charismatic leader of the KMT regime. He never led any well-structured faction and his relations with the regional militarists were weak.

Son of Sun Yat-sen

Sun Ke was the only son of Sun Yat-sen. He received his college education at the University of California and obtained a master's degree from Columbia University in New York City, but he did not complete his Ph.D. degree in the United States. He was awarded a Ph.D. degree by Fudan University after he returned to China.[58] As "The Prince" *(taizi),* Sun Ke often had an overbearing manner in the eyes of other KMT leaders and savored a political prominence that he could not have won by dint of his political skills alone.[59] Hu Hanmin presents an interesting description of Sun Ke: "Because he is the son of Sun Yat-sen, he has a revolutionary temper; because he was raised abroad, he has a foreign temper; and because he is the only son of Sun Yat-sen, he has the temper of a spoiled boy. He sometimes lost only one temper, sometimes two, and sometimes all three together."[60]

Sun Ke was appointed minister of finance by Chiang Kai-shek's Nanjing government in 1927.[61] But Sun Ke's political ambition went much higher than minister. In January 1932, taking advantage of the struggle between Chiang Kai-shek, Wang Jingwei, and Hu Hanmin, Sun Ke not only entered the CEC but also assumed the presidency of the Executive Yuan, making him the effective head of the government.[62] Because he lacked military support, however, he served in the premiership of the government for only twenty-five days and was squeezed from this position by the combined forces of Chiang Kai-shek and Wang Jingwei.

Relations with Factions and Military Forces

There is no evidence that Sun Ke led any well-structured faction. The only group that ever supported him within the KMT power center was a group of CEC members from Shanghai, Sun Ke's hometown, known as Huwei (Shanghai Members of the Committee), during the early 1930s.[63] But this group never became well organized and its members (numbering about thirty) were also associated with other leading figures of the party such as Hu Hanmin and Wang Jingwei. Nor is there any evidence that Sun Ke had the capacity to command a military force. His sole military backing came from the military forces in Guangdong. When the Sun Ke administration fell into crisis in 1932, these military forces reverted to the more powerful leaders, Chiang Kai-shek and Wang Jingwei.[64]

Sun Ke's political stock as the only son of the charismatic leader of the KMT was obviously not strong enough for him to fight a winning battle with Chiang Kai-shek or the other leaders who had more clientele followers or could command military forces. Sun Ke could compete with Chiang and loosen his control over the regime only when that control was disorganized or faced challenges from the combined forces of other political leaders in the party.

The Relative Power Positions Compared

With the preceding discussion of the major power resources possessed by the four political players, we now have a foundation allowing us to compare their relative power positions. It is apparent that Chiang Kai-shek held a more powerful position than the other three players, since he not only held the top positions in the KMT's formal hierarchy but also led well-structured factions inside and outside the party and commanded strong military forces. The major power resources possessed by Wang Jingwei, Hu Hanmin, and Sun Ke, Chiang's leading political rivals, were their seniority in the Nationalist movement and their special relationship with Sun Yat-sen. None of them enjoyed the extensive support of factional groups or had Chiang's capacity to command military forces. Although revolutionary seniority and proximity to Sun Yat-sen were certainly important power resources—on these two points Chiang Kai-shek could not match Hu Hanmin, Wang Jingwei, or Sun Ke—military resources were Chiang's trump card, one that his rivals could never top.

Therefore, Chiang Kai-shek was the most powerful political player and the single individual who could possibly become dominant in the Nationalist regime—if he were skillful enough to draw attention to his own power resources and away from those he did not possess such as longevity in the party and ideological authority. Since legitimacy within the party distinguished the Nationalist government from the warlords, it was always important for Chiang to ally with Hu or Wang during the period of this study. As we will see in the following chapters, it was only when he tried to go against both at the same time that he got into trouble and created opportunities for his rivals to gain the upper hand in the constitution-making game. Nevertheless, while Wang Jingwei, Hu Hanmin, and Sun Ke might occasionally exercise their influence over Chiang Kai-shek in coalition efforts and by alignment with powerful regional militarists, none of them possessed his power to prevail and, ultimately, predominate.

Chapter 5

Institutional Preferences of the Major Players

This book began with two assumptions—that the institutional preferences of political actors are shaped by their relative power positions and that institutional design is determined by the power contest among leading political contenders. If a political player possesses more power resources than his rivals and anticipates becoming dominant in the regime, he will prefer the presidential form of government; if a political player possesses fewer power resources and is in the weaker position, he will prefer the cabinet form. According to this logic of institutional design, Chiang Kai-shek—who possessed more power resources than any of his political rivals (Wang Jingwei, Hu Hanmin, or Sun Ke) and who was the most powerful political player—would prefer the presidential system whereas the other three leaders would prefer the cabinet system.

The empirical findings presented in this chapter concur with this assumption. Chiang Kai-shek, standing in the most powerful position, was the only political leader in the KMT regime who expressed a strong preference for presidential government. Wang Jingwei, Hu Hanmin, and Sun Ke, in the relatively weak positions, each preferred the cabinet system. Table 5 summarizes the empirical findings. This chapter elaborates each of the four players' institutional preferences in accordance with the historical record.

Chiang Kai-shek's Institutional Preference

Chiang Kai-shek's preference for the presidential form of government emerged gradually along with his rise to the most powerful position

TABLE 5
Power Positions and Institutional Preferences of the Major Players

	Institutional Preference	
POWER POSITION	PRESIDENTIAL SYSTEM	CABINET SYSTEM
Dominant		
Chiang Kai-shek	Fifth Plenary Session of Second CEC (Aug. 1928); draft of provisional constitution (1931); Fifth Plenary Session of Fourth CEC (Dec. 1935)	No
Weak		
Hu Hanmin	No	Proposal for reorganizing national government (1925); proposal for promulgation of five-power government (1928)
Wang Jingwei	No	Letter to Chiang Kai-shek (Oct. 1931)
Sun Ke	No	First four drafts of constitution (1932–1934)

in the Nationalist regime. Chiang did not express this preference until 1928, however, when he defeated his major political rivals in the succession struggle and formally climbed to the top of the KMT hierarchy. Chiang's rise began when he became chairman of the Central Military Commission and chairman of the KMT's Central Executive Committee for the first time at the Fourth Plenary Session of the Second CEC in February 1928.[1] After the plenary session, Chiang also assumed the chairmanship of the party's Central Political Council on March 7, 1928. From this powerful position he could anticipate becoming a dominant figure in the regime.

Confident in his political future, Chiang Kai-shek called for the Fifth Plenary Session of the Second CEC only a few months after the Fourth Plenary Session. The preparatory meeting of the Fifth Plenary Session was held on August 1, 1928. Since it was convened in a hurry, more than half of the CEC members were absent. The meeting lasted only one day and was reported in newspapers not as a preparatory meeting but as an informal gathering of CEC members.[2] One week later, the Fifth Plenary Session of the Second CEC was formally convened on August 7–15, 1928. It was at this plenary session that Chiang Kai-shek requested the revision of the Organic Law and was appointed chairman of the Organic Law Drafting Committee. There were eleven members on the committee, including Chiang Kai-shek, Hu Hanmin, Sun Ke, and Dai Jitao.[3] This revision designated the president (in the person of Chiang Kai-shek) to be commander-in-chief of the armed forces. The authority of the president would not be delegated from the National Government Council. He was personally responsible only to the KMT's Central Executive Committee. The old provision that "the president should be selected by and from the members of the council" was dropped in this revision.[4] Since Chiang Kai-shek himself was chairman of the CEC, the ultimate authority of the regime would be concentrated in the hands of one person, Chiang Kai-shek, because the president was not responsible to the National Government Council but to the CEC of the party. In other words, as president Chiang was responsible only to himself as chairman of the CEC. This revision of the Organic Law established a presidential form of government and one-person rule by concentrating the three major powers of the regime—the party, the army, and the government—in the hands of one person, Chiang Kai-shek.

Although the presidential system was adopted in accordance with the revised Organic Law of 1928, Chiang Kai-shek was not yet satisfied. He wanted to consolidate the presidential power by promulgation of a provisional constitution *(linshi yufa)*. Chiang first suggested adoption of a provisional constitution in a telegram dated October 3, 1930, to the CEC in Nanjing.[5] At that time he was conducting a military campaign against Wang Jingwei and other rebels in the north and was reasonably sure of a quick victory. When the Fourth Plenary Session of the Third CEC convened in November 1930, Wu Jingyuan and a number of Chiang's strong supporters submitted a formal proposal requesting the drafting of a provisional constitution. According to the minutes of the plenary session, Hu Hanmin objected to this proposal and had a bitter quarrel with Chiang's supporters.[6] Disaffected by the wrangling, Chiang left Nanjing for Lushan (a mountain resort in Jiangxi province) at the end of December 1930 and complained that "[I] don't want to return to Nanjing. The farther away [I am] from Nanjing, the better [I feel]."[7] When Hu Hanmin refused to give in, Chiang finally had him taken into "protective custody" on February 28, 1931, because, Chiang announced, Hu Hanmin was opposing adoption of the provisional constitution that had already been approved by the KMT's Central Executive Committee. In a speech on March 2, 1931, Chiang said:

> As for the provisional constitution, *zongli* [Sun Yat-sen] mentioned it many times and never said it was unnecessary to have a provisional constitution. I consulted with other [military] generals at the front in October and sent two telegrams to the center for the adoption of *yufa*. . . . When *zongli* was still alive, he said that he adopted nine-tenths of Hu Hanmin's opinions and therefore we too tolerated Hu Hanmin's opinions in 99 percent of our decisions made after the establishment of the national government. Nevertheless, . . . the *yufa* issue should be discussed in meetings and we cannot listen only to one person's opinion. On the evening of [March] 28, the center discussed the issue. The majority agreed with the *yufa* but only Hu Hanmin disagreed. . . . He was therefore relieved of his posts.[8]

After Hu Hanmin was taken into custody, Chiang Kai-shek and the other eleven CEC members presented a resolution about the adoption of the provisional constitution to the CEC for approval. The Provisional Plenary Session of the CEC, held on March 2, 1931, approved Chiang's proposal.[9] Chiang's loyal supporter, Wu Jingyuan, was appointed to head the drafting committee of the provisional constitution. Upon the promulgation of the provisional constitution, drafted by Chiang's supporters, in May 1931, the president of the national government was empowered to appoint and dismiss the presidents of the five *yuan* and heads of ministries.[10]

The presidential system designed by Chiang Kai-shek survived for about three years. In 1931 it was replaced by the cabinet system when Chiang was forced to resign for the second time from the government after a showdown with a powerful anti-Chiang coalition.[11] Despite the failure, Chiang Kai-shek insisted on his institutional preference for the presidential form of government. When the preliminary draft of the permanent constitution was about to be finished in 1935, Sun Ke, then in charge of the group drafting the new constitution, submitted the preliminary draft for approval at the Fifth Plenary Session of the Fourth CEC, held on December 10–14, 1935. Chiang Kai-shek strongly opposed the preliminary draft and requested a major revision because the draft established the cabinet form of government.[12] On

Chiang's insistence, a Resolution on Principles for the Draft of the Constitution was passed at the CEC session on December 14. Criticizing the preliminary draft for constraining the executive authority, the resolution stated:

> Government organization should consider actual political experience in order to create a practical, efficient system that can concentrate national strength. *The executive authority should not be limited by inflexible regulations.*[13]

The Central Executive Committee, as the KMT's formal decision-making organ controlled by Chiang Kai-shek, ordered a rewriting of the draft. As a result, the presidential form of government was designed to replace the cabinet form in the final draft of the constitution, promulgated on May 5, 1936.[14] Once again the president became the true executive of the government and was vested with the authority to appoint and remove the heads of the five *yuan* in accordance with the May 5 constitution.

Hu Hanmin's Institutional Preference

Although Hu Hanmin was one of the leading political rivals of Chiang Kai-shek, he was in a weaker position and, unlike Chiang, could not anticipate becoming dominant in the regime. Therefore he never showed any interest in the presidential system. On the contrary, he expressed a strong preference for the cabinet form of government. Hu Hanmin was the first KMT leader who proposed that the Nationalist government take the cabinet system to be a collective leadership. His suggestion was first put forward as early as 1925 when he received the report that Sun Yat-sen was seriously ill. Soon after the arrival of this report, Hu told Liao Zhongkai, a potential contender in the succession struggle, that "I should not continue to be the acting generalissimo now. It's better to reform the government of the generalissimo system thoroughly and adopt a committee system that would create an opportunity for *collective responsibility* for our comrades in the party."[15]

After the death of Sun Yat-sen, Hu Hanmin immediately submitted a formal proposal to the Central Executive Committee suggesting a reorganization of the Nationalist government. Two important points were made in Hu's proposal: the first was to create a cabinet form of council system to replace the generalissimo government established by Sun Yat-sen; the second was to reorganize all armies commanded by the Guangzhou regime into a unified Nationalist Revolutionary Army.[16] According to Hu's proposal, the chairman of the national government should be merely a presiding officer elected from the members of the council. The power of the council should be concentrated in its standing committee rather than in the chairman.[17] Hu's proposal was accepted by the CEC at a meeting on June 15, 1925.[18]

It seemed a puzzle. Why would Hu Hanmin propose the cabinet system while he was acting generalissimo of the Nationalist government? The explanation could be found in the fact that Hu faced strong competition from Wang Jingwei, Chiang Kai-shek, and Liao Zhongkai in the succession struggle for leadership of the KMT when Sun Yat-sen died.[19] He was not the most powerful contender and could not anticipate prevailing in the struggle. As indicated by Zhou Bingwo and Chen Hongmin in their study of Hu's political life, "Hu Hanmin's influence was derived from his relationship to Sun Yat-sen. Although Hu Hanmin took the position of acting generalissimo, he could not keep it without the support of Sun Yat-sen."[20]

It was obvious that when the party was dominated by leftist tendencies and Soviet influence in 1925, Hu Hanmin, as the right-wing leader, was not in a powerful position to compete with his rivals. Zhou Bingwo and Chen Hongmin offer a useful insight into Hu's predicament: "Soviet advisors had occupied key positions in both the KMT and the Nationalist army prior to the death of Sun Yat-sen. The chief Soviet advisor, M. M. Borodin, had powerful influence over most of the important decisions made in the KMT. Being regarded as an opposition leader to Borodin after the death of Sun Yat-sen was certainly not an advantage to Hu Hanmin."[21] Moreover, many of the KMT's leaders had trouble accepting Hu Hanmin as the successor to Sun Yat-sen because of his stubborn personality. Li Zhongren, an influential military leader in the Nationalist army, said in his reminiscences that "Hu Hanmin was a *junzi* [gentleman]. He was sincere and decent. But Hu was not a great political leader because he was narrow-minded and stubborn. After the death of Sun Yat-sen, every person, the senior party leaders and rank-and-file party members alike, respected Hu Hanmin very much, but none of them thought that Hu could be the leader with the ability to unify the party."[22]

The most important power resource in Hu's possession was his special relationship with Sun Yat-sen. When Sun Yat-sen died suddenly and was no longer able to stand behind him, Hu Hanmin must certainly have felt that his power was in danger. In these circumstances, holding the post of acting generalissimo of the Nationalist government in Guangzhou would make him the target of attacks by other potential successors to Sun Yat-sen. Neither Wang Jingwei nor Chiang Kai-shek nor Liao Zhongkai would tolerate Hu Hanmin's continuation as acting generalissimo after the death of Sun Yat-sen. Indeed, Hu Hanmin was already under fire by other contenders for succession immediately after the death of Sun Yat-sen.[23]

It was from this weak position that, upon receiving the news that Sun Yat-sen was dangerously ill, Hu Hanmin suggested that the generalissimo government be reorganized into a council system of civilian government.[24] It was for the same reason that, after the death of Sun Yat-sen, Hu once again put forth the formal proposal to the CEC suggesting the reorganization of the Nationalist government. The cabinet form of council suggested by Hu Hanmin was established in 1925. Wang Jingwei became chairman of the National Government Council. Hu Hanmin was given three important positions in the government: as one of five members of the council's standing committee; as one of eight members of the Military Commission; and as minister of foreign affairs.

The assassination of Liao Zhongkai in August 1925 obliged Hu Hanmin to leave China for Europe for a while because he was suspected of responsibility for the murder.[25] He did not return until 1928 when he was invited by Chiang Kai-shek to rejoin the newly unified Nationalist government in Nanjing. At this point Hu Hanmin expressed his institutional preference for the cabinet form of government once again. Upon accepting Chiang's invitation, Hu Hanmin and Sun Ke in Paris drafted a formal proposal to the Central Executive Committee suggesting an immediate promulgation of the five-power government originally designed by Sun Yat-sen.[26] This proposal explicitly expressed Hu Hanmin's preference for a cabinet form of government. It suggested that the national government should consist of a council led collectively by the heads of the five *yuan*. The president of the national government should be selected from and by the members of the National Government Council. Hu's proposal suggested that the Legislative Yuan have from forty-nine to ninety-nine members, the Executive Yuan from nineteen to twenty-five, and the other three *yuan* from five to nine members each. The members of the five *yuan* were to constitute the national government; the five chairmen of the five *yuan* were to constitute a standing committee of the government; and one of these five was to be designated chairman of the national government. The five members of the standing committee were to be automatically members of the Executive and Legislative Yuan.[27]

Chien Tuan-sheng, in his comments on the proposal, maintains that Hu Hanmin "was apprehensive of the reemergence of China's old scourge, the dictatorship of one person. He was for a collegiate form of organization for the top levels of government."[28] Chien Tuan-sheng is right in saying that Hu Hanmin proposed the cabinet form of government to prevent Chiang Kai-shek from becoming a one-person dictator in the Nationalist regime. But Chien does not specify what kind of collegial form of government Hu proposed. The system advocated by Hu Hanmin was obviously not a collegial form of democratic government but a collective leadership among a group of power elites within an authoritarian framework. Hu Hanmin's proposal was rejected by the Central Executive Committee at its meeting in September 1928 when Chiang Kai-shek had already risen to the top of the KMT hierarchy and anticipated becoming dominant in the regime. It was impossible for the CEC, which was chaired by Chiang Kai-shek at that time, to accept a cabinet system that would constrain Chiang's personal power.

The third time that Hu Hanmin expressed his institutional preference for the cabinet form of government was at the Fourth Plenary Session of the Third CEC convened in November 1930. Hu submitted a proposal suggesting that the CEC appoint Chiang Kai-shek, the president of the national government, to concurrently hold the presidency of the Executive Yuan.[29] Why did Hu Hanmin submit this proposal? Considering that it was at this session that the dispute erupted between Hu Hanmin and Chiang Kai-shek over whether or not the provisional constitution should be promulgated, nobody would believe that Hu Hanmin wished to render more power to Chiang Kai-shek. But if that were the case, why did he suggest that Chiang Kai-shek be appointed to the concurrent posts of president of the national government and president of the Executive Yuan? The explanation can only be that Hu's proposal was intended to weaken Chiang's presidential power by conferring the executive power down to the Executive Yuan if Chiang Kai-shek would accept the post. Thus Hu's proposal implied that the highest executive power of government should be vested in the Executive Yuan, not in the president of the national government. The executive power transfer could lead to power sharing among Chiang Kai-shek and several other top elites in the government. For if Chiang Kai-shek exercised his executive power as president of the Executive Yuan, rather than as president of the national government, his power could be balanced by Hu Hanmin (who was president of the Legislative Yuan) and the heads of the other *yuan* within the National Government Council.

The implication of Hu's proposal became clear in the Organic Law revised in the next year when Chiang was forced to resign from the government. The revised Organic Law of 1931 designed the cabinet form of government, not only by stating that the president of the national government "should have no actual political responsibility," but also by making the National Government Council composed of all the heads of the five *yuan*. Article 17 of the revised Organic Law further stated:

> All matters that cannot be settled between two or more of the *yuan* should be referred to the meetings of the National Government Council for making decisions.[30]

Thus when executive power was exercised by the president of the Executive Yuan instead of the president of the national government, it could be legally challenged in the meeting of the National Government Council by the heads of the other *yuan,* including Hu Hanmin himself as head of the Legislative Yuan. From this perspective, it is clear that Hu Hanmin was expressing his institutional preference for the cabinet form of government in the proposal that he submitted at the Fourth Plenary Session of the Third CEC in November 1930.

Wang Jingwei's Institutional Preference

Although Wang Jingwei assumed the chairmanship of the Nationalist government and the CEC in 1925, he never gained the capacity to command military forces and his factional base was never as strong as Chiang's. Therefore, just like Hu Hanmin, Wang Jingwei was in a relatively weak position and could not anticipate becoming dominant in the political contest with his rivals.

Consequently Wang Jingwei never showed any interest in the presidential system. Instead he strongly advocated the cabinet form of government. His institutional preference was expressed systematically in a letter he sent to Chiang Kai-shek in October 1931.[31] In this letter Wang Jingwei asserted that Chiang should be only a figurehead of state if he wanted to hold the post of president of the national government. Wang suggested, moreover, that the post of commander-in-chief of the Nationalist army be abolished.[32] Wang explicitly expressed his institutional design in the letter by stating that "the president of the national government should be a figurehead, like the presidents in France and Germany, and should be assumed only by a prominent elder in the country."[33]

Wang Jingwei's letter was a response to Chiang Kai-shek's request to hold a peace conference *(heping huiyi)* in October 1931. At that time Wang was supported by a grand anti-Chiang coalition led by himself, Hu Hanmin, Sun Ke, and a number of powerful regional militarists including Feng Yuxiang, Li Zhongren, and Yan Xishan.[34] The challenge from such combined forces was too strong even for Chiang Kai-shek to confront. To seek a reconciliation with the leaders of the coalition, Chiang proposed that the peace conference be held in Shanghai. In response to Chiang's initiative, Wang Jingwei, as one of the leaders of the anti-Chiang coalition, sent a letter to Chiang Kai-shek in which he advocated structural reform of politics—including replacing the presidential system by the cabinet system—with the expectation that the reform would abolish the one-person rule of Chiang Kai-shek while bringing himself a fair share of the power with other leaders through the collective leadership system. In the letter Wang Jingwei listed seven preconditions for agreeing to hold the peace conference and for reconciliation between Chiang Kai-shek and the leaders of the coalition. The replacement of the presidential form of government by the cabinet form was the fifth precondition. Other preconditions included abolishing the position of commander-in-chief of the Nationalist army; setting up a collective leadership; and calling on all members of the First, Second and Third CECs to participate in the Fourth National Congress of the KMT.[35]

After Chiang Kai-shek agreed to negotiate with the coalition based on these preconditions, the peace conference was convened in Shanghai on October 27, 1931. Representatives of the anti-Chiang coalition, including Wang Jingwei, Sun Ke, and Zou Lu, participated in the conference. Chiang Kai-shek's representatives, including Chen Minshu, Cai Yuanpei, Chen Yuren, attended but Chiang himself did not show up.

Based on Wang Jingwei's proposal for constitutional reform expressed in his letter, a Resolution on the Reform of the Nationalist Government was passed on the last day of the peace conference (October 31, 1931).[36] The resolution laid down eleven principles for the design of a cabinet form of government. The first principle explicitly stated that the president of the Nationalist government should be only a figurehead of state:

> The president of the national government is the head of state who does not take executive responsibility. He is the president in the cabinet system. His term is two years and he may take two terms. . . . The president of the national government shall not be allowed to hold any other post concurrently.[37]

Other principles promoted collective leadership by establishing a rotation system for the chairmanship of the National Government Council. Governmental authority would be shared among a group of top elites (primarily the heads of different branches of the government) according to these principles. It was stated that:

> The National Government Council is the supreme government organ. There shall be three standing councillors who will rotate the chairmanship at the council meetings. . . . The Legislative, Judicial, Examination, and Control Yuan are collectively accountable to the National Government Council. . . . The Central Executive Committee and Central Supervisory Committee members of the KMT shall be councillors of the national government.[38]

The Executive Yuan would be established, according to the fourth principle, as the true executive:

> The Executive Yuan takes true executive responsibility and is the responsible cabinet. It is accountable to the National Government Council.[39]

Wang Jingwei's letter to Chiang Kai-shek and the resolution adopted at the peace conference clearly demonstrate that Wang Jingwei, as a political leader in the weak position, systematically advocated the cabinet system for the design of the Nationalist government during its formative period.

Sun Ke's Institutional Preference

Sun Ke's political influence came mainly from the fact that he was the only son of Sun Yat-sen. Never could he possibly become the dominant leader in KMT politics, and therefore he was never interested in the presidential system. Sun Ke formally expressed his institutional preference for the cabinet form of government for the first time in Paris in 1928 when he cosigned the proposal with Hu Hanmin for the promulgation of the five-power government.[40] Other than that, Sun Ke had an opportunity to systematically express his institutional preference when he accepted Chiang Kai-shek's offer to serve as president of the Legislative Yuan in autumn 1932 and was appointed at the same time to supervise the drafting of a permanent constitution.

The proposal to draft the permanent constitution was put forward by Sun Ke and accepted by the Third Plenary Session of the Fourth CEC in 1932. As leader of the group drafting the constitution, Sun Ke had a good chance to impose his institutional preference on the constitution. The first four drafts of the constitution, which were finished during the period 1932–1934 under his leadership, clearly designated the cabinet form for the Nationalist government.[41] Not only was the president of the national government a figurehead of state, but power sharing among the top elites was guaranteed by the constitution.

According to the four early drafts of the constitution, the president of the national government was to be endowed with little more than symbolic power. The government's executive and administrative power was to reside in the cabinet, which was to be composed of the president of the Executive Yuan (the premier) and the heads of ministries. Considerable power was vested in the two legislative organs of the government: the Legislative Yuan and the National Assembly. The Legislative Yuan, headed by Sun Ke himself, would have authority to discuss and decide matters of law, the budget, martial law, declarations of war and peace, and other important matters relating to foreign affairs. The National Assembly, a representative body elected directly by the people, would have broad-ranging authority. It was to elect most of the top-level members of the government, heads of *yuan*, and the members of the Legislative and Control Yuan. If dissatisfied with either the policies or the administration of the government, it could intervene and, if still unsatisfied, impeach the president.[42] These provisions were so congenial to Sun Ke's preferences that, despite changes in all the other articles of the various early drafts, they remained virtually untouched throughout the four early drafts of the constitution written under the leadership of Sun Ke.

It was because of the consistent design of the cabinet system that Sun Ke's fourth draft was rejected by the Fifth Plenary Session of the Fourth CEC—which, at the insistence of Chiang Kai-shek, passed the Resolution on Principles of Drafting the Constitution on the last day of the meeting (December 14, 1934), criticizing Sun Ke's cabinet design and ordered a rewriting of the draft. The resolution declared that "the executive authority should not be limited by inflexible regulations." This meant that the collective leadership—which provided power sharing among Chiang Kai-shek (as chief executive) and Sun Ke (as head of the Legislative Yuan) and other heads of the *yuan*—was not acceptable to the Central Executive Committee controlled by Chiang Kai-shek.

The Institutional Preferences Compared

In comparison, Chiang Kai-shek, the most powerful leader, was the only one who preferred the presidential form of government. Wang Jingwei, Hu Hanmin, and Sun Ke, in relatively weaker positions, all expressed their preference for the cabinet system and showed no interest whatever in presidential government during the formative period of the Nationalist government. This empirical finding concurs with the theoretical assumption that political leaders' institutional preferences are shaped by their relative power position and that the political leader anticipating to become dominance favors the singular leadership of presidential system whereas the relative weaker leaders like the collective nature of cabinet system. In the next three chapters we will see how these four political leaders in Nationalist China fought for their preferred forms of government institutions.

Chapter 6

The Succession Struggle: From Cabinet to Presidential Government, 1925–1928

The first chapter proposed that the design of government institutions is an outcome of struggle for the position of power from which such a choice can be made. Indeed, the interplay between power and preference is at the heart of constitution-making in Nationalist China. Having established the positive relationship between a political leader's power position and his institutional preference in the preceding chapter, we can now move to the next step of the empirical study: examining the actual designs of the Nationalist government in the context of the power struggle among the four leading players.

This chapter analyzes the initial design of the cabinet form of Nationalist government and its replacement by the presidential form during the period 1925–1928 when Chiang Kai-shek gradually rose to power in the KMT regime. The first Nationalist government, established in Guangzhou in 1925, was designed as a cabinet system. Although Chiang Kai-shek anticipated becoming dominant in the regime during this period, his institutional preference for the presidential system could not be implemented until he had actually defeated his political rivals. In other words, Chiang Kai-shek had to mobilize his power resources to prevail over Wang Jingwei, Hu Hanmin, and Sun Ke in order to install the presidential system. Although Chiang was the most powerful leader and his rivals could not compete with him individually, a combination of forces by Wang Jingwei, Hu Hanmin, and Sun Ke could block Chiang and install their preferred cabinet system.[1] This was especially true considering that Chiang Kai-shek rose to power in the KMT hierarchy so late and so rapidly and inevitably made many political and military enemies on his speedy way up. In fact, faced by the combined opposition forces within the KMT, Chiang was forced to resign from his positions in the party and government twice, in 1927 and 1931 respectively.[2] In order to prevail, it was always important for Chiang to ally with one of his rivals or to compete with them separately.

Thus the alternatives of a presidential versus a cabinet form of government in Nationalist China reflected changes in the balance of power between Chiang Kai-shek and his rivals. The presidential form of government did not become the final choice until Chiang Kai-shek had eliminated his rivals and become the single victor in the power contest in 1936. Table 6 summarizes this relationship between the institutional choices and the outcomes of power struggle during this period.

Establishment of the Cabinet Form in 1925

The adoption of the cabinet form of government by the first Nationalist government in Guangzhou in 1925 was an outcome of the balance of power in the succession contest following the death of Sun Yat-sen. When Sun Yat-sen died in 1925, he left a will that has since been an inspiration for the KMT. Sun Yat-sen did not, however, determine his successor in the will. Although several KMT leaders were

TABLE 6
Alternative Institutional Designs and Outcomes of the Power Struggle

Institutional Design	*Power Relations Among Players*
Cabinet system (1925–1928)	A balance of power existed among Chiang Kai-shek, Wang Jingwei, Hu Hanmin, and Sun Ke.
Presidential system (1928–1931)	Chiang Kai-shek defeated his leading rivals and anticipated becoming dominant in the regime.
Cabinet system (1931–1936)	A grand coalition, composed of Wang Jingwei, Hu Hanmin, Sun Ke, and influential regional militarists, blocked Chiang Kai-shek.
Presidential system (1936–)	Chiang Kai-shek eliminated all his leading rivals.

potential contenders for the position, Sun Yat-sen "gave no clear indication as to the identity of the man who should carry on his work as the leader. He left four outstanding lieutenants, namely, Chiang Kai-shek, Hu Hanmin, Liao Zhongkai, and Wang Jingwei."[3] Among these four "outstanding lieutenants," Liao Zhongkai was assassinated soon after the Guangzhou government was founded. Thus Wang Jingwei, Hu Hanmin, and Chiang Kai-shek became the "big three" in the bitter, even bloody, succession struggle. Wang Jingwei was regarded as the leader of the leftist wing of the KMT and an impetuous man who espoused collaboration with the Communists.[4] The right wing of the party was led by Hu Hanmin and the Western Hill Group, which distrusted the Communists.[5] Chiang Kai-shek, an ambitious newcomer to politics, cautiously maintained a centrist position in the early stages of this period.[6]

Hu Hanmin was entrusted with the position of acting generalissimo of the Nationalist government when Sun Yat-sen left Guangdong for Beijing in early 1925. "This post was not controversial until Sun Yat-sen fell seriously ill," as Zhou Binwo and Chen Hongmin's study of Hu Hanmin's political career points out.[7] While Sun was still alive, the acting generalissimo would not be regarded as his designated successor because Sun Yat-sen was always the leader of the KMT whether he was in Guangdong or in Beijing. Nevertheless, holding the post of acting generalissimo after the death of Sun Yat-sen would imply that the holder, trusted by Sun Yat-sen, could be regarded as the leader's designated successor. But Hu Hanmin was not the only potential successor to Sun Yat-sen. Wang Jingwei, as leader of the left wing of the KMT, and Chiang Kai-shek, as commander-in-chief of the Nationalist army, both sought to be Sun's successor. Hu was therefore placed in a predicament and could become a target of attack from all the other contenders if he chose to remain in the position of acting generalissimo.

As leader of the right wing in the KMT during the period of leftist dominance, Hu Hanmin could not hope to win this contest. Moreover, Hu Hanmin never had the capacity to command military forces even though he was acting generalissimo. Zhou Binwo and Chen Hongmin illuminate Hu Hanmin's difficult position in this regard. Immediately after the death of Sun Yat-sen was announced, several former warlords refused to obey Hu Hanmin's orders and moved their troops toward Guangzhou, aiming to overthrow the weakened

Guangdong regime, even though these very same men had declared allegiance to the regime when Sun Yat-sen was alive.[8]

Hu Hanmin himself knew his weak position and did not anticipate becoming the most powerful leader in the regime. It was in this situation that he proposed that the Nationalist regime under the generalissimo be reorganized into a cabinet form of civilian government. Hu Hanmin had already discussed the reorganization issue with Liao Zhongkai when he learned that Sun Yat-sen was seriously ill. He now submitted a formal proposal to the KMT's Central Executive Committee immediately after the death of Sun Yat-sen was confirmed.[9] Hu Hanmin's proposal was adopted by the CEC at its meeting on June 15, 1925, but Hu was not able to assume the chairmanship of the newly established National Government Council in Guangdong.[10] Wang Jingwei, the leader of the left wing, was selected as chairman because the party's left wing was in the dominant position at the CEC meeting.[11]

Wang Jingwei, wielding the chairmanship of the Nationalist government, might have a chance to become dominant in the party and the government so long as he could win time to consolidate his position and make his struggle with Chiang Kai-shek a contest within the party arena. The Guangzhou government was now in a crisis, however, facing a military threat from warlords in the north and troubled by leftist/rightist dissension from within. Under the circumstances, Wang was unable to resolve the crisis and the playing field shifted from the party to the military arena where Wang lacked the resources to compete with Chiang Kai-shek. At that time the military forces of the Guangzhou government were commanded by Chiang Kai-shek and a Guangdong provincial militarist, Xu Chongzhi. Hu Hanmin and Liao Zhongkai, as longtime loyal followers of Sun Yat-sen, were very influential in the party. Moreover, the rightists and leftists were soon to come to blows after the death of Sun Yat-sen, a battle that the leftists were to lose. Under the circumstances, Wang Jingwei could not anticipate prevailing over his rivals to become the single most powerful leader.

Although Wang Jingwei could not anticipate becoming dominant, his rivals could not easily defeat him at that time. Thus there was a temporary balance of power among the leading power contenders that produced the cabinet form of government: the council system.

The Nationalist government, organized according to the first Organic Law, was characterized by collective leadership.[12] The chairman of the national government was merely a presiding officer elected by and from the members of the National Government Council. The council's powers were concentrated in the standing committee rather than in the person of the chairman.[13]

The first council of sixteen formed the first cabinet of the Nationalist government. Of the sixteen, five constituted the standing committee of the council, including Wang Jingwei, Hu Hanmin, Tan Yankai, Xu Chongzhi, and Lin Sen. Three ministries were established within the council and headed by three influential figures: Xu Chongzhi as military minister, Liao Zhongkai as finance minister, and Hu Hanmin as foreign minister. Nominations of ministers were made by the Standing Committee of the National Government Council and approved by the CEC.[14] Under the circumstances, it was hard for Wang Jingwei, the chairman of the council, to make any important decisions without at least consulting members of the powerful standing committee and the ministers. This was a collegial form of cabinet government in which the sixteen councillors formed the collective leadership and the five members of the standing committee (and to a certain extent the three influential ministers) shared the ultimate authority of the government.

Liao Zhongkai's Assassination

The cabinet form of government was maintained until 1928 when Chiang Kai-shek claimed victory over his leading rivals and rose to the top of the KMT. Chiang Kai-shek's victory started from the assassination of Liao Zhongkai in Guangzhou on August 20, 1925. The assassination not only eliminated one of Chiang's leading rivals, Liao Zhongkai, but also provided an opportunity for Chiang Kai-shek to oust Hu Hanmin and, later, to defeat Wang Jingwei.

Liao Zhongkai was one of the national government councillors and the powerful financial minister in Guangdong. As a trusted follower of Sun Yat-sen and the radical leader of the party's left wing, he openly advocated close cooperation with the Communists after the death of Sun Yat-sen. Liao hence became a major target attacked by the right-wing faction of which Hu Hanmin was regarded the leader.

On August 10, 1925, ten days before the assassination, Hu Hanmin held a meeting of the rightist members of the CEC in Guangzhou, a meeting that called for convening the First Plenary Session of the Second CEC on September 15, 1925, in order to oust Liao Zhongkai from the government.[15] In the meantime, Hu Yisheng, a younger brother of Hu Hanmin, allowed his zeal to outrun his discretion to the extent of urging in print that Liao Zhongkai should be "removed."[16] This infamous counsel was followed by the assassination of Liao Zhongkai near the headquarters of the CEC on August 20, 1925. Hu Hanmin thus became one of the suspects for the assassination.

A special investigation committee was organized on the same day as the assassination. Vested with political, military, and police power and headed by Chiang Kai-shek, Wang Jingwei, and Xu Chunzhi, the committee declared martial law in Guangzhou on the evening of August 20, 1925.[17] When the investigation concluded that two army generals under Xu Chongzhi were involved, they were executed along with the actual assassins, who had been mortally wounded and arrested earlier. Seizing this sudden opportunity, Chiang Kai-shek sent his First Army Corps and Huangpu cadets to disarm Xu Chunzhi's troops by surprise attack in the middle of the night of September 20, 1925. Practically no resistance was made. Xu Chunzhi was forced to leave Guangzhou for Shanghai and his soldiers were later reorganized by Chiang and incorporated into his First Army Corps.[18] The implementation of martial law had to rely entirely on the military strength of Chiang's First Army Corps and Huangpu cadets. Chiang Kai-shek thereby became the most powerful leader in the special investigation committee.[19]

Hu Hanmin's younger brother, Hu Yisheng, was also implicated in the assassination but he was not punished since he managed to escape from Guangzhou. The assassination of Liao, allegedly at the instigation of Hu Hanmin's brother, caused a great outcry against Hu Hanmin himself.[20] In this situation, Chiang Kai-shek sent his troops and took Hu Hanmin for "protection" to a house near the Huangpu Military Academy. In September 1925, Hu Hanmin decided to leave China for Russia to observe Soviet party affairs and study social conditions.[21] Thus the assassination not only eliminated Liao Zhongkai but also ousted Hu Hanmin—thereby removing two of Chiang Kai-shek's leading rivals in the succession struggle.

Two Competing Nationalist Governments

After both Liao Zhongkai and Hu Hanmin were driven out of the succession struggle, the competition between Chiang Kai-shek and Wang Jingwei came to the forefront. The result was a stalemate that produced two Nationalist governments and three CEC headquarters in 1927. One Nationalist government, led by Wang Jingwei in Wuhan since January 1927, was regarded as a leftist government because of its cooperation with the Communists. The other Nationalist government, a rightist government, was established by Chiang Kai-shek in Nanjing in April 1927.

The open split between Chiang Kai-shek and Wang Jingwei began after the successful advance of the Northern Expedition in July 1926. Considering the rather inferior military position of the south compared with that of its enemies, as well as the internal dissension that was increasing rather than subsiding, there was some dispute as to the wisdom of such an expedition. Chiang Kai-shek advocated an immediate Northern Expedition. Since a political vacuum already existed around the Yangtze and in the north, he argued, the resistance of the northern militarists would be weak.[22] In pushing for an early launch of the Northern Expedition, Chiang Kai-shek was shifting the playing field from the party to the military arena in his competition with Wang Jingwei. In fact, Chiang's effort to define the situation in military terms was a skillful political maneuver to draw attention to his personal resources and away from those he lacked, such as ideological authority and longevity in the party. Chiang's maneuver was successful. There was indeed a vacuum to be filled in the north and the rapid success of the Northern Expedition surprised even the most sanguine. Within three months of its start, the Nationalist forces had gained control of the important city of Wuhan. By March 1927 the lower Yangtze provinces and the Nanjing–Shanghai area had fallen into the hands of the Nationalist armies. In January 1927 the Nationalist government was moved from Guangzhou to Wuhan.

Along with the advance of the Northern Expedition, Chiang Kai-shek, as commander-in-chief of the Nationalist army, believed that his military service had become "well-nigh indispensable" to the Nationalist government.[23] Realizing that Wang Jingwei and his left wing of the party were firmly in control of the Wuhan government, in February 1927 Chiang Kai-shek held several provisional CPC meetings in

Nanchang, where his military headquarters were located, and proposed to move the capital to Nanchang.[24] His proposal was rejected by leaders of the Wuhan government.[25] Indeed, Wang Jingwei's supporters scheduled the Third Plenary Session of the Second CEC in Wuhan on March 1, 1927, and proceeded to release Chiang Kai-shek from all his party and government assignments, reducing him to the rank of mere army commander.[26] Chiang Kai-shek and his supporters refused to attend this meeting, which was certain to be dominated by the left-wingers, and instead invited certain members of the CEC to stop by Nanchang on their way to Wuhan. Chiang Kai-shek tried to persuade these CEC members, including Tan Yankai, He Xiangling, Chen Gongbo, Li Liejun, and Ding Weifeng, to hold a plenary meeting in Nanchang to pass his motion proposing that the Nationalist government move to Nanchang instead of Wuhan. In the meantime, he sent a telegram to Wuhan in the name of the CEC warning that "before the party headquarters and government were all moved, Wuhan [that is, the government] could not operate in the name of the central party headquarters and the government."[27] Nevertheless, these CEC members refused Chiang Kai-shek's proposal and left Nanchang for Wuhan on March 6, 1927.[28]

Because of Chiang's interference, the Third Plenary Session was postponed. In a preparatory meeting of the CEC plenum on the evening of March 7, 1927, there was a debate about whether the plenum should wait for Chiang Kai-shek. Tan Yankai argued that the plenum should not be held until the arrival of Chiang and certain other CEC members. But most participants did not agree: "For the sake of revolution," they argued, "we should not worry about how many people show up at the meeting."[29] Thus the Third Plenary Session of the Second CEC, with thirty-three members present, was held on March 10–17, 1927.[30] It passed a resolution to expel Chiang Kai-shek and his supporters from the party leadership.

Chiang Kai-shek watched these developments from Nanchang and began to lay plans to set up a rival government. Chiang's control of military forces as commander-in-chief of the Nationalist army gave him a solid power base with which to establish the rebel government. Moreover, the military situation in the lower Yangtze had moved in favor of his Northern Expedition: Chiang Kai-shek had practically complete control of southern Jiangsu, Anhui, Zhejiang, and Fujian provinces by March 1927.[31] When Nanjing was taken by his armies in April 1927, Chiang launched the rival Nationalist government and declared that the Wuhan regime was Communist-controlled and therefore non-Nationalist.[32] The first government order issued by the Nanjing government was a *qingdang mingling* ("order to clean up the party"). This order listed 197 of the most wanted Communists and leftists in the KMT.[33] Chiang Kai-shek purged the Communists from the ranks of the KMT on April 12, 1927, immediately after the Nanjing regime was set up.[34] The Nanjing government was henceforth regarded as a rightist government.

The establishment of Chiang Kai-shek's rival government was to be approved at the Fourth Plenary Session of the Second CEC, scheduled to be held in Nanjing on April 15, 1927. Since Wang Jingwei and most CEC members remained in Wuhan, however, they would not attend the session.[35] Chiang Kai-shek therefore changed his plan and convened a "political council discussion meeting" (*tanhua hui)* in Nanjing on April 16 and 17, 1927. The political council meeting denounced the Third Plenum of the Second CEC and Wang Jingwei's Wuhan government as Communist-controlled and declared the formal establishment of Chiang Kai-shek's Nationalist government in Nanjing.[36] While the friction between Chiang Kai-shek and Wang Jingwei was coming to a head, most members of the right-wing Western Hill Group stayed in Shanghai. They were inclined to support Chiang Kai-shek when they found that he had denounced the Communists and was determined to bring them to bay. On April 8, 1927, a Provisional Political Council *(lingshi zhengzhi weiyuanhui)* of the CEC was organized in Shanghai. Fifteen extreme right-wing members of the CEC were present at this meeting. They decided to support Chiang Kai-shek and the Nanjing government.[37]

Thus two Nationalist governments and three headquarters of the KMT's central authority—in Wuhan, in Nanjing, and in Shanghai—existed side by side claiming leadership of the party in 1927. This was a typical outcome of the anarchic authority relationship: the deadlock between competing leaders of the KMT had led to the diffusion of formal party authority into different political centers. Both Chiang Kai-shek and Wang Jingwei undoubtedly hoped that the split in the party might be healed—though, of course, "in each instance at the expense of the other."[38]

An Armed Race

The split of the Nationalist government produced a state of anarchy in the regime. Both Chiang Kai-shek and Wang Jingwei were supported by their own factions and military forces. Neither could compromise on the issue of who between them should lead the Nationalist government. In these circumstances, they had no choice but to rely on their military strength as the ultimate claim to leadership. Thus an armed race between the Nanjing government and the Wuhan government was carried out immediately following the government split.

At this time Chiang Kai-shek directly commanded more than 120,000 soldiers, although most had recently come from old warlords' armies and were not committed to Chiang's leadership. And since Chiang was still at war with warlords in the north, it was difficult for him to launch an immediate military attack on Wang Jingwei's Wuhan government. Nevertheless, Chiang Kai-shek never stopped preparing for military action against the Wuhan government.[39] On Wang Jingwei's side, several leaders in his Wuhan government urged an immediate attack on the rebel Nanjing government. For example, Zhou Enlai and other Communists in the Wuhan government proposed an "Eastern Expedition" *(dongzheng)* and urged Wang Jingwei to attack Chiang Kai-shek at once.[40] But the army then under direct command of his Wuhan government was very limited and, like the Nanjing government, worried about the threat from the warlords in the northeast. Therefore, it was difficult for Wang Jingwei to mobilize armed forces against Chiang Kai-shek.[41]

Under these circumstances, both Chiang Kai-shek and Wang Jingwei decided to advance northward and eliminate the threat from the warlords—recognizing that the one who could reach Beijing first and win a striking success at the last stage of the Northern Expedition would gain enormous prestige at the expense of his rival.[42] Beijing in Chinese means "Northern Capital," and it was the final destination of the Northern Expedition. In May 1927, while the troops of Chiang Kai-shek's First Army Corps crossed the Yangtze River, Wuhan's expeditionary forces were also successful in a fierce engagement against northerners in Henan province.[43] While the armies commanded by Wuhan and Nanjing were competitively marching north, a powerful regional militarist, Feng Yuxiang, the commander of the

Second Army Corps of the Nationalist army, was fighting his way north as well and conquering several provinces located between Nanjing and Beijing. By June 1927 he had some 150,000 soldiers directly under his command.[44] Feng Yuxiang's attitude toward the Nanjing and Wuhan governments, therefore, became an important political factor influencing the military balance between Chiang Kai-shek and Wang Jingwei.[45]

Wang Jingwei tried to prevent Feng Yuxiang from cooperating with Chiang Kai-shek and took the initiative by requesting a conference with Feng. Thus it was that Wang Jingwei led a delegation of the Wuhan government to meet in conference with Feng Yuxiang in Zhenzhou on June 8, 1927. As a result of the conference, which lasted two days (June 10 and 11), Feng was appointed chairman of the KMT's Political Subcouncil for Henan, Shanxi, and Gansu provinces.[46] Feng's response was not enthusiastic, however, for what Feng needed most was not an appointment from the Wuhan government but financial resources. For Feng Yuxiang, "the most difficult problem was the shortage of military supplies because of frequent military movements."[47] But Wang Jingwei's Wuhan government was itself in a difficult financial situation and could not afford to meet Feng's huge need for financial aid. Thus Wang's mission failed.[48]

The Feng–Wang meeting alerted Chiang Kai-shek. Immediately after the Zhenzhou conference, Chiang Kai-shek made a trip to Xuzhou, a city newly conquered by his army, and sent an invitation to Feng Yuxiang requesting a conference.[49] Feng Yuxiang accepted the invitation and planned to "repeat his victory at the conference table in Zhenzhou at another conference—this time at Xuzhou."[50] On June 19, accompanied by a bodyguard of five thousand soldiers, Feng Yuxiang made a secret trip to Xuzhou. Indeed, the trip was so secret that even Feng's staff members on board his train did not know where they were heading until they arrived at Xuzhou station.[51] Chiang Kai-shek showed every courtesy to Feng, setting out in his private train to meet him and escort him back to the city.[52] The Chiang–Feng meeting lasted for two days (June 20 and 21). Feng Yuxiang told Chiang Kai-shek that he came to Xuzhou as a mediator between the two rival governments in Nanjing and Wuhan. He skillfully evaded declaring in which direction his sympathies lay until Chiang Kai-shek promised that the Nanjing government would provide Feng Yuxiang's troops 2.5 million yuan monthly for military expenses from July 1927 on.[53]

Accepting this financial offer, Feng Yuxiang then issued a circulating telegram to the Wuhan government urging Wang Jingwei to end his cooperation with the Communists.[54] Feng's action encouraged Chiang Kai-shek: on the way back from Xuzhou to Nanjing, Chiang told a foreign reporter that "an alliance has been concluded with General Feng Yuxiang, who is willing to join the Nanjing government in fighting the Northern party."[55]

When Chiang Kai-shek returned to Nanjing, he decided to drive the Northern Expedition toward Beijing immediately. At first the advance of Chiang's troops was very successful and the ascendancy of his soldiers over the enemy was complete. Indeed, Chiang Kai-shek had advanced over 300 miles and was near Jinan, the capital of Shandong province, by the end of June.[56] The soldiers of the northern warlords were thrown into a panic, but out of this desperate situation grew a measure of cooperation among the northern warlords under the leadership of Zhang Zuolin.[57] In order to hold up the advance of Chiang's troops, Zhang Zuolin issued a statement in the middle of June to the effect that he was unable to protect Japanese nationals in his territory. On the next day, 1,500 Japanese troops were sent to Jinan where they constructed a barbed wire barricade on a front several miles long and established what they called a neutral zone. This line became a significant barrier, for the zone lay in the direct line of Chiang Kai-shek's advance.[58]

The advance of Chiang's troops was brought to an abrupt halt south of Jinan by a complication of difficulties—perhaps the most important of which, apart from Japanese hostility, was the shortage of funds and supplies. By this time Chiang Kai-shek's armies were in Shandong, some 350 miles from their base in Nanjing.[59] For troops who had swept everything before them in their advance northward, the difficulties began to multiply. First of all, there were financial troubles: the Nanjing regime had not thoroughly organized its revenue-producing sources, and the northern campaign had proved a severe strain on its funds. Second, there were diplomatic entanglements that were proving embarrassing: American, British, French, and Japanese troops had been sent to reinforce the garrisons in Tianjin and Beijing. Third, Chiang's new ally, Feng Yuxiang, had failed to assist him by a flanking movement against the threatening northern allies.[60] In the meantime, Chiang Kai-shek had to prevent attack by the troops of the Wuhan government. These difficulties resulted in the defeat of Chiang's armies by the combined forces of the northern warlords, forcing him to retreat back to Nanjing early in August. The situation in Nanjing became increasingly dangerous as the army of Sun Chungfang, a warlord, threatened to occupy Nanjing. Chiang Kai-shek's prestige was badly tarnished.[61]

Seizing this opportunity, Wang Jingwei allied with two Guangdong and Guangxi regional militarists, Li Zhongren and Bai Chongxi, who were then enlisted in Chiang's Nanjing government but did not belong to Chiang's faction. This alliance started in August 1927 when Wang Jingwei's Wuhan government, following Chiang's example in Nanjing, conducted a severe purge of Communists from its own ranks.[62] One of Wang Jingwei's purposes was to appease and seek the support of the Guangdong and Guangxi regional militarists. After the purge in Wuhan, Wang Jingwei sent a telegram to Li Zhongren declaring his firm anti-Communist attitude and asking support from the powerful regional militarist.[63] Wang Jingwei's telegram, coupled with the news of Chiang's defeat by northern warlords, persuaded Li Zhongren and Bai Chongxi to accept Wang Jingwei's request to oust Chiang Kai-shek from the Nanjing government.[64]

Chiang Kai-shek's Resignation

Facing this conspiracy, Chiang Kai-shek announced his sudden resignation from the Nanjing government in August 1927.[65] Some historians believe that the resignation was one of Chiang's major political failures. Yang Shubao, for example, one of Chiang Kai-shek's biographers, says that "Chiang Kai-shek was forced to resign when he had no other choice."[66] But other scholars have suggested that Chiang Kai-shek's sudden resignation can be regarded as a counteroffensive. As Hollington K. Tong indicates, this action was "a powerful appeal" to Chiang's army and his followers in the KMT.[67]

It is true that Chiang Kai-shek's resignation came after pressure from Wang Jingwei and the Guangdong–Guangxi militarists. It is also true that this action could be construed as a strong appeal to Chiang's followers. To make his appeal both explicit and powerful, Chiang Kai-shek delivered an emotional speech announcing his retirement at a conference of the Military Commission in Nanjing on August 12, 1927. He stated that the main motive inspiring his retirement was to live up to his duty to defend the unity of the party. He then added the customary self-criticism that is usually appended to statements made by politicians in China upon their retirement. Chiang's statement, coupled with his retirement, brought him full credit for having made a personal sacrifice for the good of the nation, and his prestige, far from suffering, rose to even greater heights. Indeed, an article written by C. Y. Mong in *Guowen Zhoubao* (Guowen Weekly) said:

> Where is there any man who has been willing to give up his hard-fought-for post and voluntarily retire to private life, for no other reason than the preservation of the party and the salvation of the country from further bloody internecine warfare? . . . General Chiang's retirement sets the first example of this kind. His retirement is being praised as an act of unprecedented heroism. The act has undoubtedly surprised and dismayed most people who could not but burst into tears to see such a great leader, after having rendered so much service to the party and country, retired to private life; but at the same time, they cannot but wonder why such a leader who is so much needed by China today should retire at such a critical moment. [68]

Chiang Kai-shek issued an emotional farewell to the cadets and students of the Huangpu Military Academy. He spoke of the bravery and self-sacrifice of academy men during the Northern Expedition. Referring to his own retirement, Chiang told the students that his withdrawal from active participation did not really lose them a leader or protector, as the true revolutionary is self-reliant, and his action would bring out independence in his followers. Chiang made two important pledges in his conclusion. One was that officers and men who fell in the advance from Guangzhou to the Yangtze would have fitting funeral services, a matter of extreme importance in the Chinese mind. The second was that dependents of these fallen soldiers should be given adequate compensation by the government. In the words of a biographer: "These were pledges that were never lost sight of through the years, and were implemented when opportunity came."[69]

Chiang's appeal to his followers proved effective. Hollington K. Tong points out that when Chiang Kai-shek resigned from the government and left Nanjing for his native village, Xikou, in Zhejiang province, the morale of his Nationalist armies and factional followers in the KMT was seriously affected. Chiang Kai-shek's followers vociferously insisted on calling him back to Nanjing. Even Feng Yuxiang, the powerful regional militarist, sent Chiang a telegram urging him to come back: "You are the pillar of China today. Upon you China, as well as the party, rests her hopes of salvation." He added: "Should you disregard all this, and insist upon retiring, I, Yuxiang, cannot but do the same."[70]

The Unified Government in Crisis

After Chiang Kai-shek retired and the cooperation between the Wuhan government and the Communists ended, a unified Nationalist government was established through the mediation of the Western Hill Group. In September 1927, leaders of this faction called a meeting to which representatives from both the Wuhan and the Nanjing governments were invited. This meeting established a Special Central Committee and published a "Statement of the Special Central Committee" and a "Statement About the Establishment of the National Government" on September 17, 1927.[71]

The Special Committee held ten meetings between September 20 and November 16, 1927, reorganizing the Nationalist government.[72] The National Government Council now consisted of forty-six people representing the Nanjing and Wuhan governments and the Western Hill Group. In this new government the Guangdong and Guangxi militarists played a dominant role. In fact, the Military Commission comprised almost all of these regional militarists. Thus the members of the government had to obey orders given by Li Zhongren and Bai Chongxi, who led the Guangdong and Guangxi militarists.[73]

Nevertheless, Chiang Kai-shek's followers within the party and the military never stopped denouncing the newly unified Nationalist government in Nanjing. Ultimately an intraparty conflict between Chiang's followers and the supporters of the Special Committee culminated in a bloody incident triggered by a meeting held by the party's Nanjing city committee on November 20, 1927. The trouble began when a student from the Central School of Party Affairs (Zhongyang Dangwu Xuexiao), a KMT school affiliated with the Organization Department and controlled by the CC Clique, jumped on the table to demand the resignation of the Special Committee. He and three other students were therefore arrested by the newly organized government under the Special Committee. The next day, hundreds of students from the school took to the streets protesting the arrest. One day after the arrested students were released, Gu Zhenggang, the head of the school, organized a mass rally calling for expulsion of the Western Hill Group from the party and for the dissolution of the Special Committee.

Faced with a strong challenge from Chiang's followers, the government led by the Special Committee did not give in at first but sent troops to disperse the mass rally. In the ensuing conflict, one student and two young workers were killed and more than a dozen people were wounded. This bloody incident touched off a revolt in the party. The CEC members who had earlier maintained neutrality on the friction between Chiang Kai-shek and the Special Committee now began to denounce the committee. Li Liejun and Tan Yankai, for example, two senior CEC members who had joined the government led by the Special Committee, openly criticized the Western Hill Group and demanded the arrest of those responsible for the incident. Chiang Kai-shek, seizing this opportunity, published a statement in Shanghai saying the incident was "an issue related to the life and death of the revolution. If there is no other way to resolve it, we must appeal to a revolutionary way."[74]

On the military front, after the resignation of Chiang Kai-shek no one in the new government had the capacity to command his armies. The only military forces the Special Committee could rely upon were those commanded by the Guangdong and Guangxi militarists. This situation greatly encouraged Sun Chuanfang, a warlord in the north, who launched a new attack hoping to regain territory south of the Yangtze. The troops of the Guangdong and Guangxi militarists, under attack from the warlord, retreated across the Yangtze from Puko on August 17. Nanjing was threatened in September. Only after Feng Yuxiang's troops came to its rescue in the middle of September was the threat to Nanjing temporarily relaxed.[75]

While heavy fighting was proceeding in nearby Nanjing, friction among the Nationalist armies, led by different commanders, broke out into fights in Guangzhou and the Yangtze valley. After suppressing the Communist revolt in Jiangxi province, Zhang Fakui, a general of the Nationalist army, marched his troops into Guangzhou using the excuse of pursuing and attacking the Communists. The city at that time was under the control of Li Jisheng, another general of the Nationalist army. Jealousies immediately began to develop between the rival military commanders. After Li Jisheng left Guangzhou for

Shanghai to attend a KMT conference on November 15, Zhang Fakui took advantage of his absence and attacked his troops. Elsewhere, in the Yangtze valley, friction between generals Tang Shengzhi and Chen Qian came to a head on October 18 when Chen's Sixteenth Army Corps attacked the Thirtieth Army Corps under Tang.[76] This chaotic situation seemed to nullify Chiang Kai-shek's achievements and raised two huge questions: who could successfully meet this crisis, and who could lead the Northern Expedition to success? Chiang, at this time, became "the only logical person for this titanic task."[77]

The Victory of Chiang Kai-shek

While the Nationalist government in Nanjing was in panic, Chiang Kai-shek was honeymooning in Japan with his bride, Song Meiling. A little over a week after Chiang Kai-shek returned to China, a preliminary conference of the Fourth Plenary Session of the Second CEC was called in Shanghai on December 3, 1927. At this conference Chiang was nominated to resume control as commander-in-chief of the Nationalist army, and this nomination was unanimously approved at the meeting of December 10. Ironically the nomination was initiated by Wang Jingwei—the result of a political deal between Chiang and Wang. Before the meeting in December, Chiang Kai-shek and Wang Jingwei had already exchanged telegrams and in fact had met in Shanghai. In these telegrams and meetings they discussed the agenda for the Fourth Plenary Session: to abolish the Special Committee and end the Western Hill Group's power monopoly.[78] Why did Wang Jingwei cooperate with Chiang Kai-shek at this meeting? Perhaps he wanted to share power when he realized that Chiang Kai-shek would inevitably return to center stage.

Although Wang Jingwei had allied with the Guangdong and Guangxi militarists and successfully ousted Chiang Kai-shek from the Nanjing government in August 1927, he could not get along with the leaders of the right-wing Western Hill Group in the newly unified Nationalist government. In this new government dominated by the Western Hill faction, Wang Jingwei was actually deprived of his "legitimate" position as leader of the Wuhan government. Indeed, the right-wingers found it impossible to accept the left-winger Wang Jingwei in their new government.[79] Although Wang was one of the five standing committee members of the Special Committee (the others were Hu Hanmin, Tan Yankai, Li Liejun, and Cai Yuanpei), he and his followers were eventually forced to leave Nanjing and, in fact, were excluded by the Western Hill Group from the center of the new government soon after the Special Committee was formally established.[80] It was against this background that Wang Jingwei turned to Chiang Kai-shek and insisted on nominating him in the plenary session. Undoubtedly Wang Jingwei made this move with the expectation that Chiang Kai-shek would give him a share of power in return for his nomination.

But Chiang Kai-shek had already anticipated victory in the succession contest and did not wish to share power with Wang Jingwei at all. In fact, one of the first actions taken by Chiang Kai-shek after his return to power was to expel Wang Jingwei from the party. In February 1928, Chiang Kai-shek held the Fourth Plenary Session of the CEC (originally scheduled in January but postponed for a month). At this meeting Chiang Kai-shek not only dissolved the Special Committee, in which several factions shared power, but also expelled Wang Jingwei from the party on the charge of having supported a Communist uprising in Guangzhou on December 11, 1927.[81] Although Wang Jingwei did not have the opportunity to attend the plenary session of the revived CEC, Chiang accepted Wang's nomination to resume as commander-in-chief and made use of him to oust the Western Hill Group.

The Fourth Plenum of the CEC in February 1928 marked the victory of Chiang Kai-shek in the KMT succession struggle. At this meeting Chiang was given control of the party and the Nanjing government by virtue of his reinstatement as chairman of the resurrected Military Commission and commander-in-chief of the armies. It was at this time that the presidential form of government was adopted by the KMT regime. It was no accident that when Chiang Kai-shek took over the chairmanship of the CEC standing committee at its Fifth Plenary Session in August 1928, he requested a revision of the Organic Law. The revised Organic Law of October 8, 1928, in which the five-power system was first installed, dropped the old provision that the president of the national government should be elected by and from the members of the National Government Council. Furthermore, the revised Organic Law made the president concurrently chairman of the CEC and commander-in-chief of the armed forces.[82]

Chiang Kai-shek, as chairman of the CEC, was nominated by the party to take the presidency of the Nationalist government and was inaugurated on October 10, 1928, the National Day. Thus the president in the person of Chiang Kai-shek became the powerful chief of both the state and the government. His power now was completely different from that of his predecessors. The cabinet form of government, established in 1925, was now replaced by the presidential form.

Chapter 7

The Grand Anti-Chiang Coalition: From Presidential to Cabinet Government, 1928–1931

The change in institutional design of the Nationalist government from the cabinet to the presidential system during 1925–1928, as we have seen, was an outcome of the succession struggle in which Chiang Kai-shek defeated his rivals. In light of the theoretical concerns of this book, this change showed that constitution-making reflected the underlying distribution of power. The adoption of a particular institutional design was made not because it provided a lasting solution to the political problems of Nationalist China but because the political leaders in control decided that such a design best served their ambitions. The change in the distribution of power led to the change in institutional design.

Just as the rapid rise of Chiang Kai-shek resulted in the change from the cabinet to the presidential system in 1925–1928, the dramatic formation of an anti-Chiang coalition in 1930 led to the replacement of the presidential system by a cabinet system in 1931. This change took place because Chiang's power over his rivals in the succession struggle was only temporary in 1928: his rivals were not destroyed; they were merely defeated. Indeed, Chiang's rapid emergence induced self-interested cooperation among those threatened by his prospective dominance. Starting in 1930, the grand anti-Chiang coalition composed of Wang Jingwei, Hu Hanmin, and Sun Ke and backed by powerful regional militarists was formed in order to check Chiang Kai-shek's prospective dominance in the KMT regime. While none of these political leaders was able to block Chiang Kai-shek by strength alone, a combination of their forces could seriously challenge his dominant position. Therefore a new balance of power between Chiang and his leading rivals emerged. When this balance of power changed, the presidential form of government established by Chiang Kai-shek was changed. Threatened by combined opposition forces, Chiang Kai-shek was forced to accept the cabinet form of government designed by Wang Jingwei at the First Plenary Session of the Fourth CEC on December 30, 1931. The revised Organic Law conferred executive power exclusively on the lower organ of the government, the Executive Yuan, and the president of the national government was not allowed to concurrently hold any government post and hence became a figurehead. The new cabinet government established a collective leadership in which the ultimate governmental authority was shared among a group of standing councillors of the national government.

Repercussions of Chiang's Power Consolidation

By concurrently holding the posts of chairman of the CEC's standing committee in the KMT and commander-in-chief of the Nationalist army at the Fourth Plenary Session of the Second CEC in February 1928, and by taking over the presidency of the national government at the Fifth Plenary Session in August, Chiang Kai-shek formally climbed to the apex of the party-state hierarchy. As a further step to consolidate his power, Chiang Kai-shek decided to remove the political and military powers controlled by the regional militarists who were potentially dangerous to the central government. Chiang Kai-shek's power consolidation stirred up strong resistance from the regional militarists, however, and alienated some of his political allies.

When Chiang Kai-shek took over the presidency of the "unified" Nationalist government in 1928, China was still divided into spheres of influence under regional militarists. Although Chiang Kai-shek represented a concentration of power of the Nationalist regime by concurrently holding the highest posts of the party, the government, and the army, the area over which his central government actually ruled comprised only a few provinces in the Yangtze valley, including the national capital, Nanjing, the great financial center, Shanghai, and the provinces of Zhejiang, Anhui, Jiangsu, and Jiangxi. Feng Yuxiang, Li Zhongren, and other powerful regional militarists each controlled a cluster of provinces.[1]

The report of Song Zhiwen (T. V. Soong), the minister of finance, to the Fifth Plenary Session of the Second CEC in August 1928 reflected this fact. Of all the provinces, he said, only Jiangsu, Zhejiang, Anhui, and Jiangxi furnished financial reports that were "fairly complete or reliable"—and, he added, "many of the provinces do not furnish any reports at all, and those that do, supply data that are either incomplete or of little use." He further indicated that inasmuch as the receipts of Jiangxi and Anhui were scarcely sufficient to meet their military expenditure, the central government was forced to depend on Jiangsu (in which the capital was located) and Zhejiang. He pointed out that 78 percent of the estimated gross national revenue was absorbed by military expenditure.[2] This situation confirms Harley F. MacNair's observation that "officially the government instituted on October 10, 1928, ruled the country; actually it was no more than the only government at the time which claimed to be the legitimate ruler of all China. The territories fairly definitely controlled by Nanjing included most of the five provinces."[3] Because of the powerful influence of the regional militarists, when Chiang Kai-shek assumed the chairmanship of the Central Political Council at the Fourth Plenary Session in 1928 he was forced to give the chairmanships of four regional subcouncils to the four most powerful regional militarists: Li Jisheng was appointed as chairman of the political subcouncil in Guangzhou, Li Zhongren as chairman in Wuhan, Feng Yuxiang as chairman in Kaifeng, and Yan Xishan as chairman in Taiyuan.

Although Chiang Kai-shek prevailed over his political rivals in 1928 due to his ability to command military forces, the very first troubles he had to face were those presented by the very military leaders who had helped him seize control of the regime.[4] Chiang Kai-shek complained at the Third National Congress of the KMT, held in March 1929, that the authority of the central government had never been respected and its orders carried no weight. He raised a question: "Is China really united now?" And he gave his own answer: "A cursory view would show that it is not." Chiang criticized the provincial governments for

> acting independently in financial matters in their respective areas. They were buying arms and ammunition without the sanction of the central government, and they were recruiting troops on their own account. The central government was powerless to exercise control over the provincial chieftains and could not effectively stop

> them in their apparent determination to run their own show. Even worse, these provincial governments, taking advantage of their new military strength, were attempting to dictate to the central government on questions affecting themselves, with the result that it became necessary for the central government to consult the provincial leaders before issuing orders.[5]

It was this concern that prompted Chiang Kai-shek to take action in an effort to consolidate his power by disarming the regional militarists. Two important political decisions in this regard were made by Chiang upon seizing power at the top: the first was to disband the armies controlled by regional militarists; the second was to abolish the political subcouncils headed by the powerful regional militarists. Chiang Kai-shek began his plan to disband the armies by calling for a Reorganization and Disbandment Conference in January 1929. He proposed to divide the country into six disbandment zones and reduce the huge armies to about eighty-five divisions with a total manpower of 800,000. Military administration and command were to be consolidated in the central government.[6] The regional militarists, however, stood firmly against Chiang's plan. The Reorganization and Disbandment Conference was protracted—nearly three weeks—and a manifesto was issued in which the leading regional militarists at the conference rejected Chiang's proposal.[7] Although Chiang's plan to disband the regional militarists was aborted,[8] the regional subcouncils were abolished at the Third National Congress of the KMT held in March 1929. This action, however, provoked unrest among the regional militarists and stirred up strong resistance from the chairmen of all four political subcouncils.

The Chiang–Gui War

The anti-Chiang movement that coalesced in response to his consolidation actions spread secretly and quickly. In Central and South China, revolts by the regional militarists broke out one after another following the KMT's Third National Congress.[9] The first crisis erupted in early 1929 when an armed clash erupted between Chiang Kai-shek's central government and the Wuhan Political Subcouncil controlled by the Guangxi militarists Li Zhongren and Bai Chongxi. The battle was touched off by an order issued by the Wuhan subcouncil to dismiss Lu Diping from his office as governor of Hunan. Essentially, the political subcouncil was angry at Lu Diping for remitting tax revenues directly to the central government in Nanjing rather than through the subcouncil in Wuhan. To justify its action, the Wuhan subcouncil sent a telegram to the Central Political Council in Nanjing on February 21, 1929, listing several reasons for dismissing Lu:

> Lu Diping, the governor of Hunan province, has resisted the leadership of the political subcouncil ever since he took office as governor. Three mistakes were made by the governor. First, he perverted the law regarding government revenues and distributed the revenue without reporting to the political subcouncil. Second, Hunan province has suffered from communism but the governor has never made serious efforts to root out the communism and is unworthy of the trust the people have placed in him. Third, while people in Hunan province have suffered from disorder for years, the governor has still levied heavy taxes and cries of discontent have risen all over the province. The political subcouncil cautioned him many times but he paid no heed. . . . Therefore the political subcouncil has decided to dismiss him from the post of Hunan governor.[10]

By dismissing a governor loyal to the central government, the Wuhan political subcouncil was actually disobeying orders from Chiang Kai-shek's Central Political Council forbidding them to tamper with provincial officials appointed by Nanjing.[11] Knowing that removal of the governor violated Chiang's order, the Wuhan subcouncil set troops in motion against the central forces in Nanjing. Chiang Kai-shek, determined to fight back at this time, quickly deployed forces to dissolve the Wuhan Political Subcouncil and issued a statement on the behalf of the central government to denounce the revolt of regional militarists:

> The Wuhan Political Subcouncil has violated discipline, overstepped its authority to appoint and dismiss officials, and set troops against the central government. . . . The leaders of the Wuhan Political Subcouncil, Li Zhongren, Li Jisheng, and Bai Chongxi, have planned a rebellion. . . . They have betrayed the center and the revolution . . . and were therefore removed from their posts. If their troops refuse to adhere to the center, the center will send a punitive expedition against the rebellions troops.[12]

Chiang launched a military attack at the end of March 1929, and, after a short campaign, Li Zhongren's forces were driven out of Central China.[13] This battle, known as the Chiang–Gui War in modern Chinese history, marked the beginning of a prolonged conflict between Chiang Kai-shek and the regional militarists.[14]

The Central China War

After the Chiang–Gui War ended with Chiang Kai-shek's victory over the Guangxi militarists, Feng Yuxiang, the chairman of the political subcouncil in Kaifeng, revolted again. Feng Yuxiang is a remarkable figure in modern Chinese history. The appellation "Christian General" was conferred upon him by admiring missionaries who spread the report far and wide that Feng, upon embracing Christianity, had baptized all his soldiers in the faith.[15] By this time Feng Yuxiang had grown to be almost a legendary figure. He was strong; he had a huge army at his command; he ruled over a vast region difficult to attack. In him Chiang Kai-shek recognized a very potent antagonist.[16] Although Chiang demanded that the entire Chinese army be unified under a central command, for example, Feng was determined to maintain his forces as a private military unit, a principle Chiang regarded as not only feudalistic but intolerable.

Feng Yuxiang's revolt was triggered by Chiang Kai-shek's appointment of him as minister of war in the Nanjing government—a post Chiang had created at the Third National Party Congress. Upon arriving at Nanjing, however, Feng Yuxiang discovered that this appointment was a political trap and refused to take the post. He believed that the appointment reflected Chiang's attempt to confine him in Nanjing and separate him from his vast sphere of influence in Northwest China.[17] Indeed, Feng Yuxiang rudely turned down Chiang's appointment and left Nanjing for his northern preserves without even giving advance notice. Upon receiving the report that Feng had left Nanjing, Chiang Kai-shek was incensed but could do nothing to stop him. The communication between Chiang and Feng on this matter is reflected in a famous exchange of telegrams—possibly the lengthiest ever sent over a Chinese wire.[18] In one of the telegrams Chiang urged Feng to return to Nanjing, but Feng refused by citing the fate suffered by Li Jisheng, the leader of the Wuhan Political Subcouncil who was arrested without warning during his diplomatic mission in Nanjing at Chiang's request. This sudden maneuver had served as a warning to Feng. Chiang Kai-shek wired the following response:

> I understand it has been rumored that if you come to Nanjing you will be treated as a second Li Jisheng, but I believe that you will not be misled by such tales. We had conclusive proof of the Guangxi plan for rebellion, and when Li Jisheng came to the capital he was plotting with the rebels; his detention, therefore, was necessary. While I am a most imperfect man, since I entered the KMT I have never sold out my friends, nor have I deliberately taken the life of a comrade. . . . As for ourselves, in a public sense you are a revolutionary leader but privately we are sworn brothers, and you are the elder brother.[19]

A few days after this telegram was sent, however, Feng was formally dismissed from the party and relieved of his government posts (vice-president of the Executive Yuan and councillor of the national government).[20] Following the excommunication, the central government, controlled by Chiang, issued a punitive mandate against Feng Yuxiang:

> There are but two courses open to you: either you obey or you revolt. If you awaken to reality with your customary alertness and resolutely pull yourself out of your present evil environment, your mistakes will not be beyond repair.[21]

Chiang Kai-shek reinforced the mandate with a more decisive open telegram to the officers of Feng's army:

> Although you have long been associated with Feng, that relationship could be recognized only as long as Feng remained a revolutionary. Now that his sedition has become a matter of common knowledge and he has automatically repudiated his association with the revolution, which virtually amounted to a cancellation of his past army record, . . . Feng's downfall is inevitable. Therefore, if the officers do not care to stake their lives on Feng, you must act quickly.[22]

At the time of the excommunication Feng Yuxiang was preparing to fight Chiang's central government. On May 5, 1929, Feng had accepted the post of commander of the northwest headquarters of the Hudang Jiuguojun ("army for protecting the party and saving the nation") from Li Zhongren, who had appointed himself general commander of the Hudang Jiuguojun.[23] Upon taking up the commander's post, Feng Yuxiang sent one more telegram to Chiang Kai-shek expressing his strong hostility toward Chiang's central government.[24] Just when the shooting between Feng Yuxiang's troops and Chiang's central army was about to begin, Chiang Kai-shek bribed two of Feng's key subordinates, Han Fuqu and Shi Yushan, who issued a telegram to the public on December 2, 1929, declaring their loyalty to Chiang Kai-shek and the central government.[25] This defection was a heavy blow to Feng—suddenly he had lost some 100,000 of his best soldiers—and he was forced to retreat from armed opposition.[26]

After the revolt of Feng Yuxiang was suppressed, Yan Xishan, the chairman of the political subcouncil in Taiyuan, stood up against Chiang Kai-shek's central government on February 10, 1930. Yan Xishan issued an ultimatum to Chiang calling for his resignation.[27] In the meantime Yan Xishan offered Feng safe haven in Shanxi province and set up a military alliance with him. Yan took these measures very quickly because he knew that if Feng was eliminated he himself would have to face Chiang Kai-shek in northern China alone and his own autonomy in Shanxi would become precarious.[28] After Yan and Feng joined forces and formed an alliance against Chiang Kai-shek, Li Zhongren and Bai Chongxi, the two Guangxi militarists, reorganized their forces in southern China and joined Yan and Feng's anti-Chiang military alliance. The result was a war between Chiang's central military forces and the combined regional military forces. This war, known as *zhongyuan dazhan* (the Central China War) in modern Chinese history, lasted for about seven months in 1930 and was the biggest clash between Chiang and the regional militarists in his entire military and political career.[29]

The CEC's Enlarged Plenary Session

The fiery conflict between Chiang Kai-shek and the regional militarists created a great opportunity for Chiang's political rivals to gain political stock and weaken Chiang's dominant position. In the middle of the conflict Wang Jingwei returned to Hong Kong from Europe in March 1930. Upon his return Wang sent a long telegram to denounce the Third National Party Congress and Chiang Kai-shek.[30] The regional military leaders seized upon Wang's return with great joy. Yan Xishan and Feng Yuxiang sent a telegram together on April 20, 1930, urging Wang to go to Beijing and help organize an opposition government.[31] When Wang Jingwei arrived in Beijing by steamer, he was warmly received by local Reorganizationalists and representatives of the regional militarists. Indeed, a mass rally to welcome him was held at Zhongshan Park on August 8, 1930.[32]

The alliance between Wang Jingwei's Reorganizationalists and the powerful regional militarists is an interesting episode in Chinese political history. James E. Sheridan indicates that both the Reorganizationalists and the regional militarists "were hostile to Chiang Kai-shek, but they were not natural allies" because they had very different interests at stake.[33] The regional militarists were essentially seeking the kind of regional military and political power that was incompatible with genuine national government; the Reorganizationalists, however, were chiefly concerned with Chiang's administration of the government and feared that he had dictatorial aspirations which would exclude them from the government.

Despite these differences, Wang Jingwei and the regional militarists joined forces in 1930. Upon Wang Jingwei's suggestion,[34] an enlarged plenary session *(kuoda huiyi)* of the Second Central Executive Committee of the KMT convened on July 13, 1930.[35] Representatives of the Reorganizationalists led by Wang Jingwei and Chen Gongbo participated in the enlarged session.[36] So too did the regional military leaders, Yan Xishan, Feng Yuxiang, and Li Zhongren, who sent their representatives from the battleground.[37] The Western Hill Group represented by Xie Chi and Zou Lu was also invited to attend the session.[38] The enlarged session published a manifesto denouncing the Third National Congress and Chiang Kai-shek's Nanjing government and claiming that a new center of the KMT had been established by the enlarged session. Thirty CEC members signed the manifesto.[39]

Wang Jingwei assumed the chairmanship of the newly founded CEC Standing Committee, which consisted of seven members: Wang Jingwei, Xie Chi, Zhao Weiwen, Xu Chongzhi, Wang Faqin, Bai Wenwei, and Mao Zhuquan—a strange combination of Reorganizationalists and the Western Hill Group.[40] A rebel Nationalist government was created by the enlarged plenary session, as well. Yan Xishan assumed the presidency of the rebel government and was officially inaugurated in Beijing on September 9, 1930.[41] S. I. Hsiung, a Chinese scholar writing in the 1940s, believed that the enlarged session "was the most formidable threat to Chiang Kai-shek's authority, for it consisted of the largest number of dissatisfied politicians and soldiers gathered together in one place and at one time, and the area under the control of the soldiers concerned extended to several provinces along the valley of the Yellow River—Shanxi, Hebei and Shandong."[42]

Upon its inauguration, the rebel Beijing government immediately sent its troops south to expel the Nanjing government. In the extraordinarily stubborn fighting, however, the rebel armies were pushed northward by the Nanjing troops. At this moment, the attitude of Zhang Xueliang (the "Young Marshal" who controlled much of northeastern China) became crucial for the survival of the Beijing government. Both sides had entreated for his support ever since war broke out. When dispatching his troops to fight the rebel forces, Chiang Kai-shek had sent agents to the north to urge the Young Marshal to prove his allegiance to Chiang: if the Young Marshal could attack Yan Xishan from the rear, that is, from the north, the success of the Nanjing forces would be assured.[43] Unaware of Chiang Kai-shek's maneuver, the leaders of the Beijing government too sent their envoys with money and promises to secure the support of the Young Marshal, whose stock was skyrocketing.[44]

Ultimately the Young Marshal threw in his lot with Chiang Kai-shek. According to S. I. Hsiung, he did so because he wanted to repay a debt of gratitude to Chiang. Two years earlier, when the Young Marshal was approaching Nanjing to be appeased, most of the other generals had been jealous. Chiang Kai-shek had backed the Young Marshal, however, and nominated him as a member of the National Government Council.[45] It was for this reason that the Young Marshal made up his mind and telegraphed his support for Chiang Kai-shek while moving his forces inside the Great Wall.[46] He occupied Beijing peacefully in October 1930, as the forces of Yan Xishan saw it was useless to resist.[47] The Young Marshal was well recompensed for his support of Chiang Kai-shek. By doing a good turn for the man who had made him a member of the National Government Council, the Young Marshal added another province, Hebei, to his territory and another high office, vice-commander-in-chief of the Nationalist army, to those he already held.[48] Wang Jingwei and Yan Xishan, along with their rebel government, moved to Taiyuan, the capital of Shanxi province, where they continued their opposition to Chiang Kai-shek's central government.

The Hu Hanmin Incident

Although the combined forces of the Reorganizationalists, the Western Hill Group, and influential regional militarists at the enlarged plenary session in Beijing had started an anti-Chiang coalition, Chiang Kai-shek's power was not seriously challenged until Hu Hanmin joined this movement following his dispute with Chiang over the promulgation of a provisional constitution *(yuefa)*. When the dispute resulted in the house arrest of Hu Hanmin by Chiang Kai-shek in February 1931, Hu was pushed into the grand anti-Chiang coalition.

The relationship between Hu Hanmin and Chiang Kai-shek had always been very subtle. Though Hu had been forced to leave China for Europe after Liao Zhongkai's assassination in 1925, he returned to KMT politics and joined his political rival, Chiang Kai-shek, at the inception of the Nanjing government in April 1927. Hu Hanmin explained his action in ideological terms: Chiang Kai-shek had made an open break with the Communists in 1927 and therefore unification was necessary. Chiang Kai-shek made a special trip to Shanghai to meet Hu Hanmin upon his return and invited him to rejoin the government.[49] Hu accepted Chiang's invitation and recommended immediate adoption of the five-power system of government. When that system was established in October 1928, Chiang Kai-shek assumed the presidency of the national government and Hu Hanmin became president of the Legislative Yuan.[50]

Although Hu Hanmin and Chiang Kai-shek entered into cooperation in 1928, neither really trusted the other. Under the presidential system the ultimate authority of the government was concentrated in the hands of one person, Chiang Kai-shek, much to the distress of Hu Hanmin. One study of Hu Hanmin's political career offers a number of persuasive examples about the relationship between Hu and Chiang. Challenging Chiang Kai-shek's political power, which was based on his military strength, Hu Hanmin repeatedly emphasized the concept of "*yidang zhiguo*" (using the party to govern the nation).[51] Disaffected with Chiang Kai-shek's military power, Hu Hanmin said sarcastically that "we actually don't need any other organs; having a commander-in-chief would be enough."[52] Furthermore, Hu Hanmin openly opposed Chiang Kai-shek when Chiang offered Zhang Xueliang, the Young Marshal, high government positions to gain his personal allegiance: "From the point of view of a government," Hu said, "we should not make this kind of dirty deal."[53]

The collaboration between Chiang Kai-shek and Hu Hanmin finally broke down over the adoption of a provisional constitution in 1931. This controversy began with Chiang's circulating telegram of October 3, 1930, to the Central Executive Committee in Nanjing requesting that it convene a national people's convention for the adoption of a provisional constitution for the period of political tutelage.[54] He had not consulted Hu Hanmin before making this sudden departure from his customary position. At the time of the adoption of the five-power system of government in 1928, both Chiang Kai-shek and Hu Hanmin had agreed that for the period of tutelage the whole body of Sun Yat-sen's teaching formed the law of the land and no provisional constitution was necessary. Thus Hu Hanmin was taken by surprise and, a man of stubborn convictions, objected strenuously to the proposal. Chiang Kai-shek, however, was equally determined to have the provisional constitution. On February 28, 1931, Chiang had Hu Hanmin taken into protective custody in Tangshan, a mountain resort near Nanjing, lest he withdraw to join the grand anti-Chiang coalition,[55] "thus destroying his prestige and long record of faithfulness to the revolutionary cause," as Chiang himself formally stated on March 9, 1931.[56]

Why did Chiang Kai-shek take the action of promulgating a provisional constitution in 1930 even at the expense of alienating Hu Hanmin? He did so because the political legitimacy of Chiang's Nanjing regime was put at risk after Wang Jingwei's government made its provisional constitution public in Taiyuan. As a book put together by anti-Chiang activists pointed out in 1934, because the Taiyuan government had promulgated a constitution, "the non-KMT intelligentsia began to challenge the legitimacy of the Nanjing government. They believed that a fundamental law binding the KMT as well as the people was necessary."[57] Chiang Kai-shek had to meet this challenge by providing such a law. This explanation is consistent with the historical facts. During the brief life of the rival government created by the enlarged session in Beijing, Wang Jingwei had insisted on having a provisional constitution as an instrument of government for the period of tutelage. Thus a group led by Wang Jingwei went to work on a draft on September 15 and completed it on October 27. When Wang Jingwei and Yan Xishan retreated from Beijing to Taiyuan, a draft provisional constitution had even received some publicity in October 1930. Taking advantage of the provisional constitution, Wang Jingwei launched a heavy attack on Chiang Kai-shek.[58] In the declaration promulgating the draft, Wang Jingwei and the "Enlarged Sessionists" accused the national government in Nanjing of delaying its own promulgating of a provisional constitution—a delay that was "contradictory to Dr. Sun's teachings and thus resulting in political tutelage in name but individual dictatorship in fact."[59]

Such an accusation could not escape the attention of the non-KMT intelligentsia, even though it was largely a political weapon in the long series of power struggles among the KMT leaders. Military resources were indeed crucial in this conflict, but legitimacy within the party and among the intelligentsia was important too if a KMT politician was to stay in power. In fact, legitimacy was what distinguished the KMT regime from that of the warlords. The fact that Chiang wanted to promulgate a constitution to legitimize his power shows that constitutionalism had already become a discourse—a way of talking about political problems—in Nationalist China. Though Chiang could shift the playing field from time to time, he had to show his adherence to Sun Yat-sen's doctrine because this doctrine remained the source of legitimacy in the Nationalist government. To distinguish himself from the warlords, therefore, Chiang Kai-shek quickly submitted his proposal for the immediate promulgation of a provisional constitution. The Fourth Plenary Session of the Third National Congress of the KMT in November 1930 adopted Chiang's proposal and decided to hold a national convention on May 5, 1931, to approve the provisional constitution. Thus the provisional constitution was not only a weapon used by Chiang Kai-shek for political competition with Wang Jingwei but also an indispensable source of legitimacy for Chiang's government. Indeed, the provisional constitution improved the competitive position of the Nanjing regime and gave Chiang Kai-shek's presidential form of government constitutional protection. The provisional constitution, promulgated at the National People's Convention in April 1931, not only reaffirmed the presidential power defined in the Organic Law of 1928 but also vested the president with the power to appoint and remove the heads of the five *yuan*.

Why did Hu Hanmin oppose the provisional constitution so stubbornly? Arguing that Sun Yat-sen, the founding father of the KMT, had said that the provisional constitution should not go into force until local self-government had been established throughout the country, Hu Hanmin insisted that the country was not yet ready for provisional constitutional rule. Beneath the ideological language, however, Hu Hanmin had his own power in mind: he could take advantage of his position as a disciple of Sun Yat-sen while holding onto the whole body of Sun Yat-sen's teaching instead of a provisional constitution as the law of the land. Moreover, having a constitution to legalize Chiang Kai-shek's presidential power was obviously not in Hu Hanmin's interest. As the author of *The Cambridge History of China* suggests, Hu Hanmin "publicly avowed that the proclamation of a Provisional Constitution would be contrary to the intention of Sun Yat-sen—although the actual cause of his objection may well have been the fear that Chiang meant to enhance his power by having himself named president under a new constitution."[60]

Thus it was that Hu Hanmin protested Chiang Kai-shek's unilateral decision to promulgate the provisional constitution and was arrested by Chiang on February 28, 1931. This incident not only alienated Hu Hanmin from Chiang's Nanjing government but also added Hu Hanmin's name to the list of the grand Anti-Chiang coalition.

The Extraordinary Session and Chiang's Second Resignation

The alienation of Hu Hanmin was followed by the formation of the grand anti-Chiang coalition. Ostensibly in protest against Hu Hanmin's arrest, the regional militarists of Guangdong and Guangxi, along with a mixed assortment of Chiang Kai-shek's political rivals including Wang Jingwei, Sun Ke, and members of the Western Hill Group, gathered in Guangzhou in May 1931. The grand coalition was created on May 27 at an extraordinary session *(feichang huiyi)* of the KMT at Guangzhou, where, ironically, Chiang Kai-shek had started his political career.[61]

The extraordinary session was launched first by Wang Jingwei in a circulating telegram sent from Hong Kong on May 1, 1931. In the telegram Wang Jingwei called for "all revolutionary comrades" to unite against Chiang Kai-shek and suggested holding a provisional national congress of the KMT to resolve the intraparty conflict.[62] In response to Wang Jingwei's suggestion, Sun Ke and two representatives of the Western Hill Group (Chen Yuren and Xu Chongzhi) left Guangzhou for Hong Kong and met Wang Jingwei on May 24. At this meeting they agreed to convene the extraordinary session of the CEC at Guangzhou three days later.

The participants at this extraordinary session included the regional militarists of Guangdong and Guangxi (Li Zhongren, Bai Chongxi, Zhang Fakui, and Chen Jitang), representatives of the Western Hill Group (Zou Lu, Xu Chongzhi, and others) and other right-wingers of the KMT, as well as Sun Ke, Wang Jingwei, and his Reorganizationalists.[64] Hu Hanmin was not able to attend the meeting, but he was represented by Gu Yingfen and other right-wing elements of the party.[65] The participants asserted that all CEC members of the previous three national congresses could be members of the extraordinary session so long as they stood up to Chiang Kai-shek.[66] Wang Jingwei personally drafted the manifesto of the extraordinary session, which denounced Chiang Kai-shek as the dictator of China:

> Chiang Kai-shek carried out a personal dictatorship in the name of political tutelage. He destroyed the democratic centralism in the party and government. . . . Chiang Kai-shek's personal dictatorship still exists. All comrades of the party and all armed men should stand up against the dictator and take revolutionary responsibility. . . . It is in this crucial time that we, the faithful party members, gathered all the previous CEC and CSC members and held the extraordinary session.[67]

On June 1, 1931, a new Nationalist government was created by the extraordinary session at Guangzhou.[68] A Government Council of seventeen members was formed. Five of the seventeen members comprised the council's standing committee: Wang Jingwei, Sun Ke, Zou Lu, Gu Yingfen, and Tang Shaoyi. The chairmanship of the council was to be rotated among the five standing members.[69] The extraordinary session and the Guangzhou government then issued a statement denouncing the illegal arrest of Hu Hanmin and asserting that it would abandon its opposition only if the dictator Chiang Kai-shek relinquished his positions in Nanjing.[70]

Unstable coalition of incompatible rivals that it was, the grand coalition did prove to be a powerful threat to Chiang Kai-shek. Had not the Japanese invaded Manchuria on September 18, 1931, "this conflict, like its predecessors, would presumably have been fought on the battlefield."[71] When the Japanese invaded, an impassioned nationwide reaction intensified pressure to terminate the intraparty squabbling and form a united government to oppose the foreign aggressor. After extraordinarily arcane negotiations and complex conferences, including three Fourth National Congresses of the KMT and a joint peace conference, an agreement between Chiang Kai-shek and the grand anti-Chiang coalition leaders was worked out. Retaining only his membership on the standing committee of the CEC, on December 15, 1931, Chiang Kai-shek resigned once again from the Nanjing government.

Chiang Kai-shek's second resignation was different from his first resignation three years earlier. It reflected the panic of Chiang's Nanjing government, which found itself forced to fight on several fronts simultaneously in 1931. The panic started when Zhang Xueliang dispatched troops upon Chiang Kai-shek's request. While the Young Marshal, Zhang Xueliang, was helping Chiang defeat the uprising of regional militarists in Central and South China, the Chinese Communists were establishing themselves in the interior parts of Jiangxi province where they had engaged a large number of Chiang Kai-shek's troops in battle. It was at this critical time that Japan invaded Manchuria. On September 18, 1931, exactly one year after Zhang Xueliang had moved his troops inside the Great Wall to help Chiang Kai-shek, Japan launched an attack on the Chinese garrison at Mukden and occupied the whole province of Liaoning, an episode known as the Mukden Incident.

Faced with domestic political unrest and Japanese aggression simultaneously, Chiang Kai-shek had no choice but to reconcile with his political rivals within the KMT. He released Hu Hanmin on September 21, 1931, immediately following his return to Nanjing from a trip to the front where KMT troops were fighting the Communists in Jiangxi province.[72] On September 29, Chiang Kai-shek sent his representatives Wu Zhihui, Chen Minshu, Cai Yuanpei, and Zhang Ji to Hong Kong to meet Wang Jingwei and the representatives of the grand anti-Chiang coalition. Chiang Kai-shek proposed a peace conference and told his rivals that he was willing to negotiate with them.[73] Thus Chiang's representatives met those of the rival coalition for a second time at Shanghai, on October 21, 1931, to negotiate the agenda of the peace conference.[74] The representatives from Guangzhou, however, brought with them a letter from Wang Jingwei listing seven preconditions for holding the peace conference.[75] One key precondition was to put the reform of government institutions on the conference agenda. Indeed, in his letter Wang Jingwei proposed a reform that would replace the presidential system with the cabinet system: "The president of the national government should be a figurehead, like the presidents in France and in Germany, and should be assumed by a prominent elder in the country. The post of commander-in-chief of the army, navy, and air force should be abolished."[76] Chiang Kai-shek had no alternative but to accept these preconditions. In a letter dated October 24, 1931, to Wang Jingwei, he replied: "At the moment, the first priority is to resist foreign aggression. . . . The fundamental issues regarding the party-state's construction . . . are our internal affair and can be discussed frankly at the Shanghai conference."[77]

The peace conference thus was convened at Shanghai from October 27 to November 7, 1931. Seven meetings were held and the whole conference stretched to ten days. Participants included representatives of the Guangzhou government (Wang Jingwei, Sun Ke, Zou Lu, and others) and those of the Nanjing government (Chen Minshu, Cai Yuanpei, Chen Yuren, and others). Although Hu Hanmin did not attend the conference, Wang Jingwei went to Hu's residence in Shanghai and consulted with him beforehand. At this meeting Wang apologized for the rivalry between them in earlier years. After the meeting Wang, Hu, and Sun Ke had a picture taken together showing unity among the three former political rivals.[78]

As a concrete outcome of the peace conference, a circulating telegram was signed by the twelve representatives agreeing on several principles guiding the reform of the central government: "(1) Each of the five *yuan* should have independent power; (2) the political system and organization should be streamlined; (3) political practice should be democratized."[79] Reform of the government's structure was in fact one of the most important subjects discussed at the conference. The primary point contained in the "Resolution on the Reform of the Central Political Structure" passed at the conference was to replace the presidential system of Chiang Kai-shek with the cabinet system.[80]

The president of the Nationalist government would be a figurehead of state and could not concurrently hold any other posts. Article 1 of the resolution asserted:

> The president of the national government is a head of state who does not take executive responsibility. He is the president in a cabinet system. His term is two years and he may have two terms. . . . The president of the national government may not be allowed to hold any other posts concurrently.[81]

Article 2 of the resolution required power sharing among the members of the National Government Council:

> The National Government Council is the supreme government organ. There shall be three standing councillors who will rotate to serve as chairman of the council's meetings.[82]

Article 3 stated:

> The CEC and CSC members of the KMT shall be councillors.[83]

The resolution provided that executive power should be exclusively exercised by the Executive Yuan in its Article 4:

> The Executive Yuan takes true executive responsibility and is the responsible cabinet. It is accountable to the National Government Council.[84]

Article 5 stated:

> The Legislative, Judicial, Examination, and Control Yuan are collectively accountable to the National Government Council.[85]

While the peace conference did not reach any agreement about Chiang Kai-shek's position in the unified government, the grand anti-Chiang coalition insisted on Chiang's immediate retirement from his official positions. When Chiang Kai-shek refused to accept this demand, the Fourth National Congress of the KMT was called upon to resolve the problem. But Chiang Kai-shek and his political rivals could not agree on where the congress should be held, so three Fourth National Congresses were convened separately in Nanjing, Guangzhou, and Shanghai in November and December 1930. The Nanjing congress was held by Chiang Kai-shek and his followers on November 12–23; the Guangzhou congress was held by Hu Hanmin and Sun

Ke from November 18 to December 5; the Shanghai congress was held by Wang Jingwei on December 7. The congresses in Guangzhou and Shanghai held by Hu Hanmin, Sun Ke, and Wang Jingwei insisted that the party would not unite unless Chiang Kai-shek resigned promptly.[86] Indeed, the CEC members in Guangzhou and Shanghai even held Chiang's resignation as a prerequisite for them to attend the unified First Plenary Session of the Fourth CEC scheduled to be held in Nanjing.[87]

Faced with this strong demand of the grand anti-Chiang coalition, Chiang Kai-shek was forced once again to announce his resignation from the posts of president of the national government, president of the Executive Yuan, and commander-in-chief of the Nationalist army. On December 15, 1931, he "retired" to his native village of Xikou in Zhejiang province.[88]

Establishment of a Cabinet System

Chiang Kai-shek's heavy-handed moves to install the presidential system with himself as president in 1927 ended with failure because of the powerful challenge from the combined forces of his political rivals. Chiang's resignation was the political price he paid for the nonconsensual adoption of a controversial institutional design when he did not prevail in the regime. Following Chiang's resignation, the First Plenary Session of the Fourth CEC was convened on December 12, 1931. A revised Organic Law was approved at the session on December 30 reforming the system of the central government and vesting the executive power exclusively in the hands of the Executive Yuan. The revised law provided that the president of the Nationalist government was not to have any practical political responsibility, appoint or remove the heads of the five *yuan*, or hold any concurrent office.[89]

The presidential form of government was thus replaced by a cabinet system. Lin Sen, an elderly CEC member in the party, was selected as acting president of the national government in the session and later was made the president. This man was a prominent elder in the country: physically he was of a dignified and stately demeanor; politically he had been a veteran of the KMT and active in the early period of the Nationalist Revolution. As one observer noted: "He understood his position well. He never tried to assert the powers that were denied to him by the Organic Law of December 1931."[90]

The new cabinet form of government was organized with the Executive Yuan at its power center. As one study of Chinese government structure published in 1934 indicated: "The group of administrative heads of the Executive Yuan is a cabinet. Like the cabinet in other countries the Executive Yuan plays an important role in legislation in that it is vested with the actual responsibility of initiating and recommending to the consideration of the Legislative Yuan such measures, in the form of bills, as it deems necessary."[91] Sun Ke took the presidency of the Executive Yuan at first; when he was replaced by Wang Jingwei, he then assumed the presidency of the Legislative Yuan.

Chapter 8

The Destruction of Chiang's Major Rivals: From Cabinet Back to Presidential Government, 1931–1937

International relations theory relies on the concept of balance of power to account for recurrent patterns of alliance as well as the causes of war. Such logic has also been employed by comparative political scientists to explain patterns of coalition formation in domestic politics.[1] The essential logic, summarized in much of the discourse on power balancing, is the frequent tendency in politics for the emergence of strong actors to induce self-interested cooperation among those threatened by their competitor's prospective dominance. This was the case with the formation of the grand anti-Chiang coalition in 1930–1931. It was because the coalition blocked Chiang Kai-shek's efforts at predominance that the presidential system which Chiang preferred was replaced by the cabinet system in 1931. The cabinet government, based on the revised Organic Law of December 1932, assured power sharing among a group of top KMT elites.

In the politics of Nationalist China—just as in any other political realm—the unity of a political coalition would weaken as the common aims of its members were accomplished. With the resignation of Chiang Kai-shek, the target that necessitated joint action by Chiang's political rivals and regional militarists lost its power and attention shifted to dividing the rewards of success. In the absence of any authoritative arbiter capable of allocating shares, each political player tried to obtain what he saw as his fair share by relying on whatever resources were at his disposal. In the fragmented political realm, the issue of fair share was aggravated by each political leader's evaluation of what share was necessary to ensure his power position. Thus the consideration of relative benefits complicated an already delicate situation and cooperation among coalition partners became competition among rivals. The conflict among the coalition leaders started with a competition for the premiership, that is, the post of president of the Executive Yuan. Sun Ke assumed the presidency of the Executive Yuan for twenty-five days in January 1931 but was squeezed out of the premiership by Wang Jingwei, who became the effective head of the administration in February.

Profiting from the new conflict between Wang Jingwei and Sun Ke, Chiang Kai-shek returned to the government and took charge of the newly created Military Affairs Commission on January 29, 1932. The collective leadership was now based on the balance of power between Chiang Kai-shek and his leading political rivals. This balance eventually broke down, however, as Chiang's leading rivals were either eliminated or dropped out, one by one, from the power competition during the period 1932–1936. Sun Ke, after his political stock was exhausted, gave up in 1934. Wang Jingwei was forced to resign from the government and leave Nanjing to go abroad and seek medical treatment after an attempt on his life on November 1, 1935. Hu Hanmin died in Hong Kong on May 12, 1936. By 1936, therefore, the power balance no longer existed. As the single victor (or survivor) dominating the regime, Chiang Kai-shek became disaffected with the cabinet form of government and refused any substantial power sharing with other leaders. The presidential system was adopted again in the 1936 constitution.

Sun Ke's Cabinet Government of 1931

In the cabinet form of government established in 1931, President Lin Sen, a venerable but ineffectual old revolutionary, was but a figurehead. It was Sun Ke who became head of the administration by assuming the presidency of the Executive Yuan. But Wang Jingwei, one of the leading figures in the anti-Chiang coalition, also wanted to become the premier. Thus a new power struggle among the leaders of the grand anti-Chiang coalition developed after their common enemy had, temporarily, disappeared. This rivalry among the coalition's leaders started at the First Plenary Session of the Fourth CEC, held in Nanjing on December 22, 1931, about one week after the second resignation of Chiang Kai-shek. In fact, Sun

Ke was the only prominent leader present at the session: Chiang Kai-shek stayed at his native village in Zhejiang province; Wang Jingwei remained ill at the hospital in Shanghai although he sent Chen Gongbo to attend the session;[2] Hu Hanmin was in Guangzhou and did not come to the plenary session either. The major items on the agenda were revision of the Organic Law and selection of the new leadership. As a result of the revised Organic Law, executive power was now vested almost exclusively in a lower organ, the Executive Yuan. Sun Ke assumed the presidency of the Executive Yuan at the session and became the effective head of the new administration on January 1, 1932. Sun Ke's administration, however, survived only for twenty-five days. The main reason was because all of the KMT's leading personalities—Wang Jingwei, Hu Hanmin, and Chiang Kai-shek—were "excluded from or refused to associate with the new government."[3]

Chiang Kai-shek was excluded from the new government because he was already "retired" from his government posts. Wang Jingwei refused to join Sun Ke's government because he had wanted to become president of the Executive Yuan himself. Chen Gongbo, a core member of the Reorganizationalist Comrades Association, recalls in his memoirs that Wang Jingwei was ill in the Shanghai hospital during the First Plenary Session of the Fourth CEC. Wang told Chen Gongbo that he wished to take over the presidency of the Executive Yuan and concurrently hold the post of minister.[4] Chen Gongbo himself agreed that it was better to have Wang Jingwei as president of the Executive Yuan because he could unite the anti-Chiang forces.[5] Thus Wang Jingwei was very disappointed indeed when the presidency was given to Sun Ke. Although Hu Hanmin supported Sun Ke's administration, he did not join Sun Ke's government. According to one source, Hu Hanmin had a tacit understanding with Chiang Kai-shek and Wang Jingwei that if they did not block Sun Ke from becoming president of the Executive Yuan, Hu Hanmin would not seek a leading position in the central government.[6]

It was in this complex situation that Sun Ke was appointed president of the Executive Yuan and mandated the organization of the new cabinet government at the First Plenary Session of the Fourth CEC. On December 28, 1931, the plenary session selected nine CEC standing committee members: Wang Jingwei, Hu Hanmin, Chiang Kai-shek, and Sun Ke along with Yu Yuren, Yi Changchu, Gu Mengyu, Ju Zhen, and Chen Guofu. The plenary session also selected three members of the standing committee of the CPC: Wang Jingwei, Hu Hanmin, and Chiang Kai-shek. To reflect the principle of collective leadership, a resolution provided that the chairmanship of the CPC should be rotated among the three standing committee members.[7] As for the organization of the government itself, Sun Ke was selected as president of the Executive Yuan, Zhang Ji as president of the Legislative Yuan, Wu Chaoshu as president of the Judicial Yuan, Dai Chuanxian as president of the Examination Yuan, and Yu Yuren as president of the Control Yuan.[8] Although Chiang Kai-shek, Wang Jingwei, and Hu Hanmin were members of the CEC and CPC, they were not included in the cabinet.[9]

The Chiang–Wang Alliance and Reorganization of Government

In fact, Sun Ke could not govern the Nationalist government without the cooperation of either Chiang Kai-shek or Wang Jingwei. While Chiang was "retired" from the government, his followers within the government and the military remained loyal to him. Faced with strong resentment, Sun Ke could not gain the cooperation of the ministers in his cabinet, let alone the support of military leaders. Song Zhiwen (T. V. Soong), for example, the minister of finance and brother-in-law of Chiang Kai-shek, refused to associate with Sun Ke's administration and took all the key documents from the Ministry of Finance with him when he resigned from his post. In the meantime, several important provinces cut their remittance of revenues to Sun Ke's government.[10] In addition to these domestic troubles, the threat of the Japanese army was steadily increasing but Sun Ke had no military forces under his command to confront it.

While the tensions between Sun Ke and the other KMT leaders became manifest, their calculations of self-interest in the context of fragmented authority not only resulted in the breakup of the grand anti-Chiang coalition but were followed by a general realignment into new political coalitions. Witnessing the sad spectacle of Sun Ke attempting to govern without the aid of strong supporters in his cabinet government, Chiang Kai-shek contacted Wang Jingwei and with him staged a comeback. On December 22, 1931, Chiang Kai-shek secretly met Chen Gongbo, Gu Mengyu, and Wang Faqing, the three leaders of the Reorganizationalists, and told them that he wished to support Wang Jingwei's claim to be president of the Executive Yuan.[11] On January 12, 1932, Chiang asked Chen Minchu to pass a letter on to Wang Jingwei inviting Wang to meet him in the resort city of Hangzhou.[12] Wang accepted the invitation and met Chiang on January 16. They reached an agreement that Chiang Kai-shek would support Wang Jingwei to replace Sun Ke as president of the Executive Yuan; in return, Wang would cooperate with Chiang's effort to return to the government.[13] Thus a strange alliance between these two political rivals was forged.

On January 17, 1932, a telegram cosigned by Chiang Kai-shek and Wang Jingwei was sent to Hu Hanmin in Hong Kong. In the telegram Chiang and Wang invited Hu Hanmin to Hangzhou to discuss how to assist the Sun Ke administration in coping with its difficulties.[14] In the meantime, they sent another telegram to Sun Ke in Nanjing stating that:

> We [Wang Jingwei and Chiang Kai-shek] have discussed the situation [of the Nanjing government] and would like to make every effort to assist you in dealing with the difficult situation. We have sent a telegram to Hu Hanmin and have invited him to come north. . . . Once Hu Hanmin arrives we will go to Nanjing together.[15]

Faced with the hardship of governing as well as the obvious conspiracy of Chiang Kai-shek and Wang Jingwei, Sun Ke had no choice but to give in. In a dramatic turn, the political rival of Chiang Kai-shek now humbly begged for Chiang's return to power. In the telegram replying to Chiang, Sun Ke said:

> As long as you [Chiang Kai-shek], Zhantang [Hu Hanmin], and Zhisheng [Wang Jingwei] are not in Nanjing, the new government is without a center of gravity. . . . It is difficult to manage the affairs of state under such circumstances. Since you love your party and your country, surely you cannot allow yourself to stand by without doing anything about it. We are anxiously awaiting your early return to steer the helm. Your presence will have a salutary effect on the psychology of the nation.[16]

Sun Ke flew from Nanjing to Hangzhou on January 18 and met Chiang Kai-shek and Wang Jingwei at Yanxiadong, a nearby mountain resort. After two days of intensive negotiations among Chiang Kai-shek, Wang Jingwei, and Sun Ke, a compromise was reached. On January 20, Sun Ke went to Shanghai and released the outcome of the Yanxiadong meeting to the press:

> I am satisfied with the outcome of the two days of conversation [with Chiang and Wang]. Both Chiang and Wang insisted on having Hu Hanmin come to Nanjing in order to achieve unity in the party. Hu Hanmin replied by telegram. Although he did not accept the offer, he expressed his good faith in supporting the government. . . . I admire his farsightedness. Nevertheless, it is indeed difficult for me alone in Nanjing to solve the problems today. We must have Chiang Kai-shek and Wang Jingwei join the government. . . . Chiang and Wang have already accepted my request. Wang will leave Shanghai for Nanjing tonight and Chiang will fly to Nanjing tomorrow.[17]

After the Yanxiadong meeting, Sun Ke and his cabinet resigned on January 25. Three days later, a provisional meeting of the CEC standing committee was held at which five committee members (Chiang Kai-shek, Wang Jingwei, Ju Zhen, Gu Mengyu, and Yi Changchu) were present. This meeting accepted Sun Ke's resignation and appointed Wang Jingwei president of the Executive Yuan and Sun Ke president of the Legislative Yuan. Chiang Kai-shek was appointed head of the newly created Military Affairs Commission.[18] This arrangement started a nearly five-year period of collective leadership with power shared among a number of leading figures in the cabinet form of government.

The collective leadership and the reorganized cabinet government were based on the balance of power among Chiang Kai-shek, Wang Jingwei, Hu Hanmin, and Sun Ke. During the period 1932–1936, however, the balance gradually tilted to the advantage of Chiang Kai-shek as his rivals either dropped out or lost leverage at the political core of the KMT regime. Eventually the cabinet government was replaced by the presidential system when the permanent constitution was promulgated by Chiang Kai-shek on May 5, 1936. The following three sections examine how each of Chiang's three leading rivals was eliminated in the process.

Wang Jingwei's Misfortunes

Wang Jingwei was squeezed out of the power competition because of his vulnerability in confronting the internal dissension with Chiang Kai-shek and in handling Japanese aggression. From February 1932 until November 1935, Wang Jingwei headed the Executive Yuan at Nanjing while Chiang Kai-shek supervised the military operations aimed at extirpating the Communist bases in Jiangxi province and elsewhere in the hinterland. Some historians, such as Howard L. Boorman, contend that Wang Jingwei's collaboration with Chiang Kai-shek made this period "the most progressive period in the history of the Nationalist Government."[19] Indeed, it appeared to some independent observers during the early 1930s that a new nation was emerging in the lower Yangtze valley. Thomas G. Rawski's recent study of the prewar economic accomplishments of the Nationalist government during this period offers positive evidence to support this view.[20]

While the economy did grow steadily in the early 1930s, the political scene during this period was characterized by a dramatic power struggle between Chiang Kai-shek and Wang Jingwei within the KMT regime. Although Wang Jingwei and Chiang Kai-shek were major partners in the cabinet government, beneath the surface there was a bitter internecine struggle between these two leaders. Chiang Kai-shek was not in Nanjing very often, but he ensured that his own relatives by marriage, Kong Xiangxi (H. H. Kung) and Song Zhiwen (T. V. Soong), held key posts at Nanjing to "guarantee appropriate checks on Wang Jingwei."[21] Irritated by this suspicion and surveillance, Wang went on leave on October 22, 1932, visiting Europe for six months, allegedly for medical reasons, while Song Zhiwen acted in his place at Nanjing.[22]

Wang resumed his portfolio as president of the Executive Yuan and served concurrently as acting foreign minister upon his return in March 1933, but he found himself in an increasingly vulnerable political position. Wang was vulnerable not only because of the increasingly aggressive attacks from Chiang Kai-shek and his followers but also because the public associated him with the policy of appeasing the Japanese rather than linking him with the patriotic groups advocating positive resistance.[23] As the executive head of government and foreign minister, Wang Jingwei was directly confronted by Japanese aggression. It was on the very night of January 28, 1932, when Wang Jingwei officially took over the presidency of the Executive Yuan, that the Japanese garrison at Shanghai launched an undeclared attack against Chinese troops in the area.[24] Consequently Wang Jingwei had to handle the issue of Japanese aggression from the very first day of his premiership. His political fortune depended heavily on his performance in dealing with the Japanese.

As a civilian leader of the government, Wang Jingwei was dubious of China's ability to sustain a protracted war against the well-trained military forces and well-mobilized industrial system of Japan. He therefore took a cautious line and pursued an appeasement policy toward Japan's aggression.[25] In May 1933, when he became involved in negotiations with Japanese diplomatic and military authorities regarding the establishment of railway and mail communications between China and Manzhouguo (Manzhou state),[26] as well as legal arrangements defining the Japanese position on the China mainland, he signed the Tanggu treaty, which in fact took the Great Wall as the border between China and Japan and recognized Japan's occupation of three provinces in Northeast China.[27] Wang Jingwei was thus called a "*hanjian*" (traitor to China) by Chinese people and lost popularity dramatically while he "shielded Chiang Kai-shek from the rising antiappeasement criticism."[28]

The climax came on November 1, 1935, when, at a meeting of the KMT's Central Executive Committee at Nanjing, Wang was shot and wounded by an assassin who had disguised himself as a photographer. The attempted assassination of Wang Jingwei has been obscured by mysterious stories in modern Chinese history. Many eyewitnesses to the event have given different versions of what actually happened on that day. Some say the attempt on Wang's life was incited by the Communists and anti-Japanese activists; others say it was done on Chiang Kai-shek's instigation.[29] Regardless of who incited the assassination, it struck a relentless blow at Wang Jingwei. When surgery in Shanghai failed to remove the bullets completely, Wang was forced to resign all of his official posts in December to seek medical treatment abroad.[30] When Wang Jingwei left for Europe in February 1936 after four years as president of the Executive Yuan, medical exigencies appeared paramount. Beneath the surface, however, lay a deeper malaise. As indicated by Howard L. Boorman, "Wang was being ruined politically by the long, agonizing process of appeasement."[31]

Taking advantage of Wang Jingwei's unpopular position and his temporary absence from Nanjing after the assassination attempt, Chiang Kai-shek denounced Wang for his appeasement policy and shifted the entire responsibility for losing the three provinces in Northeast China onto Wang Jingwei.[32] When Wang returned to China in 1936, he found that he already lost his power in the Nanjing government. Later he defected to the Japanese and headed a puppet regime sponsored by the Japanese in opposition to the government of China led by Chiang Kai-shek. Thus Wang Jingwei, one of Chiang's leading rivals within the Nationalist government for more than a decade, was eliminated from the KMT power competition by 1936.

The Death of Hu Hanmin

Hu Hanmin was another leading rival of Chiang Kai-shek. While Wang Jingwei was struggling for survival in his contest with Chiang, Hu Hanmin was excluded from Nanjing and gradually disappeared from the power center of the Nationalist regime. As Hu Hanmin was planning a return to Nanjing after the attempted assassination of Wang Jingwei, he suffered a sudden heart attack and died in Hong Kong in May 1936.

Earlier in the decade when freed from the house arrest imposed by Chiang Kai-shek in Nanjing, Hu Hanmin returned to his native Guangdong province and took up residence at Hong Kong in October 1932.[33] Although Hu Hanmin never stopped denouncing Chiang Kai-shek while he was in Guangdong, he was not as influential as he used to be in Nanjing. Having left the power center, Hu Hanmin was obliged to stake his fortunes on the regional militarists who were maneuvering to enhance their regional power. Indeed, the regional militarists in the south had grown so strong that they had organized into the Southwest Council of Political Affairs (Xinan Zhengwu Weiyuanhui) of the national government and the Southwest Executive Headquarters (Xinan Zhixingbu) of the KMT, both at Guangzhou city, an arrangement under which the provinces of Guangdong and Guangxi maintained virtual autonomy. Chen Qitong, then the Guangdong provincial military leader, received Hu Hanmin warmly at first—apparently Chen "sensed the advantages of ridding himself of a warlord image by associating with the KMT's leading theoretician."[34] The regional militarists in Guangdong and Guangxi indeed found Hu

Hanmin useful: Hu, as the KMT's leading ideologue, "lent an aura of legitimacy to their otherwise purely warlord administration."[35]

During this period Hu Hanmin's name also became linked to the famous Fujian revolt of November 1933.[36] This uprising, led by Cai Tingkai and Chen Minshu, two regional militarists in Fujian province, aimed at weakening Chiang Kai-shek's Nanjing government by building a separate people's government based in Fujian.[37] Just before the revolt, both Cai Tingkai and Chen Minshu made a special trip from Fuzhou (the capital of Fujian) to Hong Kong and visited Hu Hanmin in June 1933. At the meeting they agreed that Guangdong and Fujian should collaborate against Chiang Kai-shek. Chen Minshu even proposed that Hu Hanmin be appointed the head of a new Fujian government.[38] As the Fujian government survived for only a matter of weeks, however, Hu Hanmin did not get a chance to take the offer extended by the Fujian leaders and therefore publicly disavowed any connection with the new government. On November 22, 1933, when the Fujian revolt was in danger of being suppressed by Chiang Kai-shek's forces, Hu Hanmin, Li Zhongren, Zou Lu, Bai Chongxi, and other political leaders sent a telegram to the Fujian government denouncing the revolt for having "betrayed the KMT and colluded with the Communists and the Japanese." The telegram called for Chen Minshu to "mend your ways and make a fresh start."[39]

By lending his prestige to the regional militarists, Hu Hanmin did make an alliance with them and thereby stood in a competitive position against Chiang Kai-shek to a certain extent. Nevertheless, his influence had been declining ever since he had left Nanjing. While the regional militarists borrowed Hu's prestige to enhance their regional power, Hu Hanmin was not able to impose his will upon the regional militarists. In fact, he was personally under the control of the Guangdong militarists when he resided in Hong Kong. Chen Qitong, then the head of the Guangdong militarists, never allowed Hu to go to Guangzhou city after he resided in Hong Kong. A study by two Chinese scholars, Zhou Bingwo and Chen Hongmin, indicates that Chen Qitong was afraid Hu's political influence would threaten Chen's position as leader of Guangdong province if he lost control over Hu's actions in his personal sphere of influence.[40] Because of his suspicion, therefore, Chen Qitong never let Hu Hanmin get involved in the Guangdong government's policymaking. Moreover, after Hu Hanmin had stayed in Hong Kong for a while, Chen Qitong began to cut his stipend. According to the archives of the Nationalist government, Hu Hanmin's monthly stipend was cut in half from HK$20,000 to HK$10,000 and again to HK$5,000 during the period 1933–1935.[41] No longer could Hu Hanmin afford the lavish establishment in Hong Kong in which he reportedly employed some thirty servants, five secretaries, and two famed chefs. Ultimately Hu Hanmin accepted funds from a private donation and left for Europe in 1935.[42]

Thus when Hu Hanmin left Hong Kong in June 1935, he was filled with pique and uncertain about his political future.[43] Hu Hanmin returned from France to Hong Kong on January 19, 1936, after the attempted assassination of Wang Jingwei. In the Fifth National Congress of the KMT, held in November 1935, Hu Hanmin was selected as a standing committee member of the CEC and planned to go back to Nanjing and rejoin the political inner circle.[44] But Hu Hanmin's intention was never realized. He died of a heart attack in Hong Kong on May 12, 1936. Hu Hanmin, like Wang Jangwei once a leading political rival of Chiang Kai-shek, was thus eliminated from the KMT's power contest.

Sun Ke's Last Attempt

Sun Ke was another long-standing rival of Chiang Kai-shek. Although he was squeezed out of the presidency of the Executive Yuan in January 1932, a position he had occupied for only twenty-five days, his political career was not over. In fact, since the cabinet form of government was designed to be a collective leadership as stipulated in the compromise among Chiang Kai-shek, Wang Jingwei, and Sun Ke at the Yanxiadong meeting on January 18–19, 1932, Sun Ke was entitled to share power with the KMT's other political leaders in the reorganized government. Three days after Sun's resignation from the post of president of the Executive Yuan on January 25, 1932, he was offered the presidency of the Legislative Yuan by Wang Jingwei and Chiang Kai-shek.[45]

Sun Ke was very experienced in KMT politics. He was not going to accept the prestigious appointment as head of the Legislative Yuan without ensuring his share of power in the regime. He therefore refused to assume the office unless Chiang Kai-shek accepted his demand to convoke a plenary session of the CEC to draft a permanent constitution—which, Sun Ke hoped, would limit Chiang Kai-shek's personal power and promote the collective leadership in the cabinet form of government with a constitutional guarantee. Under the circumstances, Sun Ke became a champion of constitutionalism when he resigned as president of the Executive Yuan. In a weak political position, Sun Ke hoped that "the ripe, exploitable issue of constitutionalism could be used to loosen Chiang Kai-shek's control of the regime."[46]

To launch the constitutional movement, Sun Ke wrote a "Draft Program of National Salvation" and made it public on April 24, 1932.[47] This document, which called for the inauguration of constitutional rule in the shortest possible time, was widely reprinted.[48] Sun Ke hoped to win a broad following not only among the populace at large but also among the diverse and fragmented opponents of Chiang Kai-shek. After Sun Ke's constitutional campaign was initiated, Hu Hanmin immediately responded in Hong Kong and said in several speeches that he supported Sun Ke's proposal for the adoption of the permanent constitution.[49] Ironically, just one year before, when Chiang Kai-shek had proposed the promulgation of the provisional constitution, Hu Hanmin had opposed it stubbornly, saying that the Chinese people were not yet ready to exercise constitutional rights—a good example of how competing power contenders in Nationalist China made use of constitution-making as an instrument to legitimize or enhance their personal power.

Sun Ke met and negotiated with Chiang Kai-shek about the constitutional issue at Lushan, a famous mountain resort in Jiangxi province, in late September. Only when Chiang Kai-shek expressed his readiness to support Sun Ke's constitutional campaign at the scheduled CEC plenary session did Sun Ke agree to assume the presidency of the Legislative Yuan.[50] At the Third Plenary Session of the Fourth CEC, convened in Nanjing on December 15–22, 1932, Sun Ke and Wu Chaoshu (John C. H. Wu), then president of the Judicial Yuan, submitted a motion entitled "Concentrating the National Strength to Save the Country" in which they proposed to prepare a draft constitution as soon as possible.[51] Their motion was adopted by the plenary session as the "Resolution on Drafting the Constitution" on December 20, 1932.[52] Satisfied with his political success, Sun Ke officially assumed the presidency of the Legislative Yuan on December 18. According to the "Resolution on Drafting the Constitution" approved by the plenary session, Sun Ke, as president of the Legislative Yuan, was empowered to prepare a constitutional draft and submit it to the First National Assembly *(guomin dahui)* in March 1935.

Under Sun Ke's leadership, four drafts of the constitution were completed between 1932 and 1934.[53] The first draft, known as the "Wu Draft," was prepared by a Constitutional Drafting Committee of forty-two people appointed by Sun Ke with himself as chairman and Wu Chaoshu and Zhang Zhiban as vice-chairmen. These jurists held their first meeting on February 9, 1933, labored at the task, and commissioned Wu to produce single-handedly a draft based on the principles they set forth. This draft, consisting of 214 articles, was published under Wu's name with the committee's authorization in order to sound out opinions and form a basis for drafting a permanent constitution.[54] With the Wu Draft as a basis of discussion, a special committee of seven people produced the second draft consisting of 160 articles. This draft, published on November 16, 1933, is generally known as the "Preliminary Draft of the Constitution." The Constitutional Drafting Committee then took over the matter and, after several months' study, produced a revised draft known as the "First Draft" consisting of 150 articles in February 1934.[55] After this draft was made available to the public, the Constitutional Drafting Committee was abolished. To continue the committee's work, Sun Ke appointed a committee of thirty-six people under the chairmanship of Fu Bingchang. After seventeen meetings held by this committee, the "Revised First Draft" containing 188 articles was published on July 9, 1934.[56]

A notable feature of the first four drafts was that all four designed a National Council as the central organ of governance and the Executive Yuan as the highest organ of executive power accountable to the National Council. The members of the council were to be elected by the National Assembly. The president was only a figurehead endowed with little more than symbolic powers. The executive and administrative powers of government were to repose in a cabinet composed of the president of the Executive Yuan (like the premier in a parliamentary system) and the heads of the ministries. To guarantee a "fair" share of power for Sun Ke himself, considerable power was vested in the Legislative Yuan, which, headed by Sun Ke, would have the authority to discuss and decide matters of law, the budget, martial law, declarations of war and peace, and crucial matters relating to foreign affairs. All four drafts also provided that the National Assembly *(guomin dahui),* a representative body elected directly by the people, would be convened regularly. It was to elect most of the top-level members of the government, the heads of the five *yuan,* and the members of the Legislative and Control Yuans. If the National Assembly was dissatisfied with either the policies or the administration of the government, it could intervene and, if still dissatisfied, could impeach the president.[57]

Nevertheless, Sun Ke and his colleagues' work of the previous two years was undone within a few weeks. On October 16, 1934, a new constitutional draft was made public. Sun Ke's draft was completely revised and infused with a fundamentally different governmental design. According to the newest revision, the president would be the dominant power in government, possessed of strong centralized power and unfettered by the Legislative Yuan or the National Assembly. Moreover, the head of the Executive Yuan and ministers were to be appointed by the president and removable at his will. This was the presidential system that Sun Ke had hitherto avoided by vesting preponderant powers in the heads of the five *yuan,* especially the Executive and Legislative Yuans. This new departure from his original design showed that Sun Ke, at this point, had lost in the institutional design contest to Chiang Kai-shek.

Sun Ke never gave a clear explanation of his departure from his original stand. In an article dated October 10, 1934, Sun Ke made an ambiguous remark about the presidential/cabinet issue: "As far as we followed the instruction of Sun Yat-sen, it was unnecessary to reckon up every iota in terms of the choice between the presidential and the cabinet systems."[58] On November 3, 1934, in a speech on the constitutional issue, Sun Ke slurred the matter again: "Because the president was elected by the people, he, though very powerful, would not become a dictator."[59] Clearly Sun Ke was subjected to strong pressure from Chiang Kai-shek and his followers after he finished the fourth draft. While Sun Ke was finishing the "Revised First Draft" (the fourth draft) in 1934, Chiang Kai-shek's political stock was sharply improving. His military campaign for suppressing the Communists had come to a successful conclusion and the Red Army was forced to leave its base in Jiangxi retreating north ("the Long March"). In the power struggle within the KMT, Chiang Kai-shek was on his way to finally eliminating both Wang Jingwei and Hu Hanmin from the contest. In this situation, the constitutional draft contemplated by Sun Ke and his Legislative Yuan became unacceptable to Chiang Kai-shek, as it would have narrowly circumscribed the power of the presidency.

In fact, Sun Ke alone could never have challenged Chiang Kai-shek. He had a share of power in the government only when Chiang's personal power was challenged or constrained by Wang Jingwei and Hu Hanmin. Along with the gradual decline of Wang Jingwei and Hu Hanmin, Sun Ke's political stock declined as well. This is why Chiang Kai-shek could firmly refuse Sun Ke's fourth constitutional draft at the Fifth Plenary Session of the CEC on December 10–14, 1934. The "Resolution on Principles for the Draft of the Constitution" passed at the CEC session (dated December 14, 1934) formally denied Sun Ke's revised constitutional draft and ordered a rewriting.[60] It was political pressure, therefore, that changed Sun Ke's standing on the constitutional issue and led to the new draft of October 16, 1934. This draft, approved by the First Plenary Session of the Fifth CEC of the KMT in December 1935 and promulgated on May 5, 1936, is known as the May 5 constitution in Chinese political history. The presidential form of government was written into the final draft of the constitution. Sun Ke's last attempt to restrict Chiang Kai-shek's ambitions had failed.

Establishment of Chiang's Singular Leadership

When Wang Jingwei, Hu Hanmin, and Sun Ke were eliminated from the power struggle, Chiang Kai-shek was left as the single victor and dominant political leader. A singular leadership, in which Chiang became dictator of Nationalist China, was now designed.

The movement to install Chiang Kai-shek as dictator began as early as 1934 when Chiang initiated a program, the New Life movement *(xingshenghuo yundong)*, to assure the personal loyalty of the Chinese people. The heart of the movement was formed from Chiang's ideas about the effect of military discipline on individual and group characteristics, elements of the Japanese warrior code, and Fascist ideas. In his speech on February 19, 1934, which marked the beginning of the movement, Chiang illustrated his ideas by reference to the speedy recovery of Germany after its defeat in World War I. He made reference, too, to the discipline of the Japanese people and suggested that the Chinese would do well to learn from Germany and Japan.[61] Chiang's own words revealed the Fascist overtones of the movement when he said that its purpose was "to thoroughly militarize the lives of citizens of the entire nation so that they can cultivate courage and swiftness, and especially the habit and ability of unified action, so that they will at any time sacrifice for the nation."[62]

In the spring of 1934, Chiang dispatched a military delegation to Germany and Italy to study Fascist methods of organization and operation and to consult with Hitler and other Fascist leaders. When the delegation returned to China in the summer of 1935, Chiang Kai-shek spent quite a few days listening to the report of Zhen Jiemin, the delegation leader. In the meantime Chiang had invited some thirty German Fascists as advisors to train leaders of the Blue Shirt Society.[63] It is worth noting that the Blue Shirt Society and the CC Clique assumed the leading role in the New Life movement. In accordance with Chiang's aspiration for one-person dictatorship, hundreds of books and journal articles were published by these factions appraising the Fascist principle of obedience to a supreme leader. Through several publishing houses such as Zhongzheng Shujiu, Qiuantu Shujiu, and Xingshengmin Shudian, numerous book series were published about dictatorship, fascism, and political leaders. The titles of these books—*Fascism and Italy, On Fascism, Organizational Theory of Fascism, Economic Foundation of Fascism, The Wave of Fascism, The Life, Thought, and Career of Hitler,* and *The Successful History of Hitler*—reveal the objectives of the movement.[64]

In a speech to a group of party cadre in Jiangxi province, Chiang Kai-shek clearly expressed his ambition to become dictator of China: "The most important point of fascism is absolute trust in a sagely, able leader. . . . Now we in China do not have one leader. I believe that unless everyone has absolute trust in one man, we cannot reconstruct the nation and we cannot complete the revolution."[65] In 1934, encouraged by Chiang Kai-shek and organized by the CC Clique and the Blue Shirt Society, twenty of the provincial and municipal party headquarters in northern China formally urged Chiang Kai-shek to assume the position of *zongli* (director general) of the KMT.[66]

As noted in previous chapters, the title of *zongli* was adopted by Sun Yat-sen in 1924 when he assumed dictatorial power over the party. After the death of Sun Yat-sen in 1925, the Second National Congress of the KMT in 1926 adopted a resolution that, to do honor and reverence to the party's late leader, the position of *zongli* would be forever reserved for Sun Yat-sen. Thus the proposal that Chiang be named *zongli* was a euphemistic way of suggesting that Chiang should now, like Sun Yat-sen, become the dictator of the party and hence of the nation.[67] This movement, however, offended the regional militarists in the southwestern part of China. Guangdong and Guangxi provincial militarists, including Chen Qitong, Li Zhongren, and Bai Chongxi, allied with Feng Yuxiang in the north and tried to obstruct the installation of the *zongli* position. They claimed that the title *zongli* was reserved for the late Sun Yat-sen and nobody else should be allowed to assume that position.[68] Chiang Kai-shek and his followers then decided to avoid the term *zongli* and instituted a similar position in the KMT called *zongchai* (general arbitrator), who was to exercise the power of *zongli* in his absence.[69] *Zongchai* and *zongli* in Chinese are different terms, but they have the same meaning. As Lloyd Eastman indicates, adopting the term *zongchai* was in fact "a distinction without a difference."[70] This was a language game that reflected both the political skills of Chiang Kai-shek and his power ambition.

While Chiang Kai-shek was fighting to be named *zongchai* in the KMT, he was working hard to become the singular leader of the Nationalist government. Seizing the opportunity of the war with Japan, Chiang called for and convened a Supreme National Defense Conference in July 1937. As chairman of the Central Military Commission, Chiang Kai-shek was concurrently designated chairman of the Supreme National Defense Conference on August 12, 1937.[71] In this position Chiang was vested with the emergency presidential power to dispose of all party, government, and military affairs by decree, in accordance with expediency and regardless of normal procedures, for the duration of the war. The conference was later reorganized into a permanent institution, the Supreme National Defense Council *(zuigao guofang weiyuanhui),* which was directly responsible to the CEC. The *zongchai* of the party was concurrently designated head of the council (*weiyuan zhang*).[72] Thus Chiang had at last realized his ambitions by concurrently serving as chairman of the Supreme National Defense Council, *zongchai* of the party, and chairman of the Central Military Commission. And in his formal capacity as chairman of the Supreme National Defense Council, he had become the one-person executive of China.[73]

CHAPTER 9
Conclusion: A Comparative Perspective

THIS BOOK, as stated at the outset, is not merely a political history of Nationalist China. The design of the Nationalist government during its formative period from 1925 to 1937 has been introduced here as a case study to explain the political logic of institutional design in authoritarian settings. As we have seen in the preceding chapters, the form taken by government institutions in the authoritarian setting of Nationalist China was not, as the conventional wisdom holds, an issue of little importance. Because the constitutional movement was championed and the Western constitutional form of government was introduced as the legitimate governing pattern in twentieth-century China, seasoned politicians made full use of the constitution-making process and modern government institutions to maximize their personal power and legitimize their authoritarian positions. Recognizing the implications of different constitutional frameworks to their personal power and position, political leaders with different power resources clearly expressed their institutional preferences and fought fiercely for their preferred designs of government. Based on the theoretical and empirical exercise presented in earlier chapters, this concluding chapter summarizes the central argument and offers a comparative perspective by examining constitutional reform in Taiwan and constitution-making in three comparable authoritarian polities of Asia: the Philippines, Indonesia, and South Korea.

Summary of the Argument

The central argument of this book is based on political realism. It argues three basic points:

1. Because the constitutional movement has prevailed in most parts of the world during the twentieth century, political leaders in modern authoritarian states find it necessary to legitimize their rule by using some approximation of institutional forms developed in Western democracies and hence to be identified as "modern" despite the form's lack of resonance in the local culture and the ruler's intention to avoid true democracy.
2. Authoritarian leaders select a form more closely approximating presidential or cabinet government depending on their personal power position in the regime: the political leader who anticipates becoming dominant insists on singular leadership of the presidential system; political leaders in a weaker position prefer the collective leadership of the cabinet system.
3. Shifts between the two systems follow from the results of ongoing political struggles within the party over whether to have a singular or a collective leadership.[1]

According to the argument of political realism, constitution-making reflects the underlying distribution of power among competing authoritarian leaders who attempt to use their resources to design political institutions that will both consolidate and maximize their personal position. An institutional design is adopted not merely because it provides a lasting solution to the political problems of the country but also (and more often) because those with superior power decide that such a design best serves their political interests. From this perspective, the design of government institutions is a choice among competing preferences and an outcome of the struggle for the superior position from which such a choice can be made. The interplay between power and preference is at the heart of institutional design. In this context, the forms assumed by government institutions are not only the product of a natural evolution or simply driven by socioeconomic forces or cultural traditions; they are also the result of the choice made by political actors who seek legitimacy by choosing the set of institutions that can best serve their ambitions in the process of strategic interaction with one another.

In examining the power struggle among the four KMT leaders over institutional design, this book has shown that for the Chinese Nationalist leaders, at least, institutional form was indeed taken seriously in the formative period of the Nationalist government. Chiang Kai-shek, as the single political leader who anticipated becoming dominant in the regime, consistently advocated the presidential system; his political rivals, Wang Jingwei, Hu Hanmin, and Sun Ke, were in a weaker position and had to seek a "fair" share of power in the regime by promoting the cabinet system. The alternating sequence of the two forms of government during the period 1925–1937 is explained as a result of the shifting power balance between Chiang Kai-shek and his rivals. The final establishment of the presidential system in the 1936 constitution is therefore an outcome of Chiang Kai-shek's ultimate predominance in the regime.

By showing how ruling elites in an autocracy both cared about and fought over formal institutional design, this book challenges the conventional view that political institutions do not matter and politicians are largely indifferent to the formal design of government institutions in nondemocratic countries. The findings in this book suggest that constitution-making may be used by authoritarian leaders to fulfill their personal ambition and can be a process of establishing autocratic rule.

A Comparative Perspective: The Nationalist Government in Taiwan

This book has so far focused on a single case of China's governmental design during one historical period. "The great advantage of the case study," as Arend Lijphart observes, "is that by focusing on a single case, that case can be intensively examined even when the research resources at the investigator's disposal are relatively limited."[2] As a case study in comparative perspective, this book places institutional design in Nationalist China in a position to be systematically compared and contrasted with other cases. Having made a case here for the seriousness with which institutional form was taken in Nationalist China during 1925–1937, we can now conduct a cross-historical and cross-national extension of the case study to see if the arguments can be generalized to encompass contemporary China and other authoritarian systems.

Clearly politicians in today's China, both in Taiwan and on the mainland, are still busy making constitutions and are still confronting the problems of institutional choice. In Taiwan, after the death of Chiang Kai-shek and his son, Chiang Ching-kuo, there emerged a constitutional reform centered on the presidential system established by Chiang Kai-shek, although the recent democratization process may have altered the terms of the debate. In Mainland China, four constitutions (1954, 1975, 1978, and 1982) have been promulgated since the victory of the Communists in 1949. Although the terms "presidential" and "cabinet" systems were never officially used by the Communist leaders in their institutional controversies, government institutions have undergone changes from time to time to suit the needs of a singular or a collective leadership during different periods of the People's Republic. Because the presidential and cabinet systems took different forms in the Communist regime of Mainland China after 1949, the study of constitution-making and institutional design there represents a different project for future study. The recent constitutional reform in Taiwan, however, has clear historical links to the constitution-making politics examined in this book and hence can be taken as a longitudinal extension of the case study.

As discussed in Chapter 8, the constitution of May 5, 1936, adopted the presidential form of government for the KMT regime. Although this constitution was not put into effect immediately because of the outbreak of the Sino-Japanese War in 1937, Chiang Kai-shek established his one-person rule in the Nationalist regime by creating the Supreme National Defense Council during the war and assuming the chairmanship *(weiyuan zhang)* of the council. When war with Japan ended, the Communist forces grew rapidly and demanded a share of power in the national government. In January 1946, the National Political Consultative Conference (Quanguo Zhengzhi Xieshang Huiyi) was inaugurated. The KMT and the Communist leaders, as well as several nonpartisan leaders, all attended. While the conference was called primarily to exchange views on negotiations between the KMT and the Communists, one of its aims was to subject the constitution of May 5, 1936, to revision. On January 31, 1946, the conference reached five agreements.[3] One of the five, the Agreement on Constitution Drafting Issues, posed a number of basic principles to guide the revision. One of the principles specifically demanded "the establishment of a cabinet system."[4] An Examination Committee was set up to study the 1936 constitution but reached deadlock when the Communists put forth a proposal calling for retention of all conference points without amendment while the KMT Central Executive Committee passed a resolution in March 1946 completely repudiating the principles put forth by the conference.[5]

A civil war between the KMT armies and the Communist troops broke out in mid-1946. As his armies "outnumbered the Communist troops by four or five to one, and were far better supplied with weapons and military equipment,"[6] Chiang Kai-shek anticipated a quick victory. On December 15, 1946, while the civil war with the Communists was raging, the National Constituent Assembly was convened. Although the Communists did not attend the assembly, a new constitution was adopted on December 25 and promulgated on New Year's Day, 1947. The system of government, however, is not clear-cut in the 1947 constitution. As Chien Tuan-sheng observes, "it can be either a presidential or a cabinet system of government, depending on the development of the political situation in terms of both personalities and political parties."[7] If the president was a man who coveted power, there were provisions he could use to establish a presidential system of government, for it was the president who selected the head of the Executive Yuan. Indeed, the president could become a dictator without violating any of the constitutional provisions if he could make the Legislative Yuan a rubber stamp. If, on the other hand, the political parties were influential and the leadership was democratically selected, a cabinet government could well result, since the Legislative Yuan, through its majority, had the right to approve the president's choice of head of the Executive Yuan and held the Executive Yuan responsible for all acts and policies of the executive.[8]

The Nationalist government with the strongman Chiang Kai-shek as president was made a presidential system under the 1947 constitution. As Linebarger indicates, "the president possesses the power of the chief executive of a strong presidential type of government."[9] The president was not only the head of government and commander-in-chief of the military forces but was also conferred power to issue emergency decrees.[10] In accordance with the constitution, the president was empowered to "take emergency measures to avert imminent danger to the security of the state—without being subject to the procedural restrictions prescribed in Article 39 or Article 43 of the constitution."[11] On May 10, 1948, in the name of the ongoing civil war with the Communists, Chiang Kai-shek promulgated the Provisional Amendments for the Period of Mobilization for Suppression of the Communist Rebellion, later known in Taiwan as the "Temporary Provision" *(lingshi tiaokuan)*. This provision extended the emergency powers already given to the president and permitted his tenure in office to exceed indefinitely the two-term restriction (each term for six years) prescribed in the constitution. This strong presidential government survived the retreat of the KMT regime to Taiwan in 1949 when the Communists took over Mainland China. Under the institutional arrangement of the "Temporary Provision," Chiang Kai-shek, as unchallenged leader of the KMT regime, never left the position of president until his death in 1974 while serving his fifth term. He was succeeded by the vice-president until 1978 when his son, Chiang Ching-kuo, was elected to the presidency. He too became a lifelong president until his death in 1988.

The presidential system designed by Chiang Kai-shek survived the retreat of the KMT regime to Taiwan because both Chiang Kai-shek and Chiang Ching-kuo were powerful leaders and held dominant positions in the KMT regime. During their presidencies, therefore, the singular leadership of the presidential system was maintained in Taiwan. After these two strong personalities passed away, Lee Teng-hui took over the presidency in January 1988. Lee Teng-hui is a native Taiwanese whose power base in KMT politics has never been as strong as that of his predecessors. In a study of contemporary Taiwan politics, Hung-mao Tien has indicated that Lee Teng-hui "is not likely to match the Chiangs in the exercise of presidential power."[12] Indeed, Hung-mao Tien predicted that a collective leadership would be formed in Taiwan: "Lacking the enormous prestige of both Chiangs in the KMT and without a personalized power base in the governing institutions, President Lee will probably not become a supreme leader even though he heads both the party and the government. Most likely his power will be constrained by a collective leadership."[13] But Hung-mao Tien did not foresee that the presidential system itself would be reformed to adapt to the change from a singular to a collective leadership. In fact, the presidential system established by the Chiang family has become one of the major institutional targets of constitutional reform and democratization in Taiwan in recent years. A Taiwan scholar indicates that "among the most controversial issues [of constitutional reform] is whether the existing five-power constitutional system will be kept intact, or whether a presidential system or a cabinet system will be set up."[14] Thus the presidential system originally designed by Chiang Kai-shek has become one of the central issues of constitutional reform.

The first step toward constitutional reform was to terminate the

"Temporary Provision." Lee Teng-hui, in his inaugural speech on May 20, 1990, declared that within a year he would put an end to the "Temporary Provision."[15] Lee Teng-hui kept his word. The "Temporary Provision," which had been in effect in Taiwan for forty-three years and broadened the presidential power of both Chiang Kai-shek and Chiang Ching-kuo, was finally terminated on May 31, 1991.[16] Prior to its termination, a National Affairs Conference *(guoshi huiyi)* was convened in Taipei on June 28–July 4, 1990. The major issue on the agenda was constitutional reform. To prepare for the conference, the Institute for National Policy Research (INPR), a think tank close to Lee Teng-hui, proposed two constitutional drafts: one draft designed the cabinet system; the other, the presidential system. Raymond Chang, then president of INPR, claimed that the two drafts "aim at providing the nation a choice between the cabinet and the presidential system."[17]

Although one of the most controversial issues discussed at the conference was how to reform the presidential system and constrain the presidential power, the cabinet option was not adopted.[18] All participants agreed that the president should be "elected by the people," but they were divided on whether the president should be elected directly or by a system similar to that of the United States where voters cast ballots for electoral college delegates representing the electorate's views as proxies.[19] While the final decision on reform of the presidential system was not reached at the conference, many participants, including some of Lee Teng-hui's aides, demanded constraints on presidential power.[20] In April 1991, the Second Provisional Meeting of the First National Assembly passed a Constitutional Amendment Act setting up strict legislative constraints on the president's emergency powers. While the president may issue emergency decrees, "such emergency decrees must, within ten days after issuance, be presented to the Legislative Yuan for ratification. If the Legislative Yuan refuses consent, the emergency decrees will immediately become null and void."[21] Moreover, the president may be elected for only one term according to the act.

The reform of the presidential system has become complicated recently due to the rise of the movement of Taiwan independence from Mainland China. The demand for constraining presidential power has now been interwoven with opposition to direct election of the president because direct election might convey the impression that the president was elected only by the people of Taiwan—thus implying Taiwan independence. On the other side, the so-called mainstream faction *(zhuliupai)* in the KMT has inclined toward establishing a presidential system with a direct and popular presidential election in 1996, when Lee Teng-hui completes his term of office.[22] In any case, the ongoing constitutional reform regarding the election of the president and the constraint on presidential power indicates that Lee Teng-hui cannot match the Chiangs in the exercise of presidential power and can no longer insist on the one-person executive. And this change, of course, has taken place in the larger context of Taiwan's democratization process by which the authoritarian nature of the KMT regime has been substantially weakened.

In the new political environment, the incentives, strategies, and problems confronting political leaders have been different in many respects from those of the early Republican era and the formative period of the KMT regime. From this perspective, the theoretical framework of institutional design in authoritarian regimes that has been presented in this book will not be sufficient to explain the institutional changes in Taiwan today. Nonetheless, the Taiwan system is descended directly from the early KMT regime on the mainland and the government system examined in this book has become the target of constitutional reform and institutional designs in Taiwan. Because of the historical connection, the theory offered earlier—which sorts out the institutional preferences of political actors and the institutional solutions to the power contest in Nationalist China—can certainly serve as a starting point to help us understand the recent constitutional reform and institutional changes in Taiwan.

A Comparative Perspective: The Philippines, Indonesia, and South Korea

Looking beyond Nationalist China and Taiwan, one can find a number of other comparable cases in Asia where political leaders took institutional forms seriously and alternative designs were adopted. The constitutional form of government was championed not only in Nationalist China but in many other Asian countries during the twentieth century. Despite the authoritarian nature of the polities, seasoned politicians in these Asian countries, just like their counterparts in Nationalist China, have taken advantage of modern political institutions rather than simply ignoring them. As in Nationalist China, constitution-making in these countries is a political process in which the shift between the presidential and cabinet forms of government follows changes in the political power configuration. Strikingly, the presidential system has been the most common design. In the following pages we will examine the constitution-making and institutional design in three selected Asian polities: the Philippines, Indonesia, and South Korea.

The Philippines

A study of government and politics in the Philippines notes that "Philippine history is replete with example of indigenous attempts at constitution-making and constitutionalizing the Office of the President."[23] During the two years prior to the American annexation in 1899, five constitutions were made by the Philippines. The 1935 constitution—the first promulgated after independence from the United States—designated a presidential system in which strong political leaders exercised dominant executive authority in the constitutional form of government. The last all-powerful president was Ferdinand Marcos, who was elected in 1965. After reelection to his second four-year term in 1969, he was constitutionally barred from remaining in office beyond eight consecutive years. Marcos, however, wanted to remain in office beyond the period allowed by the constitution. There were two ways by which he could do this: by amending the constitution and suspending the constitutional prohibition; or by casting aside the constitution under the guise of a national emergency. Marcos did both. He called a constitutional convention in 1971 to draft a constitution in response to the changes demanded by the times. In the middle of the convention, he took advantage of his presidential emergency powers and proclaimed martial law in 1972. Under the martial law Marcos claimed the powers of president and prime minister despite the 1973 constitution's adoption of a cabinet system. Remigio E. Agpalo has argued that the presidency under the 1973 constitution was—as operationalized by Marcos—an all-powerful and dominant office. Indeed, Agpalo calls it a "*pangulo*" presidency.[24] Alex B. Brillantes, Jr., has called the constitutional government under Marcos "constitutional authoritarianism" because "there was a dominant executive who actually ruled for all intents and purposes as a dictator, accountable to no one."[25] Thus Marcos in the Philippines used constitution-making and the constitutional form of government to enhance his personal power.

Indonesia

Indonesia adopted the presidential form of government in its 1945 constitution, which was designed by a strong nationalist leader, Sukarno, who proclaimed independence in Jakarta at the end of Japanese colonial rule in August 1945. Although he claimed to be a democrat, Sukarno criticized liberal democracy and promoted "guided democracy," which meant concentrating executive power in the hands of the president. "Guided democracy" emphasized "authoritarian rule by a strong executive leader who would provide direction for the nation and who would create harmony and unity."[26] As one study has pointed out, "essentially, Guided Democracy was dominated by Sukarno, whose charisma made him the unchallenged leader of Indonesia."[27] As the founder of independent Indonesia and a charismatic leader, Sukarno was in the predominant position in Indonesian politics to design the government's form.[28] Therefore, as one study indicates, "Sukarno was in favor of a strong presidential form of government."[29] Sukarno's preference for the presidential system is evidenced by the 1945 constitution, which is still the fundamental legal basis for Indonesian government today. Article 5 of the constitution states that the president, with the consent of the Council of Representatives, exercises legislative powers and enacts government regulations as necessary for the proper execution of the laws. Article 10 states that the president is the commander-in-chief of the armed forces. Article 12 gives the president the power to proclaim martial law.

After a coup attempt on September 30, 1965, Sukarno was deposed and General Suharto emerged as acting president on March 12, 1966, because of his leadership in the army's countercoup.[30] Suharto dismissed and appointed his own people to the People's Consultant Assembly. He was elected to a five-year term as president in June 1968. "Since then," notes an observer, "the unitary basis of the state, with a powerful executive at its head, has remained intact and more or less unquestioned."[31] When Suharto's fifth term of presidency expired in 1993, he was chosen for a sixth term until March 1998—

even though senior leaders of the 1945 generation, such as former army chief General Nasution, have released a public letter urging limits to executive power and Muslim intellectuals have urged Suharto to reform the political system.[32] The Indonesia case shows how the presidential system can be used by authoritarian leaders to pursue their personal ambitions under "guided democracy" (in other words, constitutional authoritarianism).

South Korea

The case of South Korea is somewhat different from the Philippines and Indonesia but resembles the situation in Nationalist China in that the government has alternated between the presidential and cabinet systems. As indicated by James C. F. Wang, "a constant nagging constitutional debate in South Korea has been whether there should be a presidential system of government or parliamentary system."[33]

The first constitution, drafted under U.S. sponsorship in 1948 by Dr. Yu Chin-o, a scholar and president of the prestigious Korea University, designed a cabinet form of government in which the president served merely as titular head of state and executive power was vested in a premier elected by the National Assembly.[34] But the emergence of a strong leader, Syngman Rhee, to political power resulted in the 1952 and 1954 amendments to the 1948 constitution. These amendments provided the popularly elected Rhee with an unlimited term as president. Having served as the first president of the Provisional Government in Shanghai in the 1920s and having led (or claiming to have led) Korean independence movements in the United States, Rhee was revered as the founding father of independent Korea. Rhee, an astute politician, used his background most effectively to elicit maximum popularity and political power. Seldom in any country had one man commanded such loyal admiration and support from such an overwhelming majority of people as Syngman Rhee did on the first day of Korean national independence. Indeed, he received 92 percent of the vote cast in the National Assembly when the election was held to choose the first president of the new republic. In the words of a historian: "A man of great ability and profound familiarity with the political tradition and institutions of the West, [Rhee] nevertheless believed firmly that Korea was not yet ready for Western-style democracy and, being of a basically authoritarian temperament, he tended to behave in a high-handed way toward his own people and above all toward his rivals."[35] During the twelve years of his presidency, Rhee increased his presidential power at the expense of representative government.

Rhee was forced to resign after the 1960 election due to widespread popular discontent with his autocratic rule, election fraud, economic depression, official corruption, and student demonstrations. The immediate successor to Rhee's government of the First Republic was an interim regime headed by Ho Chung, who shared power with a new premier, Chang Myon. Both were weak leaders. The initial action taken by the new government was the revamping of the constitution to "institute a cabinet rather than a presidential form of government, the idea being that a cabinet system would be more effective in preventing a dictatorship."[36] In Korea, just as in Nationalist China, the presidential system was based on singular rule whereas the cabinet system was based on collective leadership. According to the constitutional amendments, the president of the republic once again became a figurehead devoid of real political power. Articles 50 and 53 described the president simply as "the head of the state": he could neither affiliate "with a political party nor engage in a public or private profession nor practice any business." The real executive power was vested in the State Council headed by the premier. The State Council—in other words, the cabinet—was to be "collectively responsible to the House of Representatives."[37]

On May 16, 1961, a military coup overthrew the weak interim government. The general who emerged as leader of the Third Republic was Park Chung Hee. After consolidating his military rule, Park proclaimed a *yushin* or "revitalization" constitution in 1972. Under the new constitution the president was permitted an indefinite number of six-year terms; he was to be chosen indirectly by a popularly elected electoral college, known as the National Conference for Unification, from which members of political parties were barred; and he had the power to nominate to the National Assembly one-third of its total membership (73 of 219 seats at that time). Moreover, he could dissolve the assembly at will and take emergency measures on his own authority.[38] For the next four years, the Park regime maintained its control with little trouble. In 1978, however, trouble began when Park insisted on being elected for another term, his second under the *yushin* constitution. Park was assassinated by one of his political rivals in 1979.

The 1980–1981 constitution for the Fifth Republic under Chun Doo Hwan replaced the National Conference for Unification with a presidential electoral college of more than five thousand members. From the outset of the government President Chun Doo Hwan was "beset with opposition."[39] With the increasing popular demand for democratization, the presidential power was weakened under the 1980 constitution. Although the president still had enormous executive powers—including war declaration, treaty making, cabinet appointment, and emergency measures enactment—he could now suspend habeas corpus only with the approval of the National Assembly and for only a limited duration. Such emergency measures must be withdrawn by the president if so requested by a majority in the National Assembly. The president could not disband the National Assembly without the specific consent of the speaker and the cabinet. This constraint on presidential power was similar to those that resulted from constitutional reform in Taiwan and was, in fact, a harbinger of the coming democratization in Korea. From the very beginning it was evident that the most difficult problem for Chun Doo Hwan, a military general, was "the near-universal perception of illegitimacy of his coming to power in 1980–81."[40] Disapproval of Chun's regime cut across class, gender, and generation lines throughout his seven years in office. Indeed, Chun's regime was nearly overthrown in the summer of 1988, saving itself only when it surrendered to the popular demand for a direct presidential election. In a three-way contest, Roh Tae Woo won the race with only 36 percent of the votes to become the new president for the next five years. A democratic transition had begun.

A Question of Substance, Not Form

This brief comparative study of three Asian polities indicates that, just as in Nationalist China, the constitutional form of government was adopted in all three authoritarian countries and was used by authoritarian politicians to legitimize their political power and positions. The presidential system was preferred and designed mostly by a dominant strong leader who either had military forces under his control, such as Suharto and Park Chung Hee, or had won populist support, such as Syngman Rhee and Sukarno. The result of the constitution-making and institutional design was a constitutional authoritarian regime or "guided democracy."

This comparative study highlights the finding in Chapter 1 that what distinguishes the authoritarian regime from the democratic regime is not the constitutional form of government but the actual substance of government. In light of this perspective, the recent wave of democratization in Taiwan, the Philippines, and South Korea has resulted in a change not in the existing constitutional form of government but in the substance of government, in many cases constraining and reforming presidential power. This is a process of constitutional reform from "rule by one" and "rule by the few" to "rule by many" through the design of truly democratic government institutions.

Notes

1. Introduction

1. Recent works on constitution-making and institutional choice in democratic countries include Arend Lijphart, ed., *Parliamentary versus Presidential Government* (New York: Oxford University Press, 1992); Scott Mainwaring, "Presidentialism in Latin America," *Latin American Research Review* 25 (1) (1990): 157–179; and Juan Linz, "The Perils of Presidentialism," *Journal of Democracy* 1 (1) (Winter 1990): 51–69. For an extensive analysis see Juan Linz and Arturo Valenzuela, eds., *Presidentialism or Parliamentarism: Does It Make a Difference?* (Baltimore: Johns Hopkins University Press, 1993).

2. Crawford Young, "Politics in Africa," in Gabriel A. Almond, ed., *Comparative Politics Today: A World View* (Boston: Little, Brown, 1974), p. 499.

3. For a comparative analysis of the presidential system in these Asian polities see Chapter 9 of this book.

4. For a study of the Latin American cases see Mainwaring, "Presidentialism in Latin America."

5. For a recent review of this literature see Alfred Stepan and Cindy Skach, "Constitutional Frameworks and Democratic Consolidation: Parliamentarianism Versus Presidentialism," *World Politics* 46 (October 1993): 1–22. For another work on this subject see Matthew Soberg Shugart and John M. Carey, *Presidents and Assemblies: Constitutional Design and Electoral Dynamics* (New York: Cambridge University Press, 1992). Barbara Geddes' study indicates that in recent transitions toward democracies in several Latin American countries, one of the hottest topics has been the shift from the presidential system to the parliamentary system—a shift that has been very difficult. See Geddes, "Democratic Institutions as a Bargain Among Self-Interested Politicians" (paper presented at the annual meeting of the American Political Science Association, San Francisco, 1990), pp. 13–16 and 26–29.

6. Some scholars have conceptualized a third category: the "semipresidential system," based primarily on the Gaullist model of the French Fifth Republic. For a discussion of the semipresidential system see Maurice Duverger, "A New Political System Model: Semi-Presidential Government," *European Journal of Political Research* 8 (2) (June 1980): 165–187.

7. I use the term "cabinet system," rather than parliamentary system, in this book because the parliamentary system usually refers to a set of political institutions in democratic settings whereas this book deals with authoritarian politics in which genuine representative legislatures or parliaments do not exist.

8. Leon D. Epstein, "Parliamentary Government," in David L. Sills, ed., *International Encyclopedia of the Social Sciences* (New York: Macmillan/Free Press, 1968), 11:419.

9. For a classical elaboration of the presidential system see J. W. Garner, *Political Science and Government* (New York: The New York University Press, 1928), pp. 432–433.

10. Linz, "The Perils of Presidentialism," p. 53.

11. For the eleven criteria see Douglas V. Verney, *The Analysis of Political Systems* (London: Compton, 1959), pp. 75–76. In addition to the presidential and the cabinet government, Verney also identifies a third type of governmental arrangement that he calls "assembly government" or "convention government." The conception of assembly government is much more like the cabinet system than the presidential system. Ibid., pp. 64–65.

12. Shugart and Carey, *Presidents and Assemblies,* pp. 18–24.

13. In different countries the chief executive of the cabinet system may be called a prime minister, premier, or chancellor.

14. These first two distinctions are identified in Arend Lijphart, *Democracies: Patterns of Majoritarian and Consensus Government in Twenty-One Countries* (New Haven: Yale University Press, 1984), p. 68.

15. For the third criterion see Arend Lijphart, "Presidentialism and Majoritarian Democracy: Theoretical Observations" (unpublished manuscript, 1990), p. 5.

16. Shugart and Carey, *Presidents and Assemblies,* p. 21.

17. Although most contemporary authoritarian regimes adopt a constitutional form of government, some are simply military governments in which there are no political parties that play governing roles. This book deals with authoritarian regimes governed by one political party. Examples of such regimes can be found in Republican and Nationalist China before 1949, in Taiwan and South Korea before the 1990s, and in several Latin American countries during the 1970s and the 1980s. The former Soviet Union and East European governments prior to 1991 as well as the government of Communist China may also be included in this category.

18. Following this line of thought, some modernization theorists dichotomize states into two ideal types: traditional and modern. They believe that political modernization or development is involved in the rationalization of political authority and the establishment of institutional democracy: a set of rules, procedures, and organizations that are designed to facilitate the differentiation of political structure and the increased political participation of its citizens. See, for example, Barrington Moore, Jr., *Social Origins of Dictatorship and Democracy: Lord and Peasant in the Making of the Modern World* (Boston: Beacon Press, 1966), and Lucian W. Pye, *Aspects of Political Development* (Boston: Little, Brown, 1966). Samuel P. Huntington describes the process of political development; see his *Political Order in Changing Societies* (New Haven: Yale University Press, 1968).

19. Because of its tendency to concentrate power, the presidential system in democratic regimes is criticized by some scholars. Juan Linz believes that rigidity and immobility are "two weaknesses of presidentialism." See Linz, "Democracy, Presidential or Parliamentary: Does It Make a Difference?" (paper presented at the annual meeting of the American Political Science Association, Chicago, 1987). Arend Lijphart further indicates two "major problems of presidentialism." One is "the concentration of all executive power in the hands of one person, which is incompatible with broad coalition government and power-sharing"; the second problem is that "it is based on the principle of separation and balance of executive and legislative powers but . . . in practice, most presidential systems have found it impossible to achieve this balance." See Lijphart, "The Southern European Examples of Democratization: Six Lessons for Latin America," *Government and Opposition* 25 (1) (Winter 1990): 76.

20. For Aristotle's discussion of the three forms of politics, see *Politics* III: 7 in Richard McKeon, ed., *Introduction to Aristotle* (New York: Random House, 1947), p. 591.

21. Ibid.

22. The presidential system chosen in 1936 by Chiang Kai-shek was maintained in Mainland China until the Nationalists retreated to Taiwan in 1949. Although the Nationalist regime established in Taiwan has retained the same system, the recent transition from authoritarian to democratic rule in Taiwan has provoked a debate over the viability of presidentialism as a system able to accommodate the multiple demands placed on the regime.

23. The public choice approach is one of microeconomics and has its theoretical origin in rational choice theory. For this school of thought see Mancur Olson, *The Logic of Collective Action: Public Goods and the Theory of Groups* (Cambridge, Mass.: Harvard University Press, 1965); Russell Hardin, *Collective Action* (Baltimore: Johns Hopkins University Press, 1982); Albert O. Hirschman, *Exit, Voice, and Loyalty: Responses to Decline in Firms,*

Organizations, and States (Cambridge, Mass.: Harvard University Press, 1970); Samuel L. Popkin, *The Rational Peasant: The Political Economy of Rural Society in Vietnam* (Berkeley: University of California Press, 1979). Based on rational choice theory, specialists in American politics have produced important research showing that such institutional features as single-member district elections, different modes of elections for political leaders, the constitutional division of powers between government branches, and the internal committee organization of Congress have influenced the policymaking process and its outcomes. For these works see, for example, Morris P. Fiorina, *Congress: Keystone of the Washington Establishment* (New Haven: Yale University Press, 1989), and Roderick Kiewiet and Matthew D. McCubbins, *The Logic of Delegation: Congressional Parties and Appropriations Process* (Chicago: University of Chicago Press, 1991).

24. Samuel P. Huntington, *The Common Defense* (New York: Columbia University Press, 1961), p. 146.

25. Ellen Comisso, "Introduction: State Structures, Political Processes, and Collective Choice in CMEA States," in Ellen Comisso and Laura D'Andrea Tyson, eds., *Power, Purpose, and Collective Choice: Economic Strategy in Soviet States* (Ithaca: Cornell University Press, 1986), p. 37.

26. Philip G. Roeder, "Soviet Politics and Kremlin Politics," *International Studies Quarterly* 28 (1984): 171–193.

27. Thomas A. Baylis, *Governing by Committee: Collegial Leadership in Advanced Societies* (Albany: State University of New York Press, 1989), pp. 11–12.

28. In 1927, for example, three Central Executive Committees were claiming the KMT's leadership. One was in Wuhan led by Wang Jingwei; one in Nanjing led by Chiang Kai-shek; and another in Shanghai led by the Western Hill Group in the KMT. Moreover, three separate Fourth National Congresses were held by Chiang Kai-shek, Sun Ke, and Wang Jingwei respectively in Nanjing, Guangzhou, and Shanghai in 1931. For details see Chapters 6 and 7.

29. Two types of faction provided powerful clientele support for competing political actors in the struggle for leadership of the Nationalist regime. The first type formed around functional organs of the KMT—such as the Organization Group (also known as the CC Clique) that formed around the Organization Department of the KMT. The second type formed outside the KMT's formal organization—such as the Blue Shirt Society, the Western Hill Group, and the Reorganizationalists. For details see Chapter 3.

30. For Chiang's military background see Chapter 4.

31. For details of these factions see Chapters 3 and 4.

32. The Guangzhou government established by Sun Yat-sen in 1924 was, in fact, a military government. Sun Yat-sen, as the generalissimo, led the

KMT, the government, and the Nationalist army. This system was therefore called the generalissimo system.

33. For a detailed description of this coalition see Chapter 7.

34. The lacunae in the literature are obvious to serious students of modern Chinese politics. The standard reference on the theory, practice, and structure of the KMT and the Nationalist government remains Chien Tuan-sheng's classic work, *The Government and Politics of China,* first published in 1950 and reprinted several times. In recent decades, a few students of Chinese politics have made important contributions to the study of the Nationalist regime prior to 1949. George T. Yu has examined the Chinese party movement with special emphasis on the KMT during the period 1912–1924; see Yu, *Party Politics in Republican China: The Kuomintang, 1912–1924* (Berkeley: University of California Press, 1966). Hung mao Tien has offered a comprehensive analysis of the Nationalist government's central and local administrative institutions during the period 1927–1937; see Tien, *Government and Politics in Kuomintang China, 1927–1937* (Stanford: Stanford University Press, 1972). Parks M. Coble, Jr., has provided a new view of relations between the business class and the Nationalist government in Shanghai; see Coble, *The Shanghai Capitalists and the Nationalist Government, 1927–1937* (Cambridge, Mass.: Council on East Asian Studies, Harvard University, 1986). Hsi-sheng Chi has explored the intricate relationship between the military and the Nationalist government; see Chi, *Nationalist China at War: Military Defeats and Political Collapse, 1937–1945* (Ann Arbor: University of Michigan Press, 1982). Joseph Fewsmith has examined merchant organizations and politics in Shanghai; see Fewsmith, *Party, State, and Local Elites in Republican China: Merchant Organizations and Politics in Shanghai, 1890–1930* (Honolulu: University of Hawai'i Press, 1985).

35. See, for example, Lloyd Eastman, *The Abortive Revolution: China Under Nationalist Rule, 1927–1937* (Cambridge, Mass.: Harvard University Press, 1974).

36. Avery Goldstein describes two behavioral patterns of Communist leaders in Mainland China: "bandwagon politics" and "balance-of-power politics." From 1949 to 1966, the Chinese polity displayed the structural feature that he calls "bandwagon politics" in which Mao Zedong held supreme personal authority over his rivals. During the Cultural Revolution (1966–1978), the Chinese polity showed what Goldstein calls "balance-of-power politics" in which there was a "recurrent realignment of actors into counterbalancing coalitions." Although Goldstein does not relate the singular leadership and the collective leadership to these two patterns and does not explore the different institutional arrangements that might facilitate them, his patterns are similar to the behavior of the KMT leaders in their struggle for power in 1920s and 1930s. For a summary of Goldstein's argument see his article, "Explain-

ing Politics in the People's Republic of China: The Structural Alternative," *Comparative Politics* 22 (3) (April 1990): 301–322.

2. The Rise of Constitutionalism

1. Paul M. A. Linebarger, Djang Chu, and Ardath W. Burks, *Far Eastern Governments and Politics: China and Japan* (Princeton: Van Nostrand, 1956), p. 141.

2. For an English translation of these constitutions see Pan Wei-tung, *The Chinese Constitution: A Study of Forty Years of Constitution-Making in China* (Westport, Conn.: Hyperion Press, 1945), apps. C–I, pp. 148–238.

3. Linebarger, Chu, and Burks, *Far Eastern Governments,* p. 142.

4. For an English version of the provisional constitution of March 1912 see Pan Wei-tung, *The Chinese Constitution,* app. C, pp. 150–156.

5. For an English version of the constitutional compact of May 1914 see Pan Wei-tung, *The Chinese Constitution,* app. E, pp. 170–178.

6. Article 14 of the constitutional compact; see Pan Wei-tung, *The Chinese Constitution,* app. E, p. 171.

7. Linebarger, Chu, and Burks, *Far Eastern Governments,* p. 142.

8. For an English version of the draft constitution of August 1919 see Pan Wei-tung, *The Chinese Constitution,* app. F, pp. 179–190.

9. Linebarger, Chu, and Burks, *Far Eastern Governments,* p. 142.

10. Historians at the Institute of Modern History, Academia Sinica, Taiwan, have conducted valuable research into the political history of Republican China. For example, Zhang Yufa, the director of the institute, has published rich historical data for scholarly study of the KMT's history and party politics in Republican China. See Zhang Yufa, *Minguo Chu Nian de Zhengdang* (Political parties in early Republican China) (Taipei: Institute of Modern History, Academia Sinica, 1985). Zhang has also edited several volumes on the politics of the early period of the Republic of China. Among them is *Zhongguo Xiandaishi Lunji* (Collection of essays on the modern history of China) (Taipei: Lianjing Chuban Gongsi, 1980), a collection of fifteen essays on party politics and the struggle between the revolutionary forces and the monarchical restoration movement in the early Republic of China. *Zhonghua Minguo Kaiguo Qishi nian lai de Zhengzhi* (Politics of the Republic of China in its seventy-year history), edited by Lei Feilong (Taipei: Guangwen Shuju, 1981), contains a good description of the political history of Republican China.

11. Ernest P. Young, *The Presidency of Yuan Shih-k'ai: Liberalism and Dictatorship in Early Republican China* (Ann Arbor: University of Michigan Press, 1977), p. 221.

12. Andrew J. Nathan, "Chinese Democracy: The Lessons of Failure," *The Journal of Contemporary China* 4 (Fall 1993): 3.

13. Linebarger, Chu, and Burks, *Far Eastern Governments,* p. 132.

14. Among the studies of Chinese constitutional tradition and democracy see Andrew J. Nathan, *Chinese Democracy* (New York: Knopf, 1985), and Suisheng Zhao, "Zhongguo Minzhu Beiju Tanyuan" (Origins of the Chinese democracy tragedy), *Zhishi Fenzi* (Chinese Intellectual) (Winter 1990): 3–16.

15. Ye Qizheng, "Zhongguo Zhishi Fenzi Yu Xiandaihua" (The Chinese intellectual and modernization), *Zhishi Fenzi* (Chinese Intellectual) 5 (4) (Summer 1990): 37.

16. For a historical study of Chinese government institutions influenced by the constitutional movement before the KMT came to power, see Franklin W. Houn, *Central Government of China, 1912–1928: An Institutional Study* (Madison: University of Wisconsin Press, 1959).

17. Samuel P. Huntington's study, for example, indicates that "virtually all significant regime changes were from less democracy to more democracy" in the early twentieth century. See Huntington, "Will More Countries Become Democracies?" in Roy C. Macridis and Bernard E. Brown, eds., *Comparative Politics: Notes and Readings* (Chicago: Dorsey Press, 1986), p. 68. In this study Huntington divides the evolution of democracies into four stages: first there was a world trend toward the extension of democracy from the early nineteenth to the early twentieth centuries; this trend was reversed in 1920; the aftermath of World War II marked another dramatic, if brief, spurt in the multiplication of democratic regimes; in the fourth stage, from the early 1950s to the 1980s, the trends were mixed.

18. Alexis de Tocqueville, *Democracy in America* (New York: New American Library, 1956); James Bryce, *Modern Democracies,* 2 vols. (New York: Macmillan, 1921).

19. See Lloyd E. Eastman, *The Abortive Revolution: China Under Nationalist Rule, 1927–1937* (Cambridge, Mass.: Harvard University Press, 1974), p. 140.

20. See Pan Wei-tung, *The Chinese Constitution,* p. 1.

21. See William L. Tung, *The Political Institutions of Modern China* (The Hague: Martinus Nijhoff, 1964), p. 2.

22. Hu Pingsheng, *Minguo Chuqi de Fubi Pai* (Monarchical restoration activists in the early Republic of China) (Taipei: Taiwan Xuesheng Shuju, 1985).

23. Eastman, *Abortive Revolution,* p. 169.

24. Although democracy as a value system was championed in China in the early twentieth century, Andrew Nathan correctly indicates that "democracy in its most generally accepted sense" was "never tried in China." Nathan finds that "elected legislatures were unable to exercise the authority they were supposed to enjoy under the constitution and the laws" and "freedoms of organization and expression were subject to such severe limits, either legally

or extralegally, that they could not be used with much effect in political competition." See Nathan, "Chinese Democracy," pp. 3–4.

25. For a collection of recent studies on Sun Yat-sen's doctrine see Chuyuan Cheng, ed., *Sun Yat-sen's Doctrine in the Modern World* (Boulder: Westview, 1989).

26. *Minquan Chubu* (Primer of democracy) was one of three books that constituted what Sun Yat-sen called the "Jian Guo Fanglue" (Program of National Reconstruction). See *The Collected Works of Sun Yat-sen* (Shanghai: Tai Quan Co., 1929), vol. 2.

27. The *Fundamentals* consists of twenty-five articles. Sun Yat-sen personally wrote two copies of the *Fundamentals:* one was kept at his wife's place and the other was with his son, Sun Ke. The *Fundamentals* was first published in April 1924. For the text see *Geming Wenxian* (Collection of revolutionary documents) (Taipei: Zhongguo Guomindang Danshi Weiyuanhui, 1976), 70:385–388.

28. Paul Myron Anthony Linebarger, *The Political Doctrines of Sun Yat-sen: An Exposition of the San Min Chu I* (Baltimore: Johns Hopkins University Press, 1937), p. 218.

29. See Sun Yat-sen, *San Min Zhu Yi* (The people's three principles) (Taipei: Zhongguo Guomindang Dangshi Weiyuanhui, 1985), p. 209.

30. Ibid.

31. For the five-power constitution doctrine see Sun Yat-sen's *Fundamentals,* art. 19, in *Geming Wenxian,* 70:387.

32. Ibid., art. 21.

33. For Sun's discussion of the National Assembly see his *Fundamentals,* arts. 14, 21, and 23, in *Geming Wenxian,* 70:387; see also Sun's will in *Geming Wenxian,* 69:130–134.

34. For a selected English translation of Sun Yat-sen's works see Julie Lee Wei, Ramon H. Myers, and Donald G. Gillin, eds., *Prescriptions for Saving China: Selected Writings of Sun Yat-sen* (Stanford: Hoover Institution Press, 1994).

35. Democratic government is defined here not in ideal terms but in two operational points. One is a "polyarchy." This term, borrowed from Robert Dahl's *Polyarchy: Participation and Opposition* (New Haven: Yale University Press, 1971), means that government institutions must be divided into different branches designed to have different interests and to check and balance one another. The other point, "frequent election" of government officials, was emphasized by James Madison in no. 52 of *The Federalist Papers.* In other words, the heads of government must be elected periodically by the citizens.

36. For a critical explanation of Sun Yat-sen's thought and the KMT's ideology see Joseph Fewsmith, *Party, State, and Local Elites in Republican*

China: Merchant Organizations and Politics in Shanghai, 1890–1930 (Honolulu: University of Hawai'i Press, 1985), pp. 87–114.

37. For Sun Yat-sen's doctrine of political tutelage see his *Fundamentals,* art. 5, in *Geming Wenxian,* 70:386. In 1929, after five-power government was established, the KMT, following Sun's doctrine, adopted an "Essentials of Political Tutelage" that was to guide the Nationalist government during the period of political tutelage. Article 1 of the "Essentials" stated that "the Republic of China shall, during the period of political tutelage, have the KMT's National Congress guide the people, on behalf of the People's National Congress, in the exercise of their political powers." For a text of the "Essentials" see *Geming Wenxian,* 70:388-389.

38. These authoritarian characteristics of the Nationalist regime are elaborated in the next chapter.

39. See Eastman, *Abortive Revolution,* pp. 140–180.

40. Nathan, *Chinese Democracy.*

41. See Barrington Moore, Jr., *Social Origins of Dictatorship and Democracy* (Boston: Beacon Press, 1966).

42. See Linebarger, *Political Doctrines of Sun Yat-sen,* p. 6.

43. Eastman, *Abortive Revolution,* p. 167.

44. Linebarger, *Political Doctrines of Sun Yat-sen,* p. 8.

45. Ibid., p. 218.

46. This debate is still going on in Taiwan in the 1990s with respect to constitutional reform. For one group of articles discussing constitutional reform see Xue Fusheng, "Xianzheng Tizhi, Xuanjuzhidu Yu Zhengdang Yunzuo" (Constitution structure, electoral system, and party operation); Jiang Dashu, "Shuang Shouzhangzhi Xianzheng Jiagou Jiexi" (Analysis of the constitutional form of the semipresidential system); Liu Shuhui, "Xingzheng Yu Lifa Guanxi de Xingsiwei" (New thinking on the relationship between executive and legislature); and Zhang Baomin, "Minzhu Zhengzhi de Lilun Yu Shijian" (Theory and practice of democratic politics). All these articles were published in *Lilun yu Shijian* (Theory and Policy) (Taipei), 8 (2) (Spring 1994): 5–72.

47. See Sun Yat-sen, *San Min Zhu Yi* (The people's three principles), pp. 112–113.

48. Ibid., pp. 208–213.

49. See *Fundamentals,* art. 5, in *Geming Wenxian,* 70:386.

50. See George T. Yu, *Party Politics in Republican China: The Kuomintang, 1912–1924* (Berkeley: University of California Press, 1966), p. 183.

51. To a certain extent this situation was similar to the relationship between prime minister and the majority party in a democratic parliamentary system. A recent example was the resignation of the British prime minister, Margaret Thatcher, in 1990.

52. The Organic Law and all its revisions had to be approved by the KMT's Central Executive Committee. The first Organic Law was very brief and consisted of only ten articles. For a text see Chen Dezhang et al., eds., *Zhonghua Minguo Xianfa Shiliao* (Historical documents of the constitutions of the Republic of China) (Taipei: Lianguofeng Chuban She, 1973), pp. 25–26.

53. See Article 2 of the first Organic Law of the Republic of China, approved by the CEC of the KMT on July 1, 1925, in Chen Dezhang et al., ibid., p. 25; emphasis added.

54. See Article 4 of the Organic Law of July 1, 1925, in Chen Dezhang et al., ibid., p. 25.

55. Article 2 of the revised Organic Law of March 30, 1927; see Chen Dezhang et al., ibid., p. 27.

56. See Chen Dezhang et al., ibid., pp. 29–30.

57. Article 10 of the revised Organic Law of February 11, 1928.

58. Article 2 of the revised Organic Law of February 11, 1928.

59. Article 2 of the revised Organic Law of October 3, 1928. For an English translation of the Organic Law see Wu Chao-chu, *The Nationalist Program for China* (New Haven: Yale University Press, 1929), app. 2, pp. 81–90. Wu Chao-chu (Wu Chaoshu) was formerly minister of foreign affairs for the Nationalist government.

60. Article 9 of the revised Organic Law of October 3, 1928.

61. Article 13 of the revised Organic Law of October 3, 1928.

62. Article 13 of the revised Organic Law of November 17, 1930.

63. In fact, the revised Organic Law of October 1928 was already greatly expanded into forty-eight articles and looks very much like a provisional constitution. The provisional constitution of the political tutelage period was made public on June 1, 1931. For an English translation see Pan Wei-tung, *The Chinese Constitution*, pp. 247–255.

64. Article 19 of the revised Organic Law of December 30, 1931.

65. Articles 11 and 12 of the revised Organic Law of December 30, 1931; emphasis added.

66. Article 14 of the revised Organic Law of December 30, 1931.

67. Articles 10 and 15 of the revised Organic Law of December 30, 1931.

68. Eastman, *Abortive Revolution*, p. 177.

69. See Article 14 of the revised draft of the constitution.

70. Emphasis added. See Article 55 of the draft constitution of the Republic of China in Xue Zhuoyun, *Zhonghua Minguo Xianfa Lun* (On the constitution of the Republic of China) (Taipei: Wenjing Chuban She, 1972), app. 1, pp. 277– 288. For an English translation see Pan Wei-tung, *The Chinese Constitution*, app. O, pp. 286–305.

71. Article 37 of the constitution of May 5, 1936.

72. Article 38 of the constitution of May 5, 1936.

73. Article 44 of the constitution of May 5, 1936.
74. Eastman, *Abortive Revolution,* p. 177.
75. Ibid., p. 178.

3. Power Resources and Authority Relationships

1. Robert A. Dahl, *Who Governs?* (New Haven: Yale University Press, 1961).

2. K. J. Holsti regards relevance as a variable affecting the exercise of influence in international relations. He believes that "gross quantities of resources cannot be equated with effective influence" owing to "the distinction between a state's overall capabilities and the relevance of resources to a particular diplomatic situation." See Holsti, *International Politics: A Framework for Analysis* (Englewood Cliffs, N.J.: Prentice-Hall, 1983), p. 152.

3. Hung-mao Tien, "Factional Politics in KMT China, 1928–1937: An Interpretation," in Gilbert Chan, ed., *China at the Crossroads: Nationalists and Communists, 1927–1949* (Boulder: Westview, 1980), p. 34.

4. Andrew J. Nathan, "A Factionalism Model for CCP Politics," *China Quarterly* 53 (January–March 1973): 37.

5. In a study of Chinese politics, Lucian Pye suggests that "the prime bases of factions are power constellations of clusters of officials who for some reason or other feel comfortable with each other, who believe that they can share mutual trust and loyalties, and who may recognize common foes." See Pye, *The Dynamics of Chinese Politics* (Cambridge, Mass.: Oelgeschlager, Gunn & Hain, 1981), p. 6.

6. Avery Goldstein, *From Bandwagon to Balance of Power Politics: Structure Constraints and Politics in China, 1949–1978* (Stanford: Stanford University Press, 1991), p. 29.

7. In common parlance, "anarchy" is often used interchangeably with "chaos." Its use here is more narrowly circumscribed, however, as is often the case with scientific terms borrowed from the vernacular. The term "anarchy" is defined by political scientists as the absence of a central authority. For a definition see Kenneth Waltz, *Theory of International Politics* (Menlo Park, Calif.: Addison-Wesley, 1979).

8. Kenneth Waltz takes the "ordering principle" as the first of three characteristics of an international system. See his *Theory of International Politics.*

9. In recent years scholars have begun to apply the well-crafted international relations theories to the study of domestic politics. Avery Goldstein has applied the hierarchical and anarchic principles characterizing different international systems to explain fundamental patterns of Chinese Communist politics. See Goldstein, *From Bandwagon to Balance of Power Politics.*

10. Ibid., p. 30.

11. Samuel P. Huntington discusses these three aspects of one-party states

in his "Social and Institutional Dynamics of One-Party Systems," in Samuel P. Huntington and Clement H. Moore, eds., *Authoritarian Politics in Modern Society: The Dynamics of Established One-Party Systems* (New York: Basic Books, 1970), p. 6.

12. In assuming that all actors of a certain type have the same goal I do not mean to imply there is no individual variation. Researchers who make such an assumption realize that models grow too complicated to be useful if they try to reproduce all the complexity of social reality. Thus I am simply selecting the most prevalent motivation among these political players.

13. For a brief history of the KMT see Zhou Lu, *Zhongguo Kuomintang Jianshi* (Brief history of the KMT) (Taipei: Zhongzheng Shuju, 1953).

14. Zhang Yufa, director of the Institute of Modern History in Taipei, conducted an interesting investigation of the KMT and some six hundred other political organizations in the early period of Republican China. See Zhang Yufa, *Minguo Chu Nian de Zhengdang* (Political parties in the early Republic of China) (Taipei: Institute of Modern History, Academia Sinica, 1985). For an excellent discussion of the early history of KMT politics in English see George T. Yu, *Party Politics in Republican China: The Kuomintang, 1912–1924* (Berkeley: University of California Press, 1966). Yu's work presents an in-depth examination of the party movement influenced by Western democracies with a focus on the formative period of the KMT (1912–1924). Yu's father was Yu Yuren, an elder of the KMT.

15. For a description of the early factional competition see Jerome Chen, "Defining Chinese Warlords and Their Factions," *Bulletin of the School of Oriental and African Studies* 31 (1968): 563–600.

16. For a detailed description of the politics in this period see Lei Feilong, ed., *Zhonghua Minguo Kaiguo Qishi Nian Lai de Zhengzhi* (Politics of the Republic of China in its seventy-year history) (Taipei: Guangwen Shuju, 1981), pp. 281–371.

17. Yu, *Party Politics*, p. 183.

18. Ibid., p. 160.

19. Ibid., p. 172.

20. For an overall review of the historical facts on the reorganization of the KMT see Zhongguo Dier Lishi Dangan Guan (Second Archive Library of China), ed., *Zhongguo Kuomintang Di Yi, Er Ci Quanguo Daibaodahui Huiyi Shiliao* (Collection of the archives and documents of the KMT First and Second National Congresses) (Nanjing: Jiangshu Guji Chuban She, 1986). In two lengthy volumes this book provides all the available minutes and proceedings of meetings and documents on both the principles and the process of the KMT reorganization.

21. Mainland China has published numerous articles and books criticizing the brutal purge of the Communists by Chiang Kai-shek in 1927. They call

this incident the "Four Twelve (April 12) Counterrevolutionary Coup." Taiwan for its part has published many articles and books justifying the purge. They call this action *"qingdang"* (cleaning the party). One systematic examination published in Taiwan is Li Yunhan's *Cong Ronggong dao Qingdang* (From tolerating Communists to cleaning up the party) (Taipei: Zhongguo Xueshu Zhuzuo Jiangzhu Weiyuanhui, 1966).

22. For a detailed description of the purge of the Communists in Wuhan see Liu Jizheng, *Wuhan Guomin Zhengfu Shi* (History of the Nationalist government in Wuhan) (Wuhan: Hubei Renmin Chuban She, 1986), pp. 372–433.

23. Sun Yat-sen, *Fundamentals,* art. 8, in *Geming Wenxian,* 70:386.

24. This document was important because before the promulgation of the provisional constitution in 1931 there was "tutelage constitutionalism"—in fact, at least, if not in name. For a text of the "Essentials of Political Tutelage" see *Geming Wenxian,* 70:388–389.

25. See *Geming Wenxian,* 70:388–389.

26. Ibid.

27. Ibid.

28. The party statute adopted in 1924 required the National Congress to meet once a year.

29. Max Weber defines charisma as an "extraordinary quality of a person" and charismatic authority as a rule "to which the governed submit because of their belief in the extraordinary quality of the specific person." See H. H. Gerth and C. Wright Mills, *From Max Weber: Essays in Sociology* (New York: Oxford University Press, 1958), p. 295.

30. Sun's power even included his right to approve the reentry of expelled party members. Article 22 of the statute specified the conditions under which a party member could be expelled. Article 23 stipulated that expelled party members desiring to reenter the party must present evidence of their loyalty and obtain the personal approval of the party's *zongli.*

31. William L. Tung, *The Political Institutions of Modern China* (The Hague: Martinus Nijhoff, 1964), p. 93.

32. According to the party statute, members of the CEC were chosen by delegates of the National Party Congresses; members of the CEC standing committee were chosen by members of the CEC.

33. KMT Party Constitution, art. 35, in *Geming Wenxian,* 70:83.

34. For the historical evolution of the Political Council see Secretariat of the CEC, ed., *Zhengzhi Huiyi Gongzuo Baogao* (Work report of the Political Council) (Columbia University Library, November 1935).

35. See Chen Zhimai, "KMT de Zhengzhi Weiyuan Hui" (The Political Council of the KMT), *Shehui Kexui* (Social Science), 2 (4) (1937): 608. Cited in Hung-mao Tien, *Government and Politics in Kuomintang China, 1927–1937* (Stanford: Stanford University Press, 1972), p. 36.

36. Ibid.

37. For the membership of the CPC see Chien Tuan-sheng, *The Government and Politics of China* (Cambridge, Mass.: Harvard University Press, 1961), pp. 475–476.

38. The chief functions of the CPC were to decide fundamentals and principles of legislation, to administer policies, to make general plans for national defense and financial programs, and to select the presidents and members of the five *yuan* and other specially appointed officials of the national government. For the text of the regulation see *Zhongyang Dangwu Yukan* (Central Party Monthly), June 1929.

39. For details see Chapter 7 in this book.

40. For details see Chapter 8 in this book.

41. Yu, *Party Politics,* p. 183.

42. Tai Shiaoyi, ed., *Zhonghua Minguo Zhengzhi Fazhan shi* (History of the political development of the Republic of China), vol. 2 (Taipei: Jingdai Zhongguo Chuban She, 1985).

43. See Secretariat of the CEC, *Minutes of the Fourth Plenary Session of the Third CEC, 1930.*

44. This figure is given by Chai Mongxian in his "Wuhan Shinian de Huiyi" (Reminiscences of ten years in Wuhan), in *Zhuanji Wenxue* (Biographical Literature) (March 1960): 3.

45. See Secretariat of the CEC, *Minutes of the Third Plenary Session of the Fourth CEC, 1932.*

46. In the late 1930s Chen Zhimai, a Chinese political scientist, described this state of paralysis of the KMT's top decision-making apparatus. He wrote that only two members of the standing committee stayed in Nanjing during the summer of 1935. Chiang Kai-shek spent most of his time in Sichuan directing a military campaign against the Communists. Wang Jingwei was away from Nanjing on "sick leave." Hu Hanmin was abroad, showing not the slightest interest in the party-state's affairs. Sun Ke, the head of the Legislative *Yuan,* was taking a long summer vacation in Qingdao, a summer resort on the eastern coast of China. Yu Yuren and Gu Mengyu stayed in Shanghai because of "illness." Chen Guofu, the governor of Jiangsu province, had to remain in Zhenjiang, the provincial capital. This left only Zhu Zheng and Ye Shutang, both identified as leaders of the then powerless Western Hill faction, in Nanjing. Under these circumstances various government and party bodies were forced to consult Chiang or Wang by telegram on important matters. See Hung-mao Tien, *Government and Politics in Kuomintang China,* p. 38.

47. For examples of the literature see Robert Scalapino and Junnosuke Masumi, *Parties and Politics in Contemporary Japan* (Berkeley: University of California Press, 1962); Paul R. Brass, *Factional Politics in an Indian State: The Congress Party in Uttar Pradesh* (Berkeley: University of California

Press, 1965); and Fred W. Riggs, *Thailand: The Modernization of a Bureaucratic Polity* (Honolulu: University of Hawai'i Press, 1966). For the literature on Chinese factionalism see, for example, Andrew J. Nathan, *Peking Politics, 1918–1932: Factionalism and the Failure of Constitutionalism* (Berkeley: University of California Press, 1976); Andrew J. Nathan, "A Factionalism Model for CCP Politics," *China Quarterly* 53 (January–March 1973): 34–66; and William W. Whitson, "The Field Army in Chinese Communist Military Politics," *China Quarterly* 37 (January–March 1969): 1–30.

48. Nathan, "A Factionalism Model for CCP Politics," pp. 47–48.

49. I found only one recorded exception to the consensus rule. It was a bill presented by Hu Hanmin on the second day of the Fourth Plenary Session of the Third CEC (November 14, 1930) that was "passed in principle" according to the original minutes *(jilu)* of the meeting. The phrase "passed in principle" *(yuanze tongguo)* usually means there was opposition. The original version of the minutes is handwritten and preserved at the Hoover Library at Stanford University. In the formally printed version of the minutes, the phrase "in principle" has been removed.

50. The development of the CC Clique is described in greater detail in the next chapter when Chiang's power position is analyzed.

51. For the role of the Organization Department of the KMT after the reorganization of 1924 see Chien Tuan-sheng, *The Government and Politics of China,* pp. 90 and 124–125.

52. Shen Zui's reminiscence mentions some of these assassination activities of the Bureau of Investigation and Statistics. For details see Shen Zui, *Wo de Tewu Shengya* (My life as a special agent) (Hong Kong: Jinglin Chuban She, 1985).

53. Chien Tuan-sheng's study of the KMT and the Nationalist government, which was conducted in 1948, pays special attention to the Organization Department. See Chien Tuan-sheng, *The Government and Politics of China,* p. 124.

54. The same is true in the People's Republic of China. The Central Military Commission is under the Communist Party, not under the government.

55. The Northern Expedition was a military campaign launched first in 1924 by Sun Yat-sen against the warlords in North China. It was called the Northern Expedition because Sun's base of revolutionary movement was at Guangdong, a southern province, and the warlords were mainly in the north.

56. Hung-mao Tien, "Factional Politics in KMT China, 1928–1937: An Interpretation," in Gilbert Chan, ed., *China at the Crossroads: Nationalists and Communists, 1927–1949* (Boulder: Westview, 1980), p. 24.

57. A Chinese warlord was a commander of a personal army who was ruling or seeking to rule territory and acting more or less independently. While scholars have different definitions of warlordism, they agree that warlords

dominated Chinese political life from 1916 to 1928: the "warlord period." Warlordism after 1928 derived partly from the organization of the Nationalist army, which had been formed in 1925 by bringing together several regional armies that, despite their cooperation, remained substantially independent. The new warlords, unlike their predecessors, declared their support for the Nationalist Revolution while they continued in command of their personal troops. For a discussion of the old and the new warlordism in Nationalist China see James E. Sheridan, *China in Disintegration: The Republican Era in Chinese History, 1912–1949* (New York: Free Press, 1975).

58. John K. Fairbank and Albert Feuerwerker, eds., *The Cambridge History of China* (Cambridge: Cambridge University Press, 1986), vol. 13, pt. 2, p. 177.

59. James E. Sheridan offers a detailed description of the independent financial bases of the new warlordism in the Nanjing decade. See Sheridan, *China in Disintegration,* pp. 183–206.

60. Ibid.

61. For an interesting description of the struggle in the Reorganization and Disbandment Conference see *The Reminiscence of Li Zhongren,* which was part of an oral history project conducted at Columbia University. Tang Degang recorded Li Zhongren's reminiscence and published it in Chinese. For the story of the conference see Tang Degang, *Li Zhongren Huiyi lu* (Hong Kong: Nanyue Chuban She, 1986), pp. 385–391. Chen Shiyuan, the personal secretary of Li Zhongren, also wrote an account of this story: *Zhenghai Mixing* (Mystery and hardship in the political sea) (Hong Kong: Nanyue Chuban She, 1988), pp. 2–6.

62. Zhang Xueliang was best known for his historical role in the Xian Incident in which Chiang Kai-shek was arrested and forced to announce a decision to resist the Japanese invasion.

4. Relative Power Positions of the Major Players

1. For the study of Chiang Kai-shek's political activities, at least two sets of important data are available. The first set is the various biographies of Chiang Kai-shek. The biographies published in Mainland China before the 1980s treated Chiang simply as a head of the counterrevolutionaries. More objective works have been published in recent years. Among these are two books titled *Chiang Kai-shek Zhuan* (Biography of Chiang Kai-shek), one written by Yang Shubiao and the other by Wang Fumin. The biographies published in Taiwan have mostly praised Chiang Kai-shek as a great leader or hero. Examples of these books are *The Chronology of President Chiang Kai-shek* (by Chen Bulie and Tang Zhenyiao), *The Life of Chiang Kai-shek* (by Xiong Shiyi), and *Biography of President Chiang* (by Dong Xianguang). Biographies of Chiang Kai-shek written by Westerners tend to be more objec-

tive than those published in Mainland China and Taiwan. Examples include *The Man Who Lost China: The First Full Biography of Chiang Kai-shek* (by Brian Crozier) and *The Early Chiang Kai-shek: A Study of His Personality and Politics, 1887–1924* (by Pichon P. Y. Loh).

The second set of data comprises the speeches and works of Chiang Kai-shek. The Taiwan government published *The Collection of Chiang Kai-shek's Speeches and Works* in 1956 and *Supplementary Collection* in 1959—altogether twenty-seven volumes in both Chinese and English. In addition, Mao Shichen has collected Chiang's diary, letters, and speeches before 1926 into twenty volumes. Chen Bulie added two more volumes to this collection and the date was extended to 1948. For a complete review of the historical data about Chiang Kai-shek see the transcript of Lu Peiyiong's talk, "Chiang Kai-shek Xiansheng Yishi Xingtai de Shiliao yu Menjing" (Historical material and approaches for the study of Mr. Chiang Kai-shek's thought), in Research Center of Historical Materials of the Republic of China, ed., *Zhongguo Xiandai shi Zhuanti Yanjiu Baogao* (Research reports on special topics of modern Chinese history), vol. 6 (Taipei: Research Center of Historical Materials of the Republic of China, 1977), pp. 1–12.

2. For a study of the political relationship between Chiang Kai-shek and Sun Yat-sen see Pichon P. Y. Loh, *The Early Chiang Kai-shek* (New York: Columbia University Press, 1971).

3. For this study see Parks M. Coble, Jr., *The Shanghai Capitalists and the Nationalist Government 1927–1937* (Cambridge, Mass.: Council on East Asian Studies, Harvard University, 1986).

4. See Hu Puyu, *The Military Exploits and Deeds of President Chiang Kai-shek* (Taipei: Chun Wu, 1972).

5. See Hollington K. Tong, *Chiang Kai-shek: Soldier and Statesman* (Shanghai: China Publishing Co., 1937).

6. This was a military attempt by Sun Yat-sen and his military lieutenants, Huang Xing and Chen Qimei, to check Yuan Shikai and save the newborn republic by force.

7. Chien Tuan-sheng, *The Government and Politics of China* (Cambridge, Mass.: Harvard University Press, 1961), p. 183.

8. Hung-mao Tien, *Government and Politics in Kuomintang China, 1927–1937* (Stanford: Stanford University Press, 1972), p. 53.

9. See Secretariat of the CEC, *Minutes of the Second National Congress of the KMT, 1926.*

10. Ibid.

11. The CEC consisted of thirty-six members (nine of them Communists) in that congress. For the list see Secretariat of the CEC, *Minutes of the Second National Congress of the KMT, 1926.*

12. Chiang Kai-shek's certificates of appointment in the KMT and the

Nationalist government are preserved in the National History Archival Museum in Taipei.

13. There has been no official explanation of the meaning of "CC." It could stand either for its leaders, the two Chens, or for the Central Club, the inner core of the KMT's central headquarters at the time of the Northern Expedition.

14. For a critical history of the Political Study Clique and its connection with Chiang Kai-shek see Han Si, *Kan, Zhengxuexi* (Look, the Political Study Clique) (Hong Kong: Hua Nan Chuban She, 1947).

15. See Xuan Jiexi, "Lanyi She zhi lailong qumai" (Origin and development of the Blue Shirt Society), in Gan Guoxun, *Lanyi She, Fuxing She, Lixing She* (The Blue Shirt Society, Reconstruction Society, and Vigorous Action Society) (Taipei: Zhuanji Wenxue Chuban She, 1984), p. 25.

16. Chiang resigned from his position as president of the Nationalist government and commander-in-chief of the Nationalist army under pressure from a grand anti-Chiang coalition consisting of Hu Hanmin, Wang Jingwei, Sun Ke, and several regional militarists in late 1930. For details see Chapter 8 in this book.

17. For the proposal see Gan Gouxun, "Shi Lanyi She bin Yi Liu Liqun" (Explaining the Blue Shirt Society and recalling Liu Liqun), in Gan Gouxun, *Lanyi She, Fuxing She, Lixing She,* pp. 1–14. This book collects ten reminiscences about the history and activities of the Blue Shirt Society written by those who were involved in this organization in the early years of Nationalist China.

18. For an account of the meeting of Chiang Kai-shek and Liu Liqun see Xuan Jiexi, "Lanyi she zhi lailong qumai," in Gan Guoxun, *Lanyi She, Fuxing She, Lixing She,* pp. 31–32.

19. Ibid., p. 32.

20. According to the authors of *Lanyi She, Fuxing She, Lixing She,* the Blue Shirt Society was also named the Reconstruction Society *(Fuxing She),* the Vigorously-Carry-Out Society *(Lixing She),* and the Green Shirt Society *(Qingyi She)* when it was first founded. For the different names of this organization at its founding see Chen Dunzheng, "Fuxing She, Lanyi She, Qingyi She" (The Reconstruction Society, the Blue Shirt Society, and the Green Shirt Society), in Gan Gouxun, *Lanyi She, Fuxing She, Lixing She,* pp. 45–79; and Gan Guoxun, "Shanmin Zhuyi Lixing She" (The People's Three Principles Vigorous Action Society), in Gan Guoxun, ibid., pp. 164–188.

21. Almost all publications in English have criticized the Blue Shirt Society's activities and characterized the group as a Fascist organization. These works include Chien Tuan-sheng's *Government and Politics of China,* Hungmao Tien's *Government and Politics in Kuomintang China,* and Maria Hsia Chang's *The Chinese Blue Shirt Society: Fascism and Developmental Nation-*

alism. Reminiscences published in Mainland China have also criticized the Blue Shirt Society. For one of these publications see Shen Zui's *Wo de Tewu Shengya* (My life as a special agent). Recent reminiscences written by those who were involved in this organization, however, disagree strongly with the criticism. For an article directly refuting Eastman's criticism see Gan Guoxun, "Bochi Zhongguo Guomindang Faxishi Zhuzhi—Lanyi She" (Counter-criticism of the book *The Blue Shirt Society: Fascist Organization of Kuomintang in China*), in Gan Guoxun, *Lanyi She, Fuxing She, Lixing She,* pp. 189–195.

22. In fact, none of his political rivals, even Wang Jingwei, ever had such extensive control over military power. The military resource not only brought Chiang Kai-shek to power but also gave him great room to maneuver politically. Whether as president of the national government or as commander-in-chief, Chiang Kai-shek had always held both nominal and actual control of the military administration and command of the field forces.

23. See Robert Payne, *Chiang Kai-Shek* (New York: Weybright & Talley, 1969), pp. 63–79, 81, and 257.

24. See S. I. Hsiung, *The Life of Chiang Kai-shek* (London: Peter Davies, 1948), pp. 87, 92, and 136. For the relations between Chiang and the Chens see also Loh, *The Early Chiang Kai-Shek,* pp. 26–29.

25. Tien, *Government and Politics in Kuomintang China,* pp. 49–50.

26. Howard L. Boorman, "Wang Ching-wei: A Political Profile," in Chun-tu Hsueh, ed., *Revolutionary Leaders of Modern China* (New York: Oxford University Press, 1971), p. 29.

27. Ibid.

28. For a detailed description of Wang's heroic activities see Wang Xing and Liu Hong, eds., *Nanjing Guominzhengfu Junzheng Yaoyuan Lu* (Brief chronicle of the important military and civilian officials of the Nanjing government) (Beijing: Chunqiu Chuban She, 1988), pp. 125–127.

29. There is no satisfactory critical biography of Wang Jingwei in either Chinese or English. Tang Liangli's *Wang Jingwei: A Political Biography* (Beijing, 1931) is an adulatory account by a close associate; Don Bate's *Wang Jingwei: Puppet or Patriot?* (Chicago, 1941) is a sympathetic but superficial journalistic profile. A more cynical account by a contemporary who later became a Communist depicts the youthful Wang as a gay deceiver—eloquent and attractive on the surface but underneath a "spineless man, irresolute, easy to change." See Wu Yuzhang, *The Revolution of 1911* (Beijing: Renmin Chuban She 1962), p. 80. Bibliographic guidance to basic Chinese and Western-language sources is given, respectively, in Eugene Wu, *Leaders of Twentieth-Century China* (Stanford: Stanford University Press, 1956), and T. L. Yuan, *China in Western Literature* (New Haven: Yale University Press, 1958). The most useful edition of Wang's writings for the period up to 1929 is *Wang Jingwei Wenji* (Collected works of Wang Jingwei), 4 vols. (Shanghai:

Shangwu Shuju, 1929). Many of Wang's political statements of the ensuing period were released in English by the China United Press (Beijing and Shanghai). See, for example, *The Chinese National Revolution: Essays and Documents* (1931) and *China's Problems and Their Solution* (1934); see also *China's Own Critics,* a selection of essays by Hu Shi and Lin Yutang with commentary by Wang Jingwei (Beijing, 1931).

30. Wang Jingwei's certificates of appointment to the top positions of the KMT and the Nationalist government are preserved in the National History Archival Museum in Taipei (series numbers 0321.00/6077 and 0321.02/6077).

31. T'ang Leang-li, *The Inner History of the Chinese Revolution* (New York: Dutton, 1930), provides a useful statement, intended for Western consumption, of the Reorganizationalist case against Chiang Kai-shek.

32. Concerning the founding date of the KMT Reorganizationalist Comrades Association, there are several different views. Chen Gongbo said it was in the winter of 1928; see *Geming Ribao* (Revolutionary Daily), June 15, 1931, p. 1. He Kuangwen said it was in the spring of 1928; see He's "reminiscences" of Reorganizationalists in *Wenshi Ziliao Xuanji* (Selected collection of materials of historical literature), 17:168, a collection edited by the National Consultant Conference of China. Fan Yusui said it was in May 1928; see Fan's "reminiscences" of Reorganizationalists in *Wenshi Ziliao Xuanji* 45:215–216. And Huang Yingbai said it was on November 11, 1928; see Shen Yunlong, *Huang Yingbai Xiansheng Nianpu Changbian* (A long biography of Mr. Huang Yingbai) (Taipei: Nianjing Chuban Shiyie Gongsi, 1976), 1:371.

33. This document is preserved in the Second Historical Archives Museum of China (Nanjing), "Nationalist Government Archives I," no. 6300. It was collected by Cha Jiangyu in *Guomindang Gaizhupai Ziliao Xuanbian* (Selected documents of the KMT Reorganizationalists) (Hunan: Hunan Renmin Chuban She, 1986), pp. 134–138.

34. See Cha Jianyu, *Guomindang Gaizhupai Ziliao Xuanbian.*

35. For the development of the provincial and overseas branches of the Reorganizationalists see Cha Jianyu, *Guomindang Gaizhupai Ziliao Xuanbian,* pp. 142–149 (provincial branches) and pp. 150–151 (overseas branches).

36. For the resolution see the minutes *(jilu)* of the KMT Third Congress in *Zhongguo Guomindang Nianjian, 1929* (KMT Yearbook, 1929), edited by the Editorial Committee of the CEC, pp. 73–74. For Chiang's suppression of the Reorganizationalists see Cha Jianyu, ibid., pp. 539–672.

37. See *Geming Ribao* (Revolutionary Daily), March 1, 1930, p. 1.

38. See *Xin Chen Bao* (Xin Chen News), March 26, 1930, p. 2.

39. See *Geming Ribao,* March 23, 1930, p. 1.

40. A detailed article about the expanded session of the CEC appeared in *Dagong Bao* (Dagong Daily), July 15, 1930, p. 4. The proceedings of this ses-

sion were published in this newspaper later. See *Dagong Bao,* July 29 and August 7, 8, 10, 12, 14, 16, 17, 19, 20, 22, 26, 28, 1930.

41. For the whole process of organizing the Beijing government see *Xin Chen Bao,* September 2, 1930, p. 2.

42. This war was known as the Zhongyuan Dazhan (Great Central China War) in modern Chinese history because it was fought in Central China.

43. Zhang Xueliang published an open telegram on December 29, 1928, declaring his support for Chiang Kai-shek. For the text of the telegram see *Guowen Zhoubao* (Guowen Weekly), vol. 6, no. 2, January 6, 1929.

44. In May 1936, just after Hu's death, *Hu Xiansheng Hanmin Jilian Zhuankan* (A special collection to memorialize Hu Hanmin) was published in Guangzhou; it collected nineteen reminiscences and twelve poems for the memory of Hu Hanmin. From the late 1970s to the early 1980s, Taiwan published *Hu Hanmin Zhuanji Ziliao* (Materials for studying the biography of Hu Hanmin), 12 vols. In Mainland China, *Hu Hanmin Zizhuan* (Autobiography of Hu Hanmin) was published by Zhongguo Shehui Kexue Chuban She (Beijing) in 1981. Zhou Binwo and Chen Hongmin, two young Chinese scholars, published their master's thesis, *Hu Hanmin Pingzhuan* (A study of Hu Hanmin's life), in Guangzhou in 1989. These are useful historical resources for studying Hu Hanmin's life and revolutionary activities.

45. See *Hu Hanmin Zizhuan,* p. 7.

46. See Melville T. Kennedy, Jr., "Hu Hanmin: His Career and Thought," in Chun-tu Hsueh, ed., *Revolutionary Leaders of Modern China* (London: Oxford University Press, 1971), p. 272.

47. Ibid., p. 271.

48. For Hu Hanmin's personal dignity and his contribution to Sun Yat-sen's doctrine see Zhen Yianfen, a historian in Taiwan and also an early follower of Hu Hanmin, "Hu Zhantang Xiansheng de Shengping jiqi dui Guofu Geming Sixiang de Chanyiang" (The life of Mr. Hu Zhantang and his contribution to the thought of the founding father), in Zhonghua Minguo Shiliao Yanjiu Zhongxing (Research Center of Historical Materials of the Republic of China), ed., *Zhongguo Xiandai Shi Zhuanti Yanjiu Baogao* (Research report on special topics of China's modern history) (Taipei: Research Center of Historical Materials of the Republic of China, 1979), 9:25–44.

49. Hu Hanmin's major work on the People's Three Principles was *Sanminzhuyi de lianhuan sing* (The links between the People's Three Principles) (Shanghai, 1928). Other than these works, a collection of Hu Hanmin's speeches, *Hu Hanmin Yanjang Ji,* was published in Shanghai in 1927. An English collection of his selected writings and addresses was published in Guangzhou in 1925. His personality and character were revealed in his daughter's reminiscences published in *Zhongyang Ribao* (Central Daily News), Taipei, February 8, 1969.

50. George F. Bother, *A Short History of Nationalist China, 1919–1949* (New York: Putnam's, 1979), p. 85.

51. For a detailed description of Hu's activities in this period see Zhou Binwo and Chen Hongmin, *Hu Hanmin Pingzhuan* (Study of Hu Hanmin's life) (Guangzhou: Guangdong Renmin Chuban She, 1989), pp. 168–175.

52. Shi Qiansheng, *Nanjing Guominzhengfu de Jianli* (Establishment of the Nationalist government in Nanjing) (Zhengzhou: Henan Renmin Chuban She, 1987), p. 77.

53. Xie Yiutien, Xie Chi's grandson, was a visiting scholar in the Hoover Institution in 1990–1991. (He came from the Institute of History Studies at the Chinese Academy of Social Sciences.) When I interviewed him at the Hoover Institution in June 1990, he gave me valuable information about the Western Hill Group and its relations with Hu Hanmin and Chiang Kai-shek.

54. For example, Xie Yiutien told me that his grandfather, Xie Chi, was a close friend of Hu Hanmin. For the relationship between Xie Chi and the Western Hill Group see also Xie Yiutien, *Xie Huisheng Xiansheng Shiji Jizhuan* (Biography of Mr. Xie Huisheng) (Taipei: Jindai Zhongguo Chuban She, 1991).

55. See Zhou Binwo and Chen Hongmin, *Hu Hanmin Pingzhuan,* pp. 179–180.

56. For an account of this historical event see Huang Jilu, "Hu Xiansheng yu Xishan Huiyi" (Mr. Hu and the Western Hill meeting), in *Zhuanji Wenxue* (Biography Literature), 28 (6) (June 1989): 18–20.

57. For a description of the relations between Hu Hanmin and Chen Jitang see Zhou Bingwo and Chen Hongmin, *Hu Hanmin Pingzhuan,* pp. 280–284.

58. See Xiao Jizhong, ed., *Geming Renwu Zhi* (Biography of revolutionaries) (Taipei: Zhongguo Guomindang Dangshi Weiyuanhui, 1976), 13:19.

59. Eastman, *Abortive Revolution,* p. 154.

60. Quoted from Yang Shubiao, *Chiang Kai-shek Zhuan* (Biography of Chiang Kai-shek) (Beijing: Tuanjie Chuban She, 1989), p. 190.

61. Sun Ke's certificates of appointment to the top positions in the KMT and the Nationalist government can be found in the National History Archival Museum in Taiwan (series numbers 0321.70/0037, 0321.03/0034, and 0321.03/0034.2).

62. For the details see Chapter 8 in this book.

63. Eastman, *Abortive Revolution,* p. 164.

64. The biographies of Sun Ke published in Taiwan tried to avoid discussing the short life of Sun Ke's government. Yang Shubiao, *Chiang Kai-shek Zhuan,* pp. 187–192, offers interesting historical data about the relations of this government with Chiang Kai-shek, Wang Jingwei, and Hu Hanmin.

5. Institutional Preferences of the Major Players

1. The minutes *(jilu)* of this session can be found in the library of the Hoover Institution at Stanford University.

2. See Li Shonglin, eds., *Zhongguo Guomindang Dashi Ji* (Chronology of the KMT) (Beijing: Jiefangjun Chuban She, 1988), p. 180.

3. See Secretariat of the CEC, *Minutes of the Fifth Plenary Session of the Second CEC, 1928.*

4. For the text of the revised Organic Law see Chen Dezhang et al., eds., *Zhonghua Minguo Xianfa Shiliao* (Historical documents of the constitutions of the Republic of China) (Taipei: Lianguofeng Chuban She, 1973), pp. 29–30.

5. For Chiang's telegram see *Guowen Zhoubao* (Guowen Weekly), October 3, 1930.

6. See Secretariat of the CEC, *Minutes of the Fourth Plenary Session of the Third CEC, 1930.*

7. Tai Shiaoyi, ed., *Zhonghua Minguo Zhengzhi Fazhan Shi* (History of the political development of the Republic of China) (Taipei: Jindai Zhongguo Chuban She, 1985), 2:990.

8. Although it was reported that Chiang's speech was made on the morning of March 2, in fact reporters were told during the afternoon that they were not allowed to report the speech. For the story and Chiang's speech see *Guowen Zhoubao,* March 9, 1931.

9. Since the provisional session of the CEC was a meeting that only some CEC members attended, it was therefore not a formal session. Even decisions as important as a constitution could be made at such provisional sessions—evidence of the lack of institutionalization in the KMT's decision-making organs. For the *yufa* proposal and the provisional session see Tai Shiaoyi, *Zhonghua Minguo Zhengzhi Fazhan Shi,* p. 991.

10. Article 74 of the provisional constitution stated: "The presidents of the five *yuan* and the heads of the various ministries and commissions shall be appointed or dismissed in accordance with law by the national government at the insistance of the president of the national government." For an English translation see William L. Tung, *The Political Institutions of Modern China* (The Hague: Martinus Nijhoff, 1964), pp. 344–349.

11. In Chapter 8 this institutional change is explained by analyzing the shift in the balance of power.

12. Lloyd E. Eastman, *The Abortive Revolution: China Under Nationalist Rule, 1927–1937* (Cambridge, Mass.: Harvard University Press, 1974), p. 171.

13. This is point five, the key point, of the resolution's five points of instructions for the draft of the constitution; emphasis added.

14. For the process of drafting the constitution and the CEC's resolution see Sun Ke's report in Hu Chunhui, ed., *Zhongguo Xiandai Shiliao Xuanji:*

Minguo Xianzheng Yundong (Collected materials of modern Chinese history: The constitutional movement in the Republic of China) (Taipei: Zhenzhong Shuju, 1978), pp. 829–834.

15. Hu Hanmin, "Dao Tan Zhuan Xiansheng" (Mourning Mr. Tan Zhuan), quoted in Zhou Bingwo and Chen Hongmin, *Hu Hanmin Pingzhuan* (Study of Hu Hanmin's life) (Guangzhou: Guangdong Renmin Chuban She, 1989), p. 167; emphasis added.

16. For the details see Zhou Bingwo and Chen Hongmin, *Hu Hanmin Pingzhuan,* p. 167.

17. For the proposal submitted by Hu Hanmin in 1925 see Zhou Bingwo and Chen Hongmin, *Hu Hanmin Pingzhuan,* pp. 167–168.

18. For a historical account see Zhang Xianwen, ed., *Zhonghua Minguo Shigang* (Outline history of the Republic of China) (Zhengzhou: Henan Renmin Chuban She, 1985), p. 231.

19. Zhou Bingwo and Chen Hongmin, *Hu Hanmin Pingzhuan,* p. 165.

20. Ibid.

21. Ibid., p. 166.

22. See Tang Degang, *Li Zhongren Huiyi Lu* (Reminiscences of Li Zhongren) (Hong Kong: Nanyu Chuban She, 1986), p. 52.

23. For the pressure on Hu after the death of Sun Yat-sen see Zhou Bingwo and Chen Hongmin, *Hu Hanmin Pingzhuan,* p. 169.

24. Ibid., p. 167.

25. The assassination has been obscured by historical myth. (The murderer has never been found.) It is difficult to decide, according to the evidence now available, whether or not Hu Hanmin was indeed responsible for this murder. Wang Jingwei made an interesting statement: "Hu Hanmin was politically responsible for the assassination but not legally responsible for it." Quoted in Zhou Bingwo and Chen Hongmin, *Hu Hanmin Pingzhuan,* p. 171.

26. For a description of this proposal see Chien Tuan-sheng, *The Government and Politics of China* (Cambridge, Mass.: Harvard University Press, 1961), pp. 153–154.

27. Ibid., p. 153.

28. Ibid.

29. Hu Hanmin's proposal was submitted on the second day of the session (November 14, 1930). It was passed unanimously. See Secretariat of the CEC, *Minutes of the Fourth Plenary Session of the Third CEC, 1930.*

30. For an English translation of the revised Organic Law of December 29, 1931, see Pan Wei-tung, *The Chinese Constitution* (Westport, Conn.: Hyperion Press, 1945), pp. 256–262.

31. For a text of Wang's letter see Yang Shubiao, *Chiang Kai-shek Zhuan* (Biography of Chiang Kai-shek) (Beijing: Tuanjie Chuban She, 1989), pp. 182–183.

32. For details see Yang Shubiao, *Chiang Kai-shek Zhuan,* p. 184.

33. Ibid.

34. For a detailed description of this coalition see Chapter 8 of this book.

35. For details see Yang Shubiao, *Chiang Kai-shek Zhuan,* pp. 182–183.

36. For a text of the resolution see Yang Shubiao, *Chiang Kai-shek Zhuan,* pp. 183–184. See also *Guowen Zhoubao,* November 16, 1931.

37. Yang Shubiao, *Chiang Kai-shek Zhuan,* p. 183.

38. Ibid.

39. Ibid., p. 184.

40. See the discussion of Hu Hanmin's institutional preference elsewhere in this chapter.

41. The fourth draft, known as the "revised preliminary draft of the constitution" and made public in July 1934, was the last draft written under the leadership of Sun Ke. It fully expressed Sun Ke's institutional preference for a cabinet form of government.

42. For an English translation of the revised draft of the constitution of July 1934 see Pan Wei-tung, *The Chinese Constitution,* pp. 263–285.

6. The Succession Struggle

1. Several scholars of Nationalist politics have indicated this fact. See, for example, Chien Tuan-sheng, *The Government and Politics of China* (Cambridge, Mass.: Harvard University Press, 1961), p. 99; Parks M. Coble, Jr., *The Shanghai Capitalists and the Nationalist Government, 1927–1937* (Cambridge, Mass.: Council on East Asian Studies, Harvard University, 1986), pp. 7-8.

2. These events are discussed later in this chapter and in Chapter 8.

3. Hollington K. Tong, *Chiang Kai-shek: Soldier and Statesman* (Shanghai: China Publishing Co., 1937), 1:80.

4. All the Taiwan publications on Wang Jingwei blamed him for his collaboration with Communists at that time. Zhou Fuhai, for example, an elder of the KMT, called Wang's Wuhan government a "red government" in his reminiscences; see Zhou, "Tao Chule Chiduo Wuhan" (Escaping from the Red Capital: Wuhan), in Chiang Yongjing, ed., *Beifa Shiqi de Zhengzhi Shiliao* (Historical materials on politics during the Northern Expedition) (Taipei: Zhongzheng Shuju, 1981). Publications in Communist China recognized that Wang Jingwei led the left wing of the KMT and began collaborating with the Communists immediately after the death of Sun Yat-sen. See, for example, Liu Jizhen, *Wuhan Guomin Zhengfu Shi* (History of the Nationalist government in Wuhan) (Wuhan: Hubei Renmin Chuban She, 1986), pp. 4–21. Two articles on the left-wing group are Jerome Chen's "The Left Wing Kuomintang—a Definition," *Bulletin of the School of Oriental and African Studies* 25 (pt. 3) (1962): 557–574; and James Shirley's "Factionalism and the Left Kuomintang," *Studies on Asia* (University of Nebraska at Lincoln) 5 (1965): 97–104.

5. For a detailed description of the development of the Western Hill Group and the right wing of the KMT during this period see Huang Jilu, "Hu Xiansheng yu Xishan Huiyi" (Mr. Hu and the Western Hill meeting), in *Zhuanji Wenxue* (Biography Literature) 28 (6) (1989): 18–20; and S. I. Hsiung, *The Life of Chiang Kai-shek* (London: Peter Davies, 1948), pp. 235–303.

6. For an excellent study of Chiang's change of position during this period see Li Yunhan, *Cong Ronggong dao Qingdang* (From tolerating Communists to cleaning up the party) (Taipei: Zhongguo Xueshe Zhuzuo Jiangzhu Weiyuanhui, 1966).

7. Zhou Bingwo and Chen Hongmin, *Hu Hanmin Pingzhuan* (Study of Hu Hanmin's life) (Guangzhou: Guangdong Renmin Chuban She, 1989), p. 165.

8. Ibid., p. 167.

9. Ibid.

10. For a historical record of this meeting see Zhang Xianwen, ed., *Zhonghua Minguo Shigang* (Outline history of the Republic of China) (Zhengzhou: Henan Renmin Chuban She, 1985), p. 231.

11. Zhou Bingwo and Chen Hongmin, *Hu Hanmin Pingzhuan,* p. 169.

12. The first Organic Law consisted of only ten articles outlining the fundamentals of organization of the national government. It was approved by the KMT's Central Executive Committee on July 1, 1925.

13. For the text of the first Organic Law see Chen Dezhang et al., eds., *Zhonghua Minguo Xianfa Shiliao* (Historical documents of the constitutions of the Republic of China) (Taipei: Lianguofeng Chuban She, 1973), pp. 25–26.

14. See Chen Gongbo, *Kuxao Lu* (A record of forced smiles) (Beijing: Xiandai Shiliao Biankan She, 1981), p. 19.

15. Shi Quansheng, *Nanjing Guominzhengfu de Jianli* (Establishment of the Nationalist government in Nanjing) (Zhengzhou: Henan Renmin Chuban She, 1987), p. 20.

16. Tong, *Soldier and Statesman,* 1:80.

17. Shi Quansheng, *Nanjing Guominzhengfu de Jianli,* p. 21.

18. Ibid., pp. 21–22.

19. Ibid., p. 22.

20. Tong, *Soldier and Statesman,* 1:81.

21. See George F. Bother, *A Short History of Nationalist China, 1919–1949* (New York: Putnam's, 1979), p. 85.

22. Chien Tuan-sheng, *The Government and Politics of China,* p. 93.

23. Ibid., p. 180.

24. These meetings were called "provisional meetings" because the participants constituted less than half of all the CPC members. For a description of these meetings and Chiang's proposal see Liu Jingzhen, *Wuhan Guomin Zhengfu Shi,* pp. 258–262.

25. Ibid., p. 267.

26. Shi Quansheng, *Nanjing Guominzhengfu de Jianli,* p. 48.

27. Liu Jingzhen, *Wuhan Guomin Zhengfu Shi,* p. 272.

28. Shi Quansheng, *Nanjing Guominzhengfu de Jianli,* p. 49.

29. See the minutes of the preparatory meeting recorded by the Secretariat of the CEC on March 7, 1927. Shi Quansheng and Liu Jingzhen also described this story: see Shi Quansheng, *Nanjing Guominzhengfu de Jianli,* p. 49; Liu Jingzhen, *Wuhan Guomin Zhengfu Shi,* pp. 287–288.

30. Hubei Zhengfashi Bainji Weiyunhui (Editorial Committee of Hubei Legal History), *Wuhan Guo Gong Lianhe Zhengfu Fazhi Wenxian Xuanbain* (Collection of legal documents of the Nationalist-Communist coalition government in Wuhan) (Wuhan: Nongchun Duwu Chuban She, 1984), p. 20.

31. Tang Degang, *Li Zhongren Huiyi Lu* (Reminiscences of Li Zhongren) (Hong Kong: Nanyue Chuban She, 1986), p. 296.

32. Shi Quansheng, *Nanjing Guominzhengfu de Jianli,* p. 75.

33. For this order see *Guominzhengfu Gongbao* (Bulletin of the Nationalist government), May 1, 1927.

34. On April 20, 1927, the Communist Party of China issued a statement protesting the purge. For the text of this statement see *Xiangdao Zhoubao* (Xiangdao Weekly), May 1, 1927. Chinese Communists criticized the brutal purge of the Communists by Chiang Kai-shek and called this incident the "April 12 Counterrevolutionary Coup" of 1927.

35. Shi Quansheng, *Nanjing Guominzhengfu de Jianli,* p. 76.

36. This "discussion meeting" is recorded as the seventy-third and seventy-fourth meetings of the CPC in the KMT archives. See Liu Jingzhen, *Wuhan Guomin Zhengfu Shi,* p. 333; see also Guo Tingyi, ed., *Zhonghua Minguo Shishi Rizhi, 1926–1930* (Daily chronology of the history of the Republic of China, 1926–1930) (Taipei: Institute of Modern History, 1984), 2:183.

37. For an account of the Provisional Political Council see Li Shongling, eds., *Zhongguo Guomindang Dashi Ji* (Chronology of the KMT) (Beijing: Jiefangjun Chuban She, 1988), p. 163.

38. Tong, *Soldier and Statesman,* 1:157.

39. Shi Quansheng, *Nanjing Guominzhengfu de Jianli,* p. 89.

40. For this plan see Zhou Enlai, *Zhou Enlai Xuanji* (Selected works of Zhou Enlai) (Beijing: Renmin Chuban Shi, 1986), 1:6–7.

41. See Liu Jingzhen, *Wuhan Guomin Zhengfu Shi,* p. 359; also see Shi Quansheng, *Nanjing Guominzhengfu de Jianli,* pp. 92–93.

42. Tong, *Soldier and Statesman,* p. 157.

43. Guo Tingyi, *Zhonghua Minguo Shishi Rizhi, 1926–1930,* pp. 205–206.

44. Gao Xingya, *Feng Yuxiang Jiangjun* (General Feng Yuxiang) (Beijing: Beijing Chuban She, 1982), p. 88.

45. For Feng Yuxiang's position toward both Wang Jingwei and Chiang

Kai-shek see Feng, *Wo de Shenghuo* (My life) (Harbin: Heilongjiang Renmin Chuban She, 1984), pp. 35–37.

46. For a detailed description of the Zhengzhou conference see Liu Jingzhen, *Wuhan Guomin Zhengfu Shi,* pp. 422–429.

47. Jian Yuwen, *Feng Yuxiang Zhuan* (Biography of Feng Yuxiang) (Taipei: Zhuanji Wenxue Chuban She, 1982), p. 268.

48. Liu Jingzheng, *Wuhan Guomin Zhengfu Shi,* p. 428.

49. Feng Yuxiang, *Wo de Shenghuo,* p. 560.

50. Tong, *Soldier and Statesman,* p. 159.

51. According to several Chinese historians Feng took a railroad train, accompanied by his headquarters staff, to meet Chiang in Xuzhou. The train started off in the opposite direction of Xuzhou and only later turned back toward its real destination. Nobody in the train knew where they were going. See Shi Quansheng, *Nanjing Guominzhengfu de Jianli,* p. 101.

52. Feng Yuxiang's autobiography, *Wo de Shenghuo,* describes in great detail the Chiang–Feng meeting. Li Zhongren, as a witness, also describes this event in detail in his reminiscences; see Tang Degang, *Li Zhongren Huiyi Lu* (Reminiscences of Li Zhongren) (Hong Kong: Nanyue Chuban She, 1966), pp. 313–314. For this meeting see also Gao Xingya, *Feng Yuxiang Jiangjun* (General Feng Yuxiang) (Beijing: Beijing Chuban She, 1982), pp. 103–104.

53. Shi Quansheng, *Nanjing Guominzhengfu de Jianli,* pp. 103–104.

54. For a text of the telegram see *Guowen Zhoubao* (Guowen Weekly), July 1, 1927. Feng Yuxiang himself has described the process of drafting the telegram; see Feng, *Wo de Shenghuo,* p. 561.

55. Cited in Tong, *Soldier and Statesman,* p. 160.

56. Tang Degang, *Li Zhongren Huiyi Lu,* p. 315.

57. Ibid., p. 164.

58. Ibid.

59. Ibid., p. 318.

60. Tong, *Soldier and Statesman,* p. 165.

61. Tang Degang, *Li Zhongren Huiyi Lu,* p. 318.

62. For a detailed description of the purge of Communists in Wuhan see Liu Jingzheng, *Wuhan Guomin Zhengfu Shi,* pp. 372–433.

63. For the text of the telegram see *Geming Wenxian,* vol. 17.

64. For Li Zhongren's telegram to Wang Jingwei see *Geming Wenxian,* vol. 17. See also Peng Min, ed., *Zhongguo Xiandai Shi Ziliao Xuanji, 1927–1931* (Collection of historical documents of modern China, 1927–1931) (Beijing: Zhongguo Renmin Daxue Chuban She, 1988), 3:1–2.

65. For a detailed account of Chiang Kai-shek's resignation from the Nanjing government see "Chiang Kai-shek Xiayie Jingguo" (The story of Chiang Kai-shek's resignation), *Guowen Zhoubao* (Guowen Weekly), August 28, 1927.

66. See Yang's *Chiang Kai-shek Zhuan* (Biography of Chiang Kai-shek) (Beijing: Tuanjie Chuban She, 1989), p. 113.

67. Tong, *Soldier and Statesman,* 1:176.

68. Quoted in Tong, *Soldier and Statesman,* 1:178–179.

69. Ibid., p. 191.

70. Ibid., p. 179.

71. For the text of the first statement see *Guowen Zhoubao,* August 28, 1927; for the second one see *Guowen Zhoubao,* October 10, 1927.

72. Tang Degang, *Li Zhongren Huiyi Lu,* pp. 344–345.

73. For the construction of this government under the Special Central Committee see Tang Degang, *Li Zhongren Huiyi Lu,* pp. 340–349.

74. For the whole story see Shi Quansheng, *Nanjing Guominzhengfu de Jianli,* pp. 144–147.

75. Feng Yuxiang, *Wo de Shenghuo,* pp. 570–571.

76. For these military conflicts see Tang Degang, *Li Zhongren Huiyi Lu,* pp. 350–358.

77. Tong, *Soldier and Statesman,* p. 196.

78. See Yang Shubiao, *Chiang Kai-shek Zhuan,* pp. 124–125.

79. Tang Degang, *Li Zhongren Huiyi Lu,* pp. 345–346.

80. Wang Jingwei left for Wuhan and his followers (Guo Mengyu and Chen Gongbo) for Guangzhou. See Tang Degang, *Li Zhongren Huiyi Lu,* p. 4.

81. Since a number of Wang Jingwei's followers were implicated in the Communist uprising of Guangzhou, Wang himself was denounced by the Nanjing regime for having tolerated the Communists in this incident. See Yang Shubiao, *Chiang Kai-shek Zhuan,* p. 125.

82. For the text of the 1928 Organic Law see Chen Dezhang et al., *Zhonghua Minguo Xianfa Shiliao,* pp. 30–36.

7. The Grand Anti-Chiang Coalition

1. For a detailed study of developing regionalism in the late 1920s see Chen Lenzhi, "Beifahou Zhongguo Difangzhuyi de Fazhan: 1926–1937" (Development of regionalism in China after the Northern Expedition, 1926–1937), in Zhang Yufa, ed., *Zhongguo Xiandaishi Lunji* (Collected works on modern Chinese history) (Taipei: Lianjing Chuban Shiye Gongshi, 1982), 8:153–174. See also James E. Sheridan, *China in Disintegration: The Republican Era in Chinese History, 1912–1949* (New York: Free Press, 1975).

2. The text of the report was published in *Huabei Ribao* (North China Daily), January 16, 1929; see also *Zhongguo Nianjian* (China Yearbook), 1929–1930, pp. 637–641.

3. Harley F. MacNair, *China in Revolution: An Analysis of Politics and Militarism Under the Republic* (New York: Howard Fertig, 1968), p. 159.

4. S. I. Hsiung, *The Life of Chiang Kai-shek* (London: Peter Davies, 1948), p. 291.

5. See Secretariat of the CEC, *Minutes of the Third National Congress of the KMT, 1929.*

6. For this plan see Chiang Kai-shek's speech to the Beijing press on July 13 in *Guowen Zhoubao* (Guowen Weekly), July 22, 1928.

7. For the text of the "Manifesto of the Reorganization and Disbandment Conference" see *Guowen Zhuobao,* August 18, 1929.

8. For a detailed discussion of the conference see Hsi-sheng Chi, *Nationalist China at War* (Ann Arbor: University of Michigan Press, 1982), p. 9.

9. For a detailed description of these rebellions see a book titled *Fan Chiang Yundong Shi* (History of the anti-Chiang movement) published in 1934 by the Qinglian Junren She (Young Military Men's Association), a group of young militarists who were against Chiang Kai-shek. This book is over 500 pages.

10. For the text of the telegram see *Guowen Zhoubao,* March 3, 1929.

11. See the "Outline of the Reorganization and Disbandment Procedure" issued by the national government on January 5, 1929, in *Guowen Zhoubao,* January 13, 1929.

12. *Guowen Zhoubao,* March 31, 1929. In the same issue of the newspaper Chiang Kai-shek himself also published a statement denouncing the Wuhan Political Subcouncil for its action against the center.

13. For this battle Li Zhongren himself offers a description in great detail. See Tang Degang, *Li Zhongren Huiyi Lu* (Reminiscences of Li Zhongren) (Hong Kong: Nanyue Chuban She, 1986), pp. 391–402.

14. "Gui" stands for Guilin, the capital of Guangxi province. For the history see Zhang Xianwen, ed., *Zhonghua Minguo Shigang* (Outline history of the Republic of China) (Zhengzhou: Henan Renmin Chuban She, 1985), pp. 358–361.

15. Gao Xingya, *Feng Yuxiang Jiangjun* (General Feng Yuxiang) (Beijing: Beijing Chuban She, 1982).

16. For Feng Yuxiang's political life see his autobiography, *Wo de Shenghuo* (My life) (Harbin: Heilongjiang Renmin Chuban She, 1984). For an excellent study of Feng Yuxiang in English see James Sheridan, *Chinese Warlord: The Career of Feng Yu-hsiang* (Stanford: Stanford University Press, 1966).

17. Hollington K. Tong, *Chiang Kai-shek: Soldier and Statesman* (Shanghai: China Publishing Co., 1937), p. 267.

18. For the texts of these important telegrams between Chiang Kai-shek and Feng Yuxiang in May 1929 see *Guowen Zhoubao,* May 26–June 2, 1929.

19. For the entire text of the telegram see *Guowen Zhoubao,* May 26, 1929.

20. This decision was made at a meeting of the standing committee of the CEC on May 23, 1930. See Qing Xiaoyi, ed., *Zhonghuaminguo Zhengzhi Fazhanshi* (History of the political development of the Republic of China) (Taipei: Jindai Zhongguo Chuban She, 1985), p. 950.

21. For the entire text of the telegram see *Guowen Zhoubao,* May 27, 1929.

22. For the entire text of the telegram see *Guowen Zhoubao,* June 2, 1929.

23. Li Zhongren published a circulating telegram announcing the appointments and denouncing Chiang Kai-shek's Nanjing government. For the text see Peng Min, ed., *Zhongguo Xiandai Shi Ziliao Xuanji, 1927–1931* (Collection of historical documents of modern China) (Beijing: Zhongguo Renmin Daxue Chuban She, 1988), 3:183–184.

24. For the text of the telegram see Pong Min, ibid., pp. 186–188.

25. For the text of the telegram see *Guowen Zhoubao,* December 12, 1929.

26. Gao Xingya, *Feng Yuxiang Jiangjun,* p. 135.

27. This ultimatum was announced through a circulating telegram on February 10, 1930. For the text of the telegram see *Guowen Zhoubao,* February 17, 1930.

28. Sheridan, *China in Disintegration,* p. 185.

29. For the history see Zhang Xianwen, *Zhonghua Minguo Shigang,* pp. 361–365.

30. For the text of the telegram see Peng Min, *Zhongguo Xiandai Shi Ziliao Xuanji,* 3:244–245.

31. For the text of the telegram see *Geming Ribao* (Revolutionary Daily), May 8, 1930. See also Cha Jianyu, ed., *Guomindang Gaizhupai Ziliao Xuanbian* (Selected documents of the KMT Reorganizationalists) (Hunan: Hunan Renmin Chuban She, 1986), p. 321.

32. For a detailed report on the mass rally see *Dagong Bao* (Dagong News), August 9, 1930.

33. Sheridan, *China in Disintegration,* p. 185.

34. Wang Jingwei published a long article on June 19, 1930, suggesting the enlarged plenary session of the CEC: "Zhongyang Dangbu Kuodahuiyi zhi Biyiao" (The necessity of the enlarged session of the party's central headquarters). See *Geming Zhanxian* (Revolutionary Front), June 25, 1930, pp. 1–4.

35. For a detailed discussion of the enlarged plenary session see Sheng Yunlong, "Kuoda Huiyi zhi Youlai ji Jingguo" (Origin and process of the enlarged plenary session), in Zhang Yufa, *Zhongguo Xiandaishi Lunji,* pp. 101–126.

36. Chen Gongbo devotes one chapter to the enlarged plenary session in

his reminiscences; see Chen Gongbo, *Kuxiao Lu* (A record of forced smiles) (Beijing: Xiandai Shiliao Biankan She, 1981), pp. 149–177.

37. Li Zhongren's reminiscence describes the enlarged session; see Tang Degang, *Li Zhongren Huiyi Lu,* pp. 410–413.

38. For the position of the Western Hill Group in the anti-Chiang coalition see an article written by Zuo Lu, one of the leaders of the faction: "Dui Dangshi Guoshi zhi Yijian" (An opinion on the affairs of party and government), dated April 7, 1930, in Peng Min, *Zhongguo Xiandai Shi Ziliao Xuanji,* 3:241–243.

39. For the text of the manifesto and its signers see *Guowen Zhoubao,* July 21, 1930.

40. For the organization of the enlarged session see *Guowen Zhuobao,* August 11, 1930.

41. For a news report of the inauguration see *Guowen Zhuobao,* September 15, 1930.

42. Hsiung, *The Life of Chiang Kai-shek,* pp. 301–302.

43. Ibid., p. 302.

44. In a brief to the press Wang Jingwei admitted that Chen Gongbo met Zhang Xueliang in August 1930. See *Dagong Bao* (Dagong News), August 28, 1930.

45. Hsiung, *The Life of Chiang Kai-shek,* p. 302.

46. Zhang Xueliang's circulating telegram was sent out on September 18, 1930. For the text of the telegram see *Xin Chen Bao* (Xin Chen News), September 19, 1930.

47. For a report on the military situation see *Xin Chen Bao,* September 22, 1930.

48. Hsiung, *The Life of Chiang Kai-shek,* p. 303.

49. For an account of the Chiang–Hu meeting in Shanghai see Zhou Bingwo and Chen Hongmin, *Hu Hanmin Pingzhuan* (Study of Hu Hanmin's life) (Guangzhou: Guangdong Renmin Chuban She, 1989), p. 206.

50. See Wu Xiangxiang, *Minguo Renwu Liezhuan* (Biographies of personages in Republican China) (Taipei: Juanji Wenxue Chuban She, 1986), 5:163.

51. Zhou Bingwo and Chen Hongmin, *Hu Hanmin Pingzhuan,* p. 215.

52. Hu Hanmin, "Gemin Guochen Zhong de Jijian Shishi" (Several historical facts in the process of the revolution), *Shanminzhuyi Yuekan* (Shanminzhuyi Monthly), vol. 2, no. 6, p. 108; quoted in Zhou Bingwo and Chen Hongmin, *Hu Hanmin Pingzhuan,* p. 216.

53. Ibid.

54. For the text of the telegram see *Guowen Zhoubao,* October 3, 1930.

55. For an early account of this incident see Qinglian Junren She, *Fan Chiang Yundong Shi,* pp. 254–259. Ever since, many reminiscences published in both Taiwan and Mainland China have discussed the Hu Hanmin Incident.

A dozen reminiscences published in Taiwan were collected in *Newspaper Clippings for Studying the Biography of Hu Hanmin.* In Mainland China, *Wenshi Ziliao* (Materials of historical literature) published a number of reminiscences on this incident. Bian Yiashan's reminiscence, for example, was published in *Jiangsu Wenshi Ziliao Xuanji* (Selected collection of historical literature in Jiangsu), vol. 20. The reminiscence of Chen Shiyuan, secretary to Li Zhongren, was written and published in Mainland China in 1983. See Chen Shiyuan, *Zhengtan Huiyi* (Reminiscence of my political life) (Guiling: Guangxi Renmin Chuban She, 1983).

56. Quoted from Qingnian Junren She, *Fan Chiang Yundong Shi,* p. 259.

57. Chien Tuan-sheng, *Government and Politics of China,* p. 98.

58. For Wang's attack see his speech in Taiyuan on the provisional constitution (October 27, 1930), *Dagong Bao* (Dagong Daily), November 4, 1930, p. 4.

59. See *Dagong Bao,* November 29, 1930.

60. Lloyd Eastman, "Nationalist China During the Nanjing Decade 1927–1937," in John K. Fairbank and Albert Feuerwerker, eds., *The Cambridge History of China,* vol. 13, pt. 2 (Cambridge: Cambridge University Press, 1986), p. 128.

61. Numerous reminiscences about the extraordinary session were published in *Wenshi Ziliao Xuanji* (Select collection of historical literature) in Mainland China. Among these are Li Gunning, "Wang Jingwei yu Kuodahuiyi" (Wang Jingwei and the extraordinary session), in *Wenshi Ziliao Xuanji,* 16:92–106; He Hanwen's reminiscence in 17:78–180; Xue Dubi's reminiscence in 16:124–129; and Wu Hexuan's reminiscence in 36:139–151. Historians in Taiwan also published several works on this event. See, for example, Shen Yunlong, "Kuodahuiyi Zhi Youlai Ji Jingguo" (Origin and process of the extraordinary session), in Zhang Yufa, *Zhongguo Xiandaishi Lunji,* 8:101–126.

62. For the text of the telegram see Qinglian Junren She, *Fan Chiang Yundong Shi,* pp. 301–302.

63. For the meeting of Sun Ke, Wang Jingwei, and the Western Hill Group see the news report in *Guowen Zhoubao,* May 26, 1931.

64. Wang Jingwei sent telegrams from Hong Kong to all provincial branches of the Reorganizationalist Comrades Association urging them to send representatives to the extraordinary session. Several reminiscences are collected in Cha Jianyu, ed., *Guomindang Gaizhupai Ziliao Xuanbian* (Selected documents of the KMT Reorganizationalists) (Hunan: Hunan Renmin Chuban She, 1986), pp. 459–461.

65. See the report describing the process of the extraordinary session in *Zhongyang Daobao* (Central Herald), July 15, 1931.

66. See the extraordinary session's "Circulating Letter to All KMT Branches," in *Zhongyang Daobao,* July 1, 1931.

67. For the text of the manifesto see *Zhongyang Daobao,* July 1, 1931.

68. For the "Manifesto Establishing the Guangzhou National Government" see Qinglian Junren She, *Fan Chiang Yundong Shi,* pp. 395–397.

69. For the organization of the Guangzhou government see ibid., pp. 393–400.

70. See *Zhongyang Daobao,* July 15, 1931.

71. Fairbank and Feuerwerker, *Cambridge History of China,* vol. 13, pt. 2, p. 129.

72. Zhou Bingwo and Chen Hongmin, *Hu Hanmin Pingzhuan,* p. 233.

73. For a report on the meeting in Hong Kong see *Dagong Bao* (Dagong News), September 30, 1931.

74. See *Guowen Zhoubao,* November 2, 1931.

75. For the text of Wang Jingwei's letter see *Lishi Dangan* (Historical Archives), no. 1, 1982. See also Cha Jiangyu, *Guomindang Gaizhupai Ziliao Xuanbian,* pp. 482–483.

76. Ibid., p. 483.

77. This letter was published in *Dagong Bao,* October 27, 1931, p. 3.

78. For this story see Yang Shubiao, *Chiang Kai-shek Zhuan,* p. 183.

79. For the text of the telegram see *Guowen Zhoubao,* November 16, 1931.

80. For the text of the resolution see Yang Shubiao, *Chiang kai-shek Zhuan,* pp. 183–184.

81. Ibid., p. 183.

82. Ibid.

83. Ibid., p. 184.

84. Ibid.

85. Ibid.

86. For Sun Ke's speech in the Guangzhou congress see *Zhongyang Daobao,* November 25, 1931. For Wang Jingwei's position in the Shanghai congress see Qingnian Junren She, *Fan Chiang Yundong Shi,* pp. 519–524.

87. Qingnian Junren She, *Fan Chiang Yundong Shi,* p. 530.

88. Chiang Kai-shek published a telegram announcing his resignation. For the text of the telegram see Qingnian Junren She, *Fan Chiang Yundong Shi,* pp. 534–535.

89. For the text of the revised Organic Law of 1931 see Chen Dezhang et al., *Zhonghua Minguo Xianfa Shiliao,* pp. 43–50.

90. Chien Tuan-sheng, *Government and Politics of China,* p. 158.

91. Chih-Fang Wu, *Chinese Government and Politics* (Shanghai: The Commercial Press, 1934), p. 176.

8. The Destruction of Chiang's Major Rivals

1. For a general theoretical exercise see Barbara Hinckley, *Coalitions and Politics* (New York: Harcourt Brace Jovanovich, 1981). For an excellent

work applying international relations theory to the study of Chinese domestic politics see Avery Goldstein, *From Bandwagon to Balance of Power Politics: Structural Constraints and Politics in China, 1949–1978* (Stanford: Stanford University Press, 1991).

2. Chen Gongbo has described his conversation with Wang Jingwei in the hospital before the First Plenary Session of the Fourth CEC. See Chen Gongbo, *Kuxiao Lu* (A record of forced smiles) (Beijing: Xiandai Shiliao Biankan She, 1981), p. 268.

3. John K. Fairbank and Albert Feuerwerker, eds., *The Cambridge History of China* (Cambridge: Cambridge University Press, 1986), vol. 13, pt. 2, p. 129.

4. Zhou Yizhi, "Feichang Huiyi Qianho" (Before and after the extraordinary session of the CEC), in Cha Jianyu, ed., *Guomintang Gaizhupai Ziliao Xuanbian* (Selected documents of the KMT Reorganizationalists) (Hunan: Hunan Renmin Chuban She, 1986), p. 524.

5. Ibid., pp. 524–525.

6. This explanation is provided by Zhou Bingwo and Chen Hongmin, *Hu Hanmin Pingzhuan* (Study of Hu Hanmin's life) (Guangzhou: Guangdong Renmin Chuban She, 1990), p. 243.

7. The organizational principle of the CEC passed at the First Plenary Session of the Fourth CEC. See Secretariat of the CEC, *Minutes of the First Plenary Session of the Fourth CEC, 1931.*

8. Ibid.

9. Guo Tingyi, ed., *Zhonghua Minguo Shishi Rizhi, 1931–1937* (Daily chronicle of the history of the Republic of China, 1931–1937) (Taipei: Institute of Modern History, 1984), 3:121.

10. Yang Shubiao, *Chiang Kai-shek Zhuan* (Biography of Chiang Kai-shek) (Beijing: Tuanjie Chuban She, 1989), p. 190.

11. For the news report see *Guowen Zhoubao* (Guowen Weekly), January 3, 1932.

12. Chen Minshu, "Linyue Hezuo Qinliji" (Personal experience of Nanjing-Guangzhou cooperation), in Cha Jianyu, *Guomintang Gaizhupai Ziliao Xuanbian,* p. 527.

13. Many news reports about the Hangzhou meeting between Chiang Kai-shek and Wang Jingwei were published in journals and newspapers in January 1932. See, for example, *Shishi Xingbao* (Shishi News Daily), January 18–23, 1932.

14. For the text of the telegram see *Guowen Zhoubao,* January 25, 1932.

15. *Shishi Xingbao,* January 18, 1932, p. 2.

16. Quoted in Keiji Furuya, *Chiang Kai-shek: His Life and Times* (New York: St. John's University Press, 1981), p. 346.

17. For Sun Ke's speech see Cha Jianyu, *Guomindang Gaizhupai Ziliao Xuanbian,* p. 530.

18. For the news report of this meeting see *Shishi Xingbao,* January 29, 1932, p. 1.

19. Howard L. Boorman, "Wang Ching-wei: A Political Profile," in Chun-tu Hsueh, ed., *Revolutionary Leaders of Modern China* (New York: Oxford University Press, 1971), p. 307.

20. See Thomas G. Rawski, *Economic Growth in Prewar China* (Berkeley: University of California Press, 1989).

21. Boorman, "Wang Ching-wei: A Political Profile," p. 307.

22. Guo Tingyi, *Zhonghua Minguo Shishi Rizhi,* p. 201.

23. Boorman, "Wang Ching-wei: A Political Profile," p. 308.

24. The attack is known as the "1/28 Incident" in modern Chinese history. See Zhang Xianwen, ed., *Zhonghua Minguo Shigang* (Outline history of the Republic of China) (Zhengzhou: Henan Renmin Chuban She, 1985), pp. 381–384.

25. Huang Meizheng and Zhang Yun, *Wang Jingwei Jituan Panguo Toudi Ji* (Wang Jingwei's road: Turning renegade from China) (Zhengzhou: Henan Renmin Chuban She, 1987), p. 12.

26. Manzhouguo was located in northeastern China. Japan occupied this area and established a puppet government in 1932. For a brief history of this puppet regime described by a Japanese scholar see Keiji Furuya, *Chiang Kai-shek: His Life and Times,* pp. 614–615.

27. Huang Meizheng and Zhang Yun, *Wang Jingwei Jituan Panguo Toudi Ji,* p. 12.

28. Boorman, "Wang Ching-wei: A Political Profile," p. 308.

29. For a collection of eyewitness stories and analyses published in China see Qiang Jianzhong, ed., *Ci Wang Neimu* (Inside stories about the assassination of Wang) (Jilin: Jilin Wenshi Chuban She, 1986).

30. Boorman, "Wang Ching-wei: A Political Profile," p. 308.

31. Ibid.

32. Huang Meizheng and Zhang Yun, *Wang Jingwei Jituan Panguo Toudi Ji,* p. 14.

33. For a description of Hu Hanmin's life in Hong Kong see Zhou Bingwo and Chen Hongmin, *Hu Hanmin Pingzhuan,* pp. 230–244.

34. See Lloyd Eastman, *The Abortive Revolution* (Cambridge, Mass.: Harvard University Press, 1974), p. 113.

35. Fairbank and Feuerwerker, *Cambridge History of China,* vol. 13, pt. 2, p. 131.

36. See Cheng Siyuan's reminiscence, *Zhengtan Huiyi* (Reminiscence of my political life) (Guilin: Guangxi Renmin Chuban She, 1983), p. 65. Several studies mention the relation between Hu Hanmin and the Fujian revolt. See, for example, Wang Sunsheng and Yang Dawei, *Fujian Shibian* (Fujian Incident) (Fuzhou: Fujian Renmin Chuban She, 1983), p. 47; Zhou Bingwo and Chen

Hongmin, *Hu Hanmin Pingzhuan,* p. 274. See also Melville T. Kennedy, Jr., "Hu Hanmin: His Career and Thought, in Chun-tu Hsueh, ed., *Revolutionary Leaders of Modern China* (London: Oxford University Press, 1971), p. 284.

37. The revolt is known to most students of modern China primarily as the result of Mao Zedong's remark to Edgar Snow that "in this period [of the Fifth Extermination Campaign] we made two important errors. The first was the failure to unite with Chai Tingkai's army in 1933 during the Fujian revolt." See Edgar Snow, *Red Star Over China* (New York: Grove Press, 1938), p. 166.

38. This meeting is recorded in the Executive Yuan Archives in Nanjing, file II-1208. See Zhou Bingwo and Chen Hongmin, *Hu Hanmin Pingzhuan,* p. 274.

39. Ibid., p. 276. See also Tang Degang, *Li Zhongren Huiyi Lu,* p. 432.

40. See Zhou Bingwo and Chen Hongmin, *Hu Hanmin Pingzhuan,* p. 281.

41. Executive Yuan Archives in Nanjing, file II-1208. See Zhou Bingwo and Chen Hongmin, *Hu Hanmin Pingzhuan,* p. 282.

42. Ibid., p. 282. See also "Hu Hanmin Chuguo Ji" (Hu Hanmin's departure from the country), June 19, 1935, Yokota Collection in Japan; quoted in Eastman, *Abortive Revolution,* pp. 251–252.

43. For the last days of Hu Hanmin see Zhou Bingwo and Chen Hongmin, *Hu Hanmin Pingzhuan,* pp. 290–297.

44. Kennedy, "Hu Hanmin: His Career and Thought," p. 284.

45. For a news report see *Shishi Xingbao,* January 29, 1932, p. 1.

46. See Eastman, *Abortive Revolution,* p. 164.

47. For the text of the document see *Shishi Xingbao,* April 27, 1932, in Hu Chunhui, ed., *Zhongguo Xiandai Shiliao Xuanji: Minguo Xianzheng Yundong* (Collected materials of modern Chinese history: The constitutional movement in the Republic of China) (Taipei: Zhenzhong Shuju, 1978), pp. 662–664.

48. Liu Zhengkai, *Zhongguo Xianzheng Shihua* (History of China's constitutionalism) (Taipei: Xianzheng Luntan She, 1960), p. 146.

49. In an article summarizing the constitutional movement in the early 1930s, Hu Shi mentions Hu Hanmin's speeches supporting Sun Ke's constitutional campaign. See Hu Shi, "Xianzheng Wenti" (On the issue of constitutionalism), in Hu Chunhui, *Zhongguo Xiandai Shiliao Xuanji,* p. 665.

50. See Eastman, *Abortive Revolution,* p. 165.

51. For the text of the bill see Hu Chunhui, *Zhongguo Xiandai Shiliao Xuanji,* pp. 669–673.

52. For the text of the resolution see Hu Chunhui, ibid., pp. 673–676.

53. Sun Ke himself described the process of the constitutional drafting in a report to the Legislative Yuan on May 4, 1936. For the text of Sun's report see *Zhongyang Ribao* (Central Daily News), May 5, 1936.

54. For a description of the drafting process of the Wu Draft see Yang Jialuo, ed., *Dalu Lunxian Qian Zhi Zhonghua Minguo* (The Republic of China before the mainland was occupied by Communists) (Taipei: Dinwen Shujiu, 1973), p. 158.

55. For the drafting process of these two drafts see Su Shongfen, "Xianfa Qichao Guochen" (The process of drafting the constitution), in Hu Chunhui, *Zhongguo Xiandai Shiliao Xuanji,* pp. 780–792.

56. For an illustration of the Revised First Draft see Sun Ke, "Lifa Yuan Zhiding Xianfa Chaoan Gailei" (An illustration of drafting the constitution by the Legislative Yuan), in Hu Chunhui, *Zhongguo Xiandai Shiliao Xuanji,* pp. 829–834.

57. For an English translation of the revised draft of the constitution of July 1934 see Pan Wei-tung, *The Chinese Constitution* (Westport, Conn.: Hyperion Press, 1945), pp. 263–285.

58. Sun Ke, "Zhongguo Xianfa de Jige Wenti" (Several issues on the Chinese constitution), in *Sun Zhesheng Wenji* (Collected works of Sun Ke) (Taipei: Zhongguo Guomintang Dangshihui, 1980), 1:257.

59. Sun Ke, "Zhongguo Xianfa de Jige Genben Wenti" (Several fundamental issues on the Chinese constitution), in *Sun Zhesheng Wenji* (Collected works of Sun Ke) (Taipei: Zhongguo Guomintang Dangshihui, 1980), 2:232.

60. Sun Ke's report on drafting the constitution quoted all the important points of the CEC's resolution. For the text see Hu Chunhui, *Zhongguo Xiandai Shiliao Xuanji,* pp. 833–834.

61. Keiji Furuya, *Chiang Kai-shek: His Life and Times,* pp. 434–435.

62. Quoted from James E. Sheridan, *China in Disintegration: The Republic Era in Chinese History, 1912–1949* (New York: Free Press, 1975), p. 218.

63. Ibid., p. 201.

64. For a list of Fascist publications in Chinese during this period see Yang Shubiao, *Chiang Kai-shek Zhuan,* pp. 200–201.

65. Quoted from Eastman, *Abortive Revolution,* p. 43.

66. Ibid., p. 176.

67. For the movement to install Chiang Kai-shek as dictator prior to the Sino-Japanese War see Chen Ruiyun, "Lun Minguo Zhengzhi" (On the political system of Republican China), *Zhonggou Xiandai Shi* (Modern History of China Monthly) 10 (1988): 111.

68. For the conflict between Chiang Kai-shek and the Guangdong and Guangxi regional militarists see Tang Degang, *Li Zhongren Huiyi Lu,* pp. 414–418.

69. The position of *zongchai* was finally installed in the Extraordinary Congress of the KMT at Wuchang, March 29–April 1, 1938.

70. Eastman, *Abortive Revolution,* p. 178.

71. Guo Tingyi, *Zhonghua Minguo Shishi Rizhi,* p. 715.

72. William L. Tung, *The Political Institutions of Modern China* (The Hague: Martinus Nijhoff, 1964), p. 180.

73. Chiang Kai-shek did not officially take over the presidency of the national government until the death of Lin Sen in 1943.

9. Conclusion

1. In arguing the third point I recognize that it is possible to hide singular leadership behind a collegial form as happened in China under Deng Xiaoping and in the USSR early in Stalin's rule.

2. Arend Lijphart, "Comparative Politics and Comparative Method", *American Political Science Review* 65 (3) (September 1971): 691.

3. They were the Agreement on Government Organization; the Agreement on Peaceful National Reconstruction; the Agreement on Military Issues; the Agreement on a National Assembly; and the Agreement on Constitution Drafting Issues. For the texts of the five agreements see *Xinghua Ribao* (Xinghua Daily News), February 1, 1946. See also *Guo Gong Tanpan Wenxian Ziliao Xianji* (Selected documents and materials of negotiations between the Communists and the Nationalists) (Nanjing: Jiangsu Renmin Chuban She, 1980), pp. 70–82.

4. P. M. A. Linebarger et al., *Far Eastern Governments and Politics* (Princeton: Van Nostrand, 1956), p. 175. For the Agreement on Constitution Drafting Issues passed by the conference on January 31, 1946, see *Xinghua Ribao,* February 1, 1946. See also *Guo Gong Tanpan Wenxian Ziliao Xianji,* pp. 80–82.

5. See Zhou Enlai's speech on March 18, 1946, in *Xinghua Ribao,* March 19; see also *Guo Gong Tanpan Wenxian Ziliao Xianji,* pp. 128–133.

6. James E. Sheridan, *China in Disintegration: The Republican Era in Chinese History, 1912–1949* (New York: Free Press, 1975), p. 270.

7. Chien Tuan-sheng, *The Government and Politics of China* (Cambridge, Mass.: Harvard University Press, 1961), p. 325.

8. Ibid., pp. 325–326.

9. Linebarger et al., *Far Eastern Governments and Politics,* p. 176.

10. Article 43 of the 1947 constitution. For an English translation see Chien Tuan-sheng, *Government and Politics of China,* p. 450.

11. Article 1, the "Temporary Provision."

12. Hung-mao Tien, *The Great Transition* (Stanford: Hoover Institution Press, 1989), p. 114.

13. Ibid.

14. David C. L. Auw, "Political Evolution in Post–Martial Law Taiwan: Issues, Problems, and Prospects," *Issues and Studies* 30 (6) (June 1994): 6.

15. *Zhongyang Ribao (Guojiban)* (Central Daily News [International Edition]), May 21, 1990.

16. Ibid., June 1, 1991.

17. "Xuyan" (Preface), in *Gongshi: Guoshihuiyi Changkao Ziliao, Xilie 3* (Consensus: Reference materials for the Constitutional Conference, series 3) (Taipei: Institute for National Policy Research, 1990), p. 3.

18. For the discussion see the special issue of *Zhongyang Yuekan* (Central Monthly) (Taipei), August 1990. See also Harvey J. Feldman, ed., *Constitutional Reform and the Future of the Republic of China* (Almonk, N.Y.: M. E. Sharpe, 1991).

19. Hungdah Chiu, "Constitutional Development and Reform in the Republic of China," *Occasional Papers/Reprints Series in Contemporary Asian Studies* 115 (1993): 28.

20. Jiang Yanshi, "Guoshihuiyi Baogao" (Report to the Constitutional Conference), *Zhongyang Yuekan,* August 1990, p. 17.

21. Ji Chensheng, "Maixiang Minzhu Xianzheng Xingjumian" (Striving toward a new stage of democratic constitutionalism), *Zhongyang Yuekan,* May 1991, p. 16.

22. Hungdah Chiu, "Constitutional Development and Reform," p. 28.

23. Alex B. Brillantes, Jr., "The Executive," in Raul P. de Guzman and Mila A. Reforma, eds., *Government and Politics of the Philippines* (Singapore: Oxford University Press, 1988), p. 114.

24. The term "*pangulo*" is derived from the Filipino prefix "*pan*" meaning "one which is used for" and the root word "*ulo*" meaning "head." See Remigio E. Agpalo, "The Philippine Executive," in Froilan Bacungan, ed., *The Powers of the Philippine President* (Quezon City: University of Philippines Law Center, 1983), p. 156.

25. Brillantes, "The Executive," p. 123.

26. James C. F. Wang, *Comparative Asian Politics: Power, Policy, and Change* (Englewood Cliffs, N.J.: Prentice-Hall, 1994), pp. 254–255.

27. Ulf Sundhaussen, "Indonesia: Past and Present Encounters with Democracy," in Larry Diamand, Juan J. Linz, and Seymour Martin Lipset, eds., *Democracy in Developing Countries: Asia* (Boulder: Lynne Rienner, 1988), p. 436.

28. For a comparative study of Sukarno's charismatic leadership see Ann Ruth Willner, *The Spellbinders: Charismatic Political Leadership* (New Haven: Yale University Press, 1984).

29. Wang, *Comparative Asian Politics,* p. 254.

30. Michael R. J. Vatikiotis, *Indonesian Politics Under Suharto: Order, Development and Pressure for Change* (London: Routledge, 1993), p. 1.

31. Ibid., p. 2.

32. Wang, *Comparative Asian Politics,* p. 259.

33. Ibid., p. 118.

34. Se-jin Kim, *The Politics of Military Revolution in Korea* (Chapel Hill: University of North Carolina Press, 1971), p. 153.

35. Harold C. Hinton, *Korea Under New Leadership: The Fifth Republic* (New York: Praeger, 1983), p. 28.

36. Ibid., p. 30.

37. The entire text of the 1960 constitution can be found in the Secretariat of the Supreme Council for National Reconstruction, *Military Revolution in Korea* (Seoul: Dong-A, 1961), pp. 115–148.

38. Hinton, *Korea Under New Leadership,* p. 35.

39. Sung-Joo Han, "South Korea: Politics in Transition," in Larry Diamand, Juan J. Linz, and Seymour Martin Lipset, eds., *Democracy in Developing Countries: Asia* (Boulder: Lynne Rienner, 1988), p. 283.

40. Manwoo Lee, *The Odyssey of Korean Democracy: Korean Politics, 1987–1990* (Westport, Conn.: Greenwood, 1990), p. 7.

Selected Bibliography

Books and Journal Articles

Agpalo, Remigio E. "The Philippine Executive." In Froilan Bacungan, ed., *The Powers of the Philippine President*. Quezon City: University of Philippines Law Center, 1983.

Aristotle. "Politics." In Richard McKeon, ed., *Introduction to Aristotle*. New York: Random House, 1947.

Auw, David C. L. "Political Evolution in Post–Martial Law Taiwan: Issues, Problems, and Prospects." *Issues and Studies* 30 (6) (June 1994): 1–15.

Baylis, Thomas A. *Governing by Committee: Collegial Leadership in Advanced Societies*. Albany: State University of New York Press, 1989.

Boorman, Howard L. "Wang Ching-wei: A Political Profile." In Chun-tu Hsueh, ed., *Revolutionary Leaders of Modern China*. New York: Oxford University Press, 1971.

Bother, George F. *A Short History of Nationalist China, 1919–1949*. New York: Putnam's, 1979.

Brass, Paul R. *Factional Politics in an Indian State: The Congress Party in Uttar Pradesh*. Berkeley: University of California Press, 1965.

Brillantes, Alex B., Jr. "The Executive." In Raul P. de Guzman and Mila A. Reforma, eds., *Government and Politics of the Philippines*. Singapore: Oxford University Press, 1988.

Bryce, James. *Modern Democracies*. 2 vols. New York: Macmillan, 1921.

Carey, John M. "Semi-Presidentialism: The Third Alternative." Unpublished manuscript, 1990.

Cha Jianyu, ed. *Guomindang Gaizhupai Ziliao Xuanbian* (Selected documents of the KMT Reorganizationalists). Hunan: Hunan Renmin Chuban She, 1986.

Chai Mongxian. "Wuhan Shinian de Huiyi" (Reminiscences of ten years in Wuhan). In *Zhuanji Wenxue* (Biographical literature), March 1960.

Chen Dezhang et al., eds. *Zhonghua Minguo Xianfa Shiliao* (Historical documents of the constitutions of the Republic of China). Taipei: Lianguofeng Chuban She, 1973.

Chen Gongbo. *Kuxao Lu* (A record of forced smiles). Beijing: Xiandai Shiliao Biankan She, 1981.

Chen, Jerome. "The Left Wing Kuomintang—a Definition." *Bulletin of the School of Oriental and African Studies* 25 (1962): 557–574.

———. "Defining Chinese Warlords and Their Factions." *Bulletin of the School of Oriental and African Studies* 31 (1968): 563–600.

Chen Ruiyun. "Lun Minguo Zhengzhi" (On the Political system of Republican China). *Zhonggou Xiandai Shi* (Modern History of China Monthly), 10 (1988): 103–113.

Cheng, Chu-yuan, ed. *Sun Yat-sen's Doctrine in the Modern World.* Boulder: Westview, 1989.

Cheng, Maria Hsia. *The Chinese Blue Shirt Society: Fascism and Developmental Nationalism.* Berkeley: Institute of East Asian Studies, University of California, 1985.

Cheng Siyuan. *Zhengtan Huiyi* (Reminiscence of my political life). Guilin: Guangxi Renmin Chuban She, 1983.

———. *Zhenghai Mixing* (Mystery and hardship in the political sea). Hong Kong: Nanyue Chuban She, 1988.

Chi, Hsi-sheng. *Nationalist China at War: Military Defeats and Political Collapse, 1937–1945.* Ann Arbor: University of Michigan Press, 1982.

Chien Tuan-sheng. *The Government and Politics of China.* Cambridge, Mass.: Harvard University Press, 1961.

Chiu, Hungdah. "Constitutional Development and Reform in the Republic of China." *Occasional Papers/Reprints Series in Contemporary Asian Studies* 115 (1993): 1–61.

Coble, Parks M., Jr. *The Shanghai Capitalists and the Nationalist Government, 1927–1937.* Cambridge, Mass.: Council on East Asian Studies, Harvard University, 1986.

Comisso, Ellen. "Introduction: State Structures, Political Processes, and Collective Choice in CMEA States." In Ellen Comisso and Laura D'Andrea Tyson, eds., *Power, Purpose, and Collective Choice: Economic Strategy in Soviet States.* Ithaca: Cornell University Press, 1986.

Crozier, Brian. *The Man Who Lost China: The First Full Biography of Chiang Kai-shek.* New York: Scribner, 1976.

Dahl, Robert A. *Who Governs?* New Haven: Yale University Press, 1961.

———. *Polyarchy: Participation and Opposition.* New Haven: Yale University Press, 1971.

Diamand, Larry, Juan J. Linz, and Seymour Martin Lipset, eds. *Democracy in Developing Countries: Asia.* Boulder: Lynne Rienner, 1988.

Duverger, Maurice. "A New Political System Model: Semi-Presidential Government." *European Journal of Political Research* 8 (2) (June 1980): 165–187.

Eastman, Lloyd. *The Abortive Revolution: China Under Nationalist Rule, 1927–1937*. Cambridge, Mass.: Harvard University Press, 1974.

Epstein, Leon D. "Parliamentary Government." In David L. Sills, ed., *International Encyclopedia of the Social Sciences*. New York: Macmillan/Free Press, 1968.

Fairbank, John K., and Albert Feuerwerker, eds. *The Cambridge History of China*, vol. 13, pt. 2. Cambridge: Cambridge University Press, 1986.

Fan Yusui. "Reminiscences About Reorganizationalists." In *Wenshi Ziliao Xuanji* (Selected collection of material of historical literature), vol. 45. Beijing: China National Consultative Conference, 1982.

Feldman, Harvey J. *Constitutional Reform and the Future of the Republic of China*. New York: M. E. Sharpe, 1991.

Feng Yuxiang. *Wo de Shenghuo* (My life). Harbin: Heilongjiang Renmin Chuban She, 1984.

Fewsmith, Joseph. *Party, State, and Local Elites in Republican China: Merchant Organizations and Politics in Shanghai, 1890–1930*. Honolulu: University of Hawai'i Press, 1985.

Fiorina, Morris P. *Congress: Keystone of the Washington Establishment*. New Haven: Yale University Press, 1989.

Furuya, Keiji. *Chiang Kai-shek: His Life and Times*. Abridged English edition by Chun-ming Chang. New York: St. John's University Press, 1981.

Gan Guoxun. *Lanyi She, Fuxing She, Lixing She* (The Blue Shirt Society, Reconstruction Society, and Vigorous Action Society). Taipei: Zhuanji Wenxue Chuban She, 1984.

Gao Xingya. *Feng Yuxiang Jiangjun* (General Feng Yuxiang). Beijing: Beijing Chuban She, 1982.

Garner, J. W. *Political Science and Government*. New York: The New York University Press, 1928.

Geddes, Barbara. "Democratic Institutions as a Bargain Among Self-Interested Politicians." Paper presented at the annual meeting of the American Political Science Association, San Francisco, 1990.

Gerth, H. H., and C. Wright Mills. *From Max Weber: Essays in Sociology*. New York: Oxford University Press, 1958.

Goldstein, Avery. "Explaining Politics in the People's Republic of China: The Structural Alternative." *Comparative Politics* 22 (3) (April 1990): 301–322.

———. *From Bandwagon to Balance of Power Politics: Structural Constraints and Politics in China, 1949–1978*. Stanford: Stanford University Press, 1991.

Guo Tingyi, ed. *Zhonghua Minguo Shishi Rizhi, 1926–1930* (Daily chronicle of the history of the Republic of China, 1926–1930). Vol. 2. Taipei: Institute of Modern History, 1984.

———. *Zhonghua Minguo Shishi Rizhi, 1931–1937* (Daily chronicle of the history of the Republic of China, 1931–1937). Vol. 3. Taipei: Institute of Modern History, 1984.

Guojia Zhengche Yanjiu Ziliao Zhongxing (Institute for National Policy Research). *Gongshi: Guoshihuiyi Chankao Ziliao, Xilie 3* (Consensus: Reference materials for the constitutional conference, series 3). Taipei: Institute for National Policy Research, 1990.

Guzman, Raul P. de, and Mila A. Reforma, eds. *Government and Politics of the Philippines*. Singapore: Oxford University Press, 1988.

Hamilton, Alexander, John Hay, and James Madison. *The Federalist Papers*. New York: Modern Library, 1952.

Han Si. *Kan, Zhengxuexi* (Look, the Political Study Clique). Hong Kong: Hua Nan Chuban She, 1947.

Han, Sung-Joo. "South Korea: Politics in Transition." In Larry Diamand, Juan J. Linz, and Seymour Martin Lipset, eds., *Democracy in Developing Countries: Asia*. Boulder: Lynne Rienner, 1988.

Hardin, Russell. *Collective Action*. Baltimore: Johns Hopkins University Press, 1982.

He, Kuangwen. "Reminiscences About Reorganizationalists." In *Wenshi Ziliao Xuanji* (Selected collection of material of historical literature), vol. 17. Beijing: China National Consultative Conference, 1976.

Hinckley, Barbara. *Coalitions and Politics*. New York: Harcourt Brace Jovanovich, 1981.

Hinton, Harold C. *Korea Under New Leadership: The Fifth Republic*. New York: Praeger, 1983.

Hirschman, Albert O. *Exit, Voice, and Loyalty: Responses to Decline in Firms, Organizations, and States*. Cambridge, Mass.: Harvard University Press, 1970.

Holsti, K. J. *International Politics: A Framework for Analysis*. Englewood Cliffs, N.J.: Prentice-Hall, 1983.

Houn, Franklin W. *Central Government of China, 1912–1928: An Institutional Study*. Madison: University of Wisconsin Press, 1959.

Hsiung, S. I. [Xiong Shihui] *The Life of Chiang Kai-shek*. London: Peter Davies, 1948.

Hu Chunhui, ed. *Zhongguo Xiandai Shiliao Xuanji: Minguo Xianzheng Yundong* (Collected materials of modern Chinese history: The constitutional movement in the Republic of China). Taipei: Zhenzhong Shuju, 1978.

Hu Hanmin. *Hu Hanmin Zizhuan* (Autobiography of Hu Hanmin). Beijing: Zhongguo Shehui Kexue Chuban She, 1981.

Hu Pingsheng. *Minguo Chuqi de Fubi Pai* (Monarchical restoration activists in the early Republic of China). Taipei: Taiwan Xuesheng Shuju, 1985.

Hu Puyu. *The Military Exploits and Deeds of President Chiang Kai-shek.* Translated into English by Chen Kuei-liang. Taipei: Chun Wu, 1972.

Huang Jilu. "Hu Xiansheng yu Xishan Huiyi" (Mr. Hu and the Western Hill meeting). *Zhuanji Wenxue* (Biography Literature) 28 (6) (1989): 37–47.

Huang Meizheng and Zhang Yun. *Wang Jingwei Jituan Panguo Toudi Ji* (Wang Jingwei's road: Turning renegade from China). Zhengzhou: Henan Renmin Chuban She, 1987.

Hubei Zhengfashi Bainji Weiyunhui (Editorial Committee of Hubei Legal History). *Wuhan Guo Gong Lianhe Zhengfu Fazhi Wenxian Xuanbain* (Collection of legal documents of the Nationalist-Communist coalition government in Wuhan). Wuhan: Nongchun Duwu Chuban She, 1984.

Huntington, Samuel P. *The Common Defense.* New York: Columbia University Press, 1961.

———. *Political Order in Changing Societies.* New Haven: Yale University Press, 1968.

———. "Social and Institutional Dynamics of One-Party Systems." In Samuel P. Huntington and Clement H. Moore, eds., *Authoritarian Politics in Modern Society: The Dynamics of Established One-Party Systems.* New York: Basic Books, 1970.

———. "Will More Countries Become Democracies?" In Roy C. Macridis and Bernard E. Brown, eds., *Comparative Politics: Notes and Readings.* Chicago: Dorsey Press, 1986.

Ji Chensheng. "Maixiang Minzhu Xianzheng Xinjumian" (Striving toward a new stage of democratic constitutionalism). *Zhongyang Yuekan* 24 (5) (May 1991): 14–18.

Jian Yuwen. *Feng Yuxiang Zhuan* (Biography of Feng Yuxiang). Taipei: Zhuanji Wenxue Chuban She, 1982.

Jiang Yiansi. "Guoshihuiyi Baogao" (Report to the constitutional conference). *Zhongyang Yuekan* (Central Monthly) (Taipei) 23 (8) (August 1990): 8–18.

Kennedy, Melville T., Jr. "Hu Hanmin: His Career and Thought." In Chun-tu Hsueh, ed., *Revolutionary Leaders of Modern China.* London: Oxford University Press, 1971.

Kiewiet, Roderick, and Matthew D. McCubbins. *The Logic of Delegation: Congressional Parties and Appropriations Process.* Chicago: University of Chicago Press, 1991.

Kim, Se-jin. *The Politics of Military Revolution in Korea.* Chapel Hill: University of North Carolina Press, 1971.

KMT Central Executive Committee. *Guominzhengfu gongbao* (Bulletin of the Nationalist government) (Nanjing), 1 (May 1, 1927).

———. "Essentials of Political Tutelage." In *Geming Wenxian,* vol. 70. Taipei: Zhongguo Guomindang Dangshi Weiyuanhei, 1976.

Lee, Manwoo. *The Odyssey of Korean Democracy: Korean Politics, 1987–1990*. Westport, Conn.: Greenwood, 1990.

Lei Feilong, ed. *Zhonghua Minguo Kaiguo Qishi Nian Lai de Zhengzhi* (Politics of the Republic of China in its seventy-year history). Taipei: Guangwen Shuju, 1981.

Li Shongling, eds. *Zhongguo Guomindang Dashi Ji* (Chronology of the KMT). Beijing: Jiefangjun Chuban She, 1988.

Li Yunhan. *Cong Ronggong dao Qingdang* (From tolerating Communists to cleaning up the party). Taipei: Zhongguo Xueshu Zhuzuo Jiangzhu Weiyuanhui, 1966.

Lijphart, Arend. "Comparative Politics and Comparative Method." *American Political Science Review* 65 (3) (September 1971): 682–693.

———. *Democracies: Patterns of Majoritarian and Consensus Government in Twenty-One Countries.* New Haven: Yale University Press, 1984.

———. "The Southern European Examples of Democratization: Six Lessons for Latin America." *Government and Opposition* 25 (1) (Winter 1990): 68–84.

———, ed. *Parliamentary versus Presidential Government.* New York: Oxford University Press, 1992.

———. "Presidentialism and Majoritarian Democracy: Theoretical Observations." Unpublished manuscript, 1990.

Linebarger, Paul Myron Anthony. *The Political Doctrines of Sun Yat-sen: An Exposition of the San Min Chu I.* Baltimore: Johns Hopkins University Press, 1937.

Linebargar, P. M. A., Djang Chu, and Ardath W. Burks. *Far Eastern Governments and Politics: China and Japan.* Princeton: Van Nostrand, 1956.

Linz, Juan. "The Perils of Presidentialism." *Journal of Democracy* 1 (1) (Winter 1990): 51–69.

Linz, Juan, and Arturo Valenzuela, eds. *Presidentialism or Parliamentarism: Does It Make a Difference?* Baltimore: Johns Hopkins University Press, 1993.

Liu Jingzhen. *Wuhan Guomin Zhengfu Shi* (History of the Nationalist government in Wuhan). Wuhan: Hubei Renmin Chuban She, 1986.

Liu Zhengkai. *Zhongguo Xianzheng Shihua* (History of China's constitutionalism). Taipei: Xianzheng Luntan She, 1960.

Loh, Pichon P. Y. *The Early Chiang Kai-Shek: A Study of His Personality and Politics, 1887–1924.* New York: Columbia University Press, 1971.

Lu Peiyiong. "Chiang Kai-shek Xiansheng Yishi Xingtai de Shiliao yu Menjing" (Historical material and approaches for the study of Mr. Chiang Kai-shek's thought). In Research Center of Historical Materials of the

Republic of China, ed., *Zhongguo Xiandai shi Zhuanti Yanjiu Baogao* (Research reports on special topics of modern Chinese history), vol. 6. Taipei: Research Center of Historical Materials of the Republic of China, 1977.

MacNair, Harley F. *China in Revolution: An Analysis of Politics and Militarism Under the Republic.* New York: Howard Fertig, 1968.

Mainwaring, Scott. "Presidentialism in Latin America." *Latin American Research Review* 25 (1) (1990): 157–179.

Mainwaring, Scott, and John M. Carey. *Presidents and Assemblies: Constitutional Design and Electoral Dynamics.* New York: Cambridge University Press, 1992.

Meiyuan Xinchun Jilianguan, ed. *Guo Gong Tanpan Wenxian Ziliao Xuanji* (Selected collection of documents and materials of negotiations between the Communists and the Nationalists). Nanjing: Jiangshu Renmin Chuban She, 1980.

Moore, Barrington, Jr. *Social Origins of Dictatorship and Democracy: Lord and Peasant in the Making of the Modern World.* Boston: Beacon Press, 1966.

Nathan, Andrew J. "A Factionalism Model for CCP Politics." *China Quarterly* 53 (January–March 1973): 34–66.

———. *Peking Politics, 1918–1932: Factionalism and the Failure of Constitutionalism.* Berkeley: University of California Press, 1976.

———. *Chinese Democracy.* New York: Knopf, 1985.

———. "Chinese Democracy: The Lessons of Failure." *Journal of Contemporary China* 4 (Fall 1993): 3–13.

Olson, Mancur. *The Logic of Collective Action: Public Goods and the Theory of Groups.* Cambridge, Mass.: Harvard University Press, 1965.

Pan Wei-tung. *The Chinese Constitution: A Study of Forty Years of Constitution-Making in China.* Westport, Conn.: Hyperion Press, 1945.

Payne, Robert. *Chiang Kai-Shek.* New York: Weybright & Talley, 1969.

Peng Min, ed. *Zhongguo Xiandai Shi Ziliao Xuanji, 1927–1931* (Collection of historical documents of modern China, 1927–1931). Vol. 3. Beijing: Zhongguo Renmin Daxue Chuban She, 1988.

Popkin, Samuel L. *The Rational Peasant: The Political Economy of Rural Society in Vietnam.* Berkeley: University of California Press, 1979.

Pye, Lucian W. *Aspects of Political Development.* Boston: Little, Brown, 1966.

———. *The Dynamics of Chinese Politics.* Cambridge, Mass.: Oelgeschlager, Gunn & Hain, 1981.

Qiang Jianzhong, ed. *Ci Wang Neimu* (Inside stories about the assassination of Wang). Jilin: Jilin Wenshi Chuban She, 1986.

Qing Xiaoyi, ed. *Zhonghuaminguo Zhengzhi Fazhanshi* (History of the political development of the Republic of China). Taipei: Jindai Zhongguo Chuban She, 1985.

Qingnian Junren She (Young Military Men's Association). *Fan Chiang Yundong Shi* (History of the anti-Chiang movement). Guangzhou: Qinglian Junren She, 1934.

Rawski, Thomas G. *Economic Growth in Prewar China*. Berkeley: University of California Press, 1989.

Riggs, Fred W. *Thailand: The Modernization of a Bureaucratic Polity.* Honolulu: University Press of Hawai'i, 1966.

Roeder, Phillip G. "Soviet Politics and Kremlin Politics." *International Studies Quarterly* 28 (1984): 171–193.

Scalapino, Robert, and Junnosuke Masumi. *Parties and Politics in Contemporary Japan*. Berkeley: University of California Press, 1962.

Secretariat of the CEC, ed. *Zhengzhi Huiyi Gongzuo Baogao* (Work report of the Political Council). Reserved in Columbia University Library. November, 1935.

Secretariat of the CEC of the KMT. *Minutes of the Second National Congress of the KMT, 1926.*

———. *Minutes of the Fourth Plenary Session of the Second CEC, 1928.*

———. *Minutes of the Fifth Plenary Session of the Second CEC, 1928.*

———. *Minutes of the Third National Congress of the KMT, 1929.*

———. *Minutes of the Fourth Plenary Session of the Third CEC, 1930.*

———. *Minutes of the First Plenary Session of the Fourth CEC, 1931.*

———. *Minutes of the Third Plenary Session of the Fourth CEC, 1932.*

Secretariat of the Supreme Council for National Reconstruction. *Military Revolution in Korea*. Seoul: Dong-A, 1961.

Shen Yunlong. *Huang Yingbai Xiansheng Nianpu Changbian* (A long biography of Mr. Huang Yingbai). Vol. 1. Taipei: Nianjing Chuban Shiyie Gongsi, 1976.

Shen Zui. *Wo de Tewu Shengya* (My life as a special agent). Hong Kong: Jinglin Chuban She, 1985.

Sheridan, James E. *Chinese Warlord: The Career of Feng Yu-hsiang*. Stanford: Stanford University Press, 1966.

———. *China in Disintegration: The Republican Era in Chinese History, 1912–1949*. New York: Free Press, 1975.

Shi Quansheng. *Nanjing Guominzhengfu de Jianli* (Establishment of the Nationalist government in Nanjing). Zhengzhou: Henan Renmin Chuban She, 1987.

Shirley, James. "Factionalism and the Left Kuomintang." *Studies on Asia* (University of Nebraska at Lincoln) 5 (1965): 97–104.

Shugart, Matthew Soberg, and John M. Carey. *Presidents and Assemblies:*

Constitutional Design and Electoral Dynamics. Cambridge: Cambridge University Press, 1992.

Snow, Edgar. *Red Star Over China,* New York: Grove Press, 1938.

Stepan, Alfred, and Cindy Skach. "Constitutional Frameworks and Democratic Consolidation: Parliamentarianism versus Presidentialism." *World Politics* 46 (October 1993): 1–22.

Sun Ke. "Zhongguo Xianfa de Jige Wenti" (Several issues on the Chinese constitution). In *Sun Zhesheng Wenji* (Collected works of Sun Ke). Vol. 1. Taipei: Zhongguo Guomintang Dangshihui, 1980.

———. "Zhongguo Xianfa de Jige Genben Wenti" (Several fundamental issues on the Chinese constitution). In *Sun Zhesheng Wenji* (Collected works of Sun Ke). Vol. 2. Taipei: Zhongguo Guomintang Dangshihui, 1980.

Sun Yat-sen. "Minquan Chubu"(Primer of democracy) and "Jianguo Fanglue" (Program of national reconstruction). In *The Collected Works of Sun Yat-sen,* vol. 2. Shanghai: Tai Quan Co., 1929.

———. "Jianguo Dagang" (Fundamentals of national reconstruction). In *Geming Wenxian* (Collection of revolutionary documents), vol. 70. Taipei: Zhongguo Guomindang Dangshi Weiyuanhui, 1976.

———. "Yizhua" (Will). In *Geming Wenxian,* vol. 69. Taipei: Zhongguo Guomindang Dangshi Weiyuanhui, 1976.

———. *San Min Zhu Yi* (The people's three principles). Taipei: Zhongguo Guomindang Dangshi Weiyuanhui, 1985.

Tai Shiaoyi, ed. *Zhonghua Minguo Zhengzhi Fazhan shi* (History of the political development of the Republic of China). Vol. 2. Taipei: Jindai Zhongguo Chuban She, 1985.

Tang Degang. *Li Zhongren Huiyi Lu* (Reminiscences of Li Zhongren). Hong Kong: Nanyue Chuban She, 1986.

T'ang, Leang-Li. *The Inner History of the Chinese Revolution.* New York: Dutton, 1930.

Tien, Hung-mao. *Government and Politics in Kuomintang China, 1927–1937.* Stanford: Stanford University Press, 1972.

———. "Factional Politics in KMT China, 1928–1937: An Interpretation." In Gilbert Chan, ed., *China at the Crossroads: Nationalists and Communists, 1927–1949.* Boulder: Westview, 1980.

———. *The Great Transition.* Stanford: Hoover Institution Press, 1989.

Tocqueville, Alexis de. *Democracy in America.* New York: New American Library, 1956.

Tong, Hollington K. *Chiang Kai-shek: Soldier and Statesman.* Shanghai: China Publishing Co., 1937.

Tung, William L. *The Political Institutions of Modern China.* The Hague: Martinus Nijhoff, 1964.

Vatikiotis, Michael R. J. *Indonesian Politics Under Suharto: Order, Development and Pressure for Change.* London: Routledge, 1993.

Verney, Douglas V. *The Analysis of Political Systems.* London: Compton, 1959.

Waltz, Kenneth. *Theory of International Politics.* Menlo Park, Calif.: Addison-Wesley, 1979.

Wang Fuming. *Chiang Kai-shek Zhuan.* Beijing: Zhongguo Guangbo Dienshi Chuban She, 1993.

Wang, James C. F. *Comparative Asian Politics: Power, Policy, and Change.* Englewood Cliffs, N.J.: Prentice-Hall, 1994.

Wang Jingwei. *Wang Jingwei Wenji* (Collected works of Wang Jingwei). 4 vols. Shanghai: Shangwu Shuju, 1929.

Wang Sunsheng and Yang Dawei. *Fujian shibian* (Fujian Incident). Fuzhou: Fujian Renmin Chuban She, 1983.

Wang Xing and Liu Hong, eds. *Nanjing Guominzhengfu Junzheng Yaoyuan Lu* (Brief chronicle of the important military and civilian officials of the Nanjing government). Beijing: Chunqiu Chuban She, 1988.

Wei, Julie Lee, Ramon H. Myers, and Donald G. Gillin, eds. *Prescriptions for Saving China: Selected Writings of Sun Yat-sen.* Stanford: Hoover Institution Press, 1994.

Whitson, William W. "The Field Army in Chinese Communist Military Politics." *China Quarterly* 37 (January–March 1969): 1–30.

Willner, Ann Ruth. *The Spellbinders: Charismatic Political Leadership.* New Haven: Yale University Press, 1984.

Wu, Chao-chu. *The Nationalist Program for China.* New Haven: Yale University Press, 1929.

Wu, Chih-Feng. *Chinese Government and Politics.* Shanghai: The Commercial Press, 1934.

Wu, Eugene. *Leaders of Twentieth Century China.* Stanford: Stanford University Press, 1956.

Wu Xiangxiang. *Minguo Renwu Liezhuan* (Biographies of personages in Republican China). Vol. 5. Taipei: Juanji Wenxue Chuban She, 1986.

Wu, Yuzhang. *The Revolution of 1911.* Beijing: Renmin Chuban She, 1962.

Xiao Jizhong, ed. *Geming Renwu Zhi* (Biographies of revolutionaries). Vol. 13. Taipei: Zhongguo Guomindang Dangshi Weiyuanhui, 1976.

Xie Yiutien. *Xie Huisheng Xiansheng Shiji Jizhuan.* (Biography of Mr. Xie Huisheng). Taipei: Jindai Zhongguo Chuban She, 1991.

Xue Zhuoyun. *Zhonghua Minguo Xianfa Lun* (On the constitution of the Republic of China). Taipei: Wenjing Chuban She, 1972.

Yang Jialuo, ed. *Dalu Lunxian Qian Zhi Zhonghua Minguo* (The Republic of China before the mainland was occupied by Communists). Taipei: Dinwen Shujiu, 1973.

Yang Shubiao. *Chiang Kai-shek Zhuan* (Biography of Chiang Kai-shek). Beijing: Tuanjie Chuban She, 1989.

Ye Qizheng. "Zhongguo Zhishi Fenzi Yu Xiandaihua" (The Chinese intellectual and modernization). *Zhishi Fenzi* (Chinese Intellectual), 5 (4) (Summer 1990): 35–38.

Young, Crawford. "Politics in Africa." In Gabriel A. Almond, ed., *Comparative Politics Today: A World View.* Boston: Little, Brown, 1974.

Young, Ernest P. *The Presidency of Yuan Shih-k'ai: Liberalism and Dictatorship in Early Republican China.* Ann Arbor: University of Michigan Press, 1977.

Yu, George T. *Party Politics in Republican China: The Kuomintang, 1912–1924.* Berkeley: University of California Press, 1966.

Yuan, T. L. *China in Western Literature.* New Haven: Yale University Press, 1958.

Zhang Xianwen, ed. *Zhonghua Minguo Shigang* (Outline history of the Republic of China). Zhengzhou: Henan Renmin Chuban She, 1985.

Zhang Yufa, ed. *Zhongguo Xiandaishi Lunji* (Collected works on modern Chinese history). Vols. 2, 5, and 8. Taipei: Lianjing Chuban Shiye Gongsi, 1980–1982.

———. *Minguo Chu Nian de Zhengdang* (Political parties in early Republican China). Taipei: Institute of Modern History, Academia Sinica, 1985.

Zhao, Suisheng. "Zhongguo Minzhu Beiju Tanyuan" (Origins of the Chinese democracy tragedy). *Zhishi Fenzi* (Chinese Intellectual) (Winter 1990): 3–16. A revised English version titled "A Tragedy of History: The Chinese Search for Democracy in the Twentieth Century" appeared in *The Journal of Contemporary China* 3 (Summer 1993): 18–37.

Zhen Yianfen. "Hu Zhantang Xiansheng de Shengping jiqi dui Guofu Geming Sixiang de Chanyiang" (The life of Mr. Hu Zhantang and his contribution to the thought of the founding father). In Zhonghua Minguo Shiliao Yanjiu Zhongxing (Research Center of Historical Materials of the Republic of China), ed., *Zhongguo Xiandai Shi Zhuanti Yanjiu Baogao* (Research report on special topics of China's modern history), vol. 9. Taipei: Research Center of Historical Materials of the Republic of China, 1979.

Zhongguo Dier Lishi Dangan Guan (Second Archive Library of China), ed. *Zhongguo Kuomintang Di Yi, Er Ci Quanguo Daibaodahui Huiyi Shiliao* (Collection of the archives and documents of the KMT First and Second National Congresses). Vols. 1 and 2. Nanjing: Jiangshu Guji Chuban She, 1986.

Zhou Bingwo and Chen Hongmin. *Hu Hanmin Pingzhuan* (Study of Hu Hanmin's life). Guangzhou: Guangdong Renmin Chuban She, 1989.

Zhou Enlai. *Zhou Enlai Xuanji* (Selected works of Zhou Enlai). Vol. 1. Beijing: Renmin Chuban Shi, 1986.

Zhou Fuhai. "Tao Chule Chiduo Wuhan" (Escaping from the Red Capital: Wuhan). In Chiang Yongjing, ed., *Beifa Shiqi de Zhengzhi Shiliao* (Historical materials on politics during the Northern Expedition). Taipei: Zhongzheng Shuju, 1981.

Zhou Lu. *Zhongguo Kuomintang Jianshi* (Brief history of the KMT). Taipei: Zhongzheng Shuju, 1953.

Newspapers and Yearbooks

Dagong Bao (Dagong Daily). 1930–1931.

Geming Ribao (Revolutionary Daily). 1930–1931.

Geming Zhanxian (Revolutionary Front). 1930.

Guowen Zhoubao (Guowen Weekly). 1927–1932.

Huabei Ribao (North China Daily). 1929.

Shishi Xingbao (Shishi News Daily). 1932.

Xiangdao Zhoubao (Xiangdao Weekly). 1927.

Xin Chen Bao (Xin Chen News). 1930.

Xinghua Ribao (Xinghua Daily News). 1946.

Zhongguo Guomindang Nianjian (KMT Yearbook). 1927–1935.

Zhongguo Nianjian (China Yearbook). 1926–1937.

Zhongyang Daobao (Central Herald). 1930–1931.

Zhongyang Ribao (Central Daily News). 1931–1969.

Zhongyang Ribao (Guojiban) (Central Daily News [International Edition]). 1990–1991.

Zhongyang Yuekan (Central Monthly). 1990–1991.

Index

absolute monarchies, 5
Agpalo, Remigio E., 151
Anhui Clique *(wan xi),* 21
Anti-Chiang Coalition, 15, 16, 18, 77, 83, 106, 113, 116, 117, 119, 121, 123, 124, 126, 127; breakup of, 127
Aristotle, 6–7
authoritarian regimes: constitutional, 151, 156; seasoned politicians in, 7; substance of, 7
authority relationships, 38–41; anarchic, 40, 41, 47, 51, 52, 53, 56, 95; hierarchical, 40, 41; hybrid pattern of, 40

Bai Chongxi, 99, 101, 109, 110, 113, 120, 135, 142
Bai Wenwei, 114
balance of power, 15, 88, 90, 126, 131; between Chiang Kai-shek and his rivals, 88, 107, 127, 145
Baylis, Thomas: collegial leadership vs. "monocratic" leadership, 10
Blue Shirt Society *(Lan Yi She),* 12, 39, 53, 58, 62–64, 141
Boorman, Howard L., 65, 132, 133
Borodin, Michael, 42, 79
Brillantes, Alex B., Jr., 151
Bryce, James, 24
Bureau of Investigation and Statistics. *See* party's secret service
cabinet: as a collective body, 4; as a collegial executive body, 6
Cai Tingkai, 135
Cai Yuanpei, 84, 104, 120, 122
Carey, John M., 4, 17
CC Clique or the Organization Group, 52, 53, 58, 64, 101, 104
Central China War, 111–113
Central Club, 64
Central Executive Committee (CEC), 12, 19, 29–30, 31, 36, 39, 44, 45, 46, 47, 48, 49, 50, 51, 57, 61, 66, 76, 78, 80, 81, 84, 90, 94, 117, 146
Central Military Commission, 75, 80, 99, 101, 104, 142; and Chiang's rise, 75
Central Organization Department, 12, 39, 52, 62
Central Political Council (CPC), 12, 19, 39, 44, 46, 47, 50, 57, 62, 70, 75, 108, 110; fast-growing membership of, 50; and lack of institutionalization, 48, 50; origins of, 46
Central Supervisory Committee, 44, 45, 46, 64, 84
Chang Myon, 154
Chang, Raymond, 149
Chen Gongbo, 67, 94, 114, 128; and meeting with Chiang, 130
Chen Guofu, 64, 65, 129

Chen Hongmin, 79, 89, 135
Chen Jionming, 59, 60
Chen Jitang, 70, 120
Chen Lifu, 64, 65
Chen Minshu, 84, 121, 122, 130, 135
Chen Qian, 103
Chen Qimei, 60, 64
Chen Qitong, 134, 135, 142
Chen Yuren, 84, 120, 122
Chiang Ching-kuo, 145, 148, 149
Chiang-Gui War, 109–111
Chiang Kai-shek, 18, 26, 37, 43, 46, 48, 50, 57, 61, 62, 64, 66, 67, 68, 72–73, 74, 80, 87, 94, 100, 106–109, 113, 144, 149; as Chairman of CPC, 62; and Chiang-Wang alliance, 129–131; as commander-in-chief of the Nationalist Army, 12, 60, 93, 94, 103–104, 124; as commander of the First Army Corps, 54, 92, 96; institutional preference of, 74–78, 87; military background of, 59–60; and power resources, 59–65; and preference for design of government, 13; as president, 30–31, 35; resignation of, 99–101, 121; second resignation of, 119–124
Chien Tuan-sheng, 53, 60, 81, 147
Chinese Revolutionary Party *(Zhonghua Geming Dang),* 60
Chun Doo Hwan, 155
coalition: anti-Chiang, 15–18, 77–83, formation of, 126; Grand, 88. *See also* Anti-Chiang Coalition
Coble, Parks M., 59
collective leadership, 6, 8, 9, 10, 31, 34, 36, 78, 80, 83, 84, 86, 107, 127, 129, 131, 136, 144, 148; of cabinet system, 144; among top power elites, 6; vs. singular, 8, 146
Comisso, Ellen, 10
Communists, 15, 61, 63, 65, 67, 89, 91, 99, 120; and the Communist Party, 42, 43, 45
consensus rule, 51; and a lack of consensus, 51–52
constitution: and constitutional compact, 21; draft, 7; provisional, 7, 76–77, 81; provisional of 1912, 21; provisional of 1931, 26; of 1936, 16, 18, 146; of 1945, 147
constitutional democracy, 28, 29
constitutional government, 5, 22, 23, 24, 25, 42; different forms of, 24; in modern authoritarian states, 5. *See also* absolute monarchies
constitutionalism, 18, 22, 24, 42
constitutional monarchy, 24
constitutional movement, 137, 143, 144
constitutional reform, 84, 143, 146, 148, 149, 150
constitution-making, 16, 17, 18, 73, 106, 137, 143, 144, 146, 151, 156; in Indonesia, 152–153; in Nationalist China, 22; in the Philippines, 151–152; during the Republican era, 21; in South Korea, 153–155
Control Yuan, 25, 26, 36, 86, 123, 139

Dahl, Robert, 38
Dai Chuanxian, 129
Dai Jitao, 76
democratic centralism, 120
democratic transitions, 17
de Tocqeville, Alexis, 24
Ding Weifung, 94
distribution of power, 144
Duan Qirui, 21, 22

"Eastern Expedition" *(dongzheng),* 96
Eastman, Lloyd, 17, 24, 26–27, 142
elections: competitive, 5, 6; modes of, 7; non-competitive, 1
emergency power. *See* president
Epstein, Leon D., 3
Examination Yuan, 25, 26, 36, 37, 123
executive/legislative relations, 7, 29

Executive Yuan, 25, 30, 31, 32, 36, 37, 80–81, 82, 84, 107, 112, 123, 124, 125, 128, 138, 139, 147
extraordinary session *(feichang huiyi),* 119–120

factional bargaining, 50, 51
factionalism, 51
fascism, 141
Feng Yuxiang, 54, 68, 83, 100, 107, 108, 111, 112, 113, 114, 142; as Chairman of the KMT's Political Subcouncil, 97; "Christian General", 111; commander of Second Army Corps of the Nationalist Army, 96–99; revolt of, 113
Fifth Plenary Session of the Fourth CEC, 14
figurehead of state, 84, 85, 122, 123
five power constitution doctrine, 25, 26, 80, 85, 104, 117, 148
five yuan, 14, 25, 28, 29, 30, 31, 32, 35, 36, 37, 77, 78, 80–82, 119, 122, 124, 129, 139. *See also names of individual yuan:* Control Yuan; Examination Yuan; Executive Yuan; Judiciary Yuan; Legislative Yuan
former Soviet Union, 9; collective oligarchy of, 9; Communist Party, 43; dictatorship of, 9
four sovereign powers, 25
Fourth Plenary Session of the Second CEC, 13, 34
Fu Bingchang, 138

Gan Laiguan, 67
generalissimo, 90; acting generalissimo, 89; system, 14, 78, 79
Goodnow, Frank J., 23
government: constitutional form of, 5, 7, 150, 155; functional substance of, 5; modern authoritarian, 5
Guangdong-Guangxi militarists, 99, 101, 102, 103
Guangxi militarists, 111
"Guided democracy", 152–153
Gu Mengyu, 67, 129; and meeting with Chiang, 130
Gu Yingfen, 120
Gu Zhenggang, 102

Han Fuqu, 113
He Xiangling, 94
Hitler, 141
Ho Chung, 156
"Hongxian" (Dynasty of Glorious Constitutionalism), 23
Hsiung, S. I., 64, 115
Huangpu (Whampoa) Military Academy, 43, 55, 60, 62–63, 64, 92, 100; Alumni Association of, 63; graduates of, 60, 62–63; and soldiers, 60, 92
Hu Hanmin, 12, 13, 14, 15, 18, 33, 46, 48, 50, 55, 56, 57, 76, 87, 89, 90, 92, 104, 116, 119, 128, 129, 134–135, 136, 145; as acting generalissimo, 79–80, 89; and association with Sun Yat-sen, 13, 69; death of, 134; founded Sanminzhuyi Yuckan, 70; house arrest of, 68, 116; institutional preference of, 78–82; linked to Fujian revolt, 135; and position in Western Hill Group, 13, 58; power resources of, 69–71
Huntington, Samuel P., 9–10
Hu Puyu, 59
Hu Yisheng, 92

Institute for National Policy Research (INPR), 149
institutional choice, 1, 16; consequences of, 18; between parliamentarianism and presidentialism in democratic countries, 1; political logic of, 8, 10; between the presidential and cabinet systems in non-democratic settings, 2, 20; in the Republican era, 20
institutional design, 1, 9, 16, 17, 106,

139, 143, 144, 145, 150, 151, 156; of authority relationship between the executive and the legislative branches, 3; of democratic government, 3; of Nationalist government, 11; nonconsensual adoption of a controversial, 124; political logic of, 9, 16, 18; in the Republican era, 22
institutional differences between the presidential and cabinet systems: in authoritarian settings, 4–7; in democratic settings, 3–4; in Nationalist China, 7–8, 29–32
institutional preferences, 2, 9, 11, 77, 80, 81, 143

James, C. F., 153
Judiciary Yuan, 25, 36, 123
Ju Zheng, 70, 129

Kennedy, Melville T., 69
KMT National Congress, 45, 48, 49–50; First, 45–48; Second, 45, 61, 64; Third, 45, 49; Fourth, 45, 50, 121, 123; Fifth, 45
KMT party statute, 48
Kong Xiangxi (H. H. Kung), 132
Kuomintang (KMT). *See* Nationalist Party

Lee Teng-hui, 148, 149, 150
left/right antagonism, 61, 66
Legislative Yuan, 25, 27, 31, 36, 37, 80–81, 82, 85, 86, 116, 123, 125, 138, 139, 140, 147, 149
Liao Zhongkai, 43, 78, 79, 80, 89, 90, 92; assassination of, 89, 91, 116
Li Jisheng, 102, 108, 110, 111, 112
Lijphart, Arend, 4, 6, 17
Li Liejun, 94, 102, 104
Linebarger, Paul M. A., 20, 27
Lin Sen, 33, 91, 124, 127
Lin Sheng, 70
Linz, Juan, 17
Liu Liqun, 62
Li Yuanhong, 21
Li Zhongren, 54, 79, 83, 99, 107, 108, 109, 110, 111, 113, 114, 120, 142
Lu Diping, 110

MacNair, Harley F., 108
Manzhouguo (Manzhou State), 133
Mao Tse-tung, 66
Mao Zedong, 26
Mao Zhuquan, 114
Marcos, Ferdinand, 151–152
May 5 Constitution, 140, 146
Military Affairs Commission, 131
Military Commission, 53, 60, 63
Minquan Chubu (Primer of Democracy), 25
modern authoritarian states, 5
Mong, C. Y., 100
monocratic leadership, 10
Moore, Barrington, Jr., 27

Nasution, 153
Nathan, Andrew, 23, 27, 39, 51
National Affairs Conference *(guoshi huiyi),* 149
National Assembly, 25, 26, 27, 85, 138, 139, 154, 155
National Conference for Unification, 154, 155
National Constituent Assembly, 147
National Government Council, 14, 30, 31, 32, 34, 76, 90, 115, 123
nationalism, 42
Nationalist government, 3, 11, 12, 22, 32, 33; cabinet form of, 31, 32; design of, 3, 11; as distinguished from warlords, 15; fragmentation of authority of, 12; in Guangzhou in 1925, 22; presidential form of, 29, 32; split of, 96
Nationalist Party (Kuomintang or KMT), 8, 11, 12, 13, 14, 15, 16, 17, 18, 19, 20, 22, 23, 26, 29–32, 40, 41, 42–44; diffusion of central authority in, 47, 56, 95; founded,

24; four tiers of authority in, 44–45; hierarchy of, 41, 44, 61–62; reorganization of, 42, 61; ultimate authority of, 29
Nationalist Revolution, 12, 55; of 1911, 22, 66; three stage program of, 28
National Political Consultative Conference *(Quanguo Zhengzhi Xieshang Huiyi),* 146
new institutionalism, 2
New Life Movement, 140
new warlordism, 55, 56
Northern Expedition, 53–54, 60, 93, 94, 96, 98, 100, 103
northern warlords, 98, 99

one-party: and dictatorship, 42, 43, 44; and government, 26, 41; and system, 5
one-person dictatorship, 8, 10, 76, 80, 83, 146, 150
one-person executive, 34, 142
Organic Law, 7, 14, 19, 26, 30, 31, 32, 33, 34, 35, 36, 81, 104, 124, 126, 128; Drafting Committee of, 14, 76; revised, 33–34, 76, 106, 124

Pan Wei-tung, 24
Park Chung Hee, 154–155
parliamentarianism, 42
party: legitimacy within, 118; majoritarian, 6; party-state hierarchy, 107, 122; revolutionary, 5, 6; stature, 45
party's secret service (Bureau of Investigation and Statistics), 52, 64
"patrimonialism," 10
Payne, Robert, 64
peace conference *(heping huiyi),* 83, 84, 121–123
Peking New Parliament draft, 21
People's Three Principles, 63
policy outcomes, 9, 10
Political Study Clique *(Zheng Xue Xi),* 62
political subcouncil (regional subcouncils): in Kaifeng, 111; in Taiyuan, 113; in Wuhan, 110
political tutelage, 28, 29, 43, 44, 45, 117–118, 120
power resources: relevance of, 38–39. *See also* Chiang Kai-shek; Hu Hanmin; Sun Ke; Wang Jingwei
president: chief executive, 5, 8, 32; commander-in-chief of armed forces, 35, 37; emergency power of, 142, 149; as figurehead of state, 8, 31–32, 33, 122, 138, 154; as one-person executive, 4, 37; as singular leader of the regime, 8, 30, 144, 148; as strongman, 6; as titular head, 5, 31; with ultimate authority of government, 6; as unitary executive, 8
presidentialism: origin of, 17; viability of, 2
Propaganda Department, 39–40
provisional constitution, 21, 35, 116, 117, 118, 119

Rawski, Thomas G., 132
regional militarists, 40, 54, 55, 56, 57, 65, 67–68, 71, 73, 88, 101, 106, 107, 108, 109, 110, 114, 116, 120, 126, 134, 142; clash with Chiang Kai-shek, 113, 126
Reorganizationalist Comrades Association, 12–13, 39–40, 53, 58, 59, 65, 66, 114, 116, 120, 128, 130
Reorganization and Disbandment Conference *(bian qian huiyi),* 55, 109
Rhee, Syngman, 153–154, 156
Roeder, Philip G., 10
Roh Tae Woo, 155
"rule by one", "rule by the few", and "rule by many", 6, 7, 16, 20, 29, 156

secular political power, 5
Sheridan, James E., 114
Shi Yushan, 113

Shugart, Matthew S., 4, 17
singular leadership, 6, 9, 140, 142, 144; vs. collective leadership, 8, 146
Song Jiaoren, 42
Song Meiling, 103
Song Zhiwen (T. V. Soong), 107, 129, 132
Southwest Council of Political Affairs and Southwest Political Headquarters, 134
Special Central Committee, 101, 102, 103–104
State Council, 21, 154
Stepan, Alfred, 17
succession struggle, 88–89, 92, 104, 106
Suharto, 152–153, 155
Sukarno, 152–156
Sun Chuangfung, 99, 102
Sun Ke, 12, 15, 18, 33, 48, 57, 58, 59, 76, 77, 80, 83, 87, 120, 122, 136–140, 145; as champion of constitutionalism, 137; power resources of, 70–73; as president of Legislative Yuan, 125, 136–137; resignation of, 131
Sun Yat-sen, 12, 14, 21, 23, 24–29, 32, 39, 42, 43, 45–47, 58–59, 61, 66, 69–80, 88–91, 117; doctrine of, 26–28, 69; generalissimo government established by, 79; nationalist revolutionary movement led by, 22; paternalistic rather than democratic, 25
Sun Yat-senist Study Society, 62–63
Supreme National Defense Conference, 142
Supreme National Defense Council, 142, 146

Taiwan: democratization of, 156; independence of, 149–150
Tanggu treaty, 133
Tang Shaoyi, 120
Tang Shengzhi, 103
Tan Yankai, 33, 94, 102, 104
"temple of heaven" draft, 21
"Temporary Provision" *(lingshi tiaokuan),* 147–149
Tien Hung-mao, 148
Tong, Hollington K., 60, 99, 100
Tongmenghui, 69
traditional sacred authority, 5

Verney, Douglas, 3, 4

Waltz, Kenneth N., 40
Wang Faqing, 114; and meeting with Chiang, 130
Wang Jingwei, 12, 15, 18, 33, 46, 48, 50, 55, 56, 57, 76, 80, 83, 87, 89, 93, 94, 95, 96, 99, 103, 104, 113, 114, 115, 119, 120, 122, 128, 132, 133, 134, 145; assassination of, 133, 136; and the handling of Japanese aggression, 133; institutional preference of, 82–85; national traitor, 66; power resources of, 65–68; as president of Executive Yuan, 127, 130, 131, 132
Wang Leping, 67
warlordism, 54, 73, 89, 90, 96, 118
Western Hill Group, 39–40, 48, 53, 58, 61, 70, 71, 89, 95, 101, 102, 103, 104, 114, 116, 119, 120
Wu Chaoshu (John C. H. Wu), 129, 136, 138
Wu Jingyuan, 76, 77
Wu Zhihui, 121

Xie Chi, 70, 114
Xingzhonghui (Revive China Society), 41
Xu Chongzhi, 33, 90, 92, 114, 120
Xunzheng Yuefa (Essentials of Political Tutelage), 44

Yang Shubao, 99
Yanxiadong Meeting, 131, 136
Yan Xishan, 54, 68, 83, 108, 113, 114–115, 118

Yi Changchu, 129
Yuan Shikai, 21, 22, 23, 24, 42
Yu Chin-o, Dr., 153
Yu, George, 29
yushin or "revitalization" constitution, 154–155
Yu Yuren, 129

Zhang Fakui, 102, 103, 120
Zhang Ji, 121, 129
Zhang Xueliang (Young Marshal), 55, 68, 115, 120
Zhang Xun, 24
Zhang Zhiban, 138
Zhang Zuolin, 55, 98
Zhao Weiwen, 114
Zhejiang Revolutionary Comrades Association, 64
Zhen Jiemin, 141
Zhenzhou Conference, 97
Zhonghua Geming Dang (Chinese Revolutionary Party), 60
Zhou Bingwo, 79, 89, 135
Zhou Enlai, 96
zongchai (general arbitrator), 142
zongli (director general), 45, 46, 141–142
Zou Lu, 70, 83, 114, 120, 122, 135

About the Author

SUISHENG ZHAO is assistant professor of government and East Asian politics at Colby College, Maine, and the founder and editor of *The Journal of Contemporary China*. He received his doctorate in political science from the University of California-San Diego and his masters in economics from Beijing University. Formerly a research fellow in the Economic Research Center, State Council of China, and an assistant professor in Beijing University before coming to the United States in 1985, he is co-editor of *Decision-Making in Deng's China* (1995) and has published widely on Chinese politics and foreign policy and East Asian international relations. His articles have appeared in *Asian Survey, Journal of Northeast Asian Studies, Asian Affairs, Issues and Studies*, and elsewhere.

to a reader many years hence,
I hope this finds you well...

-RC 2020